TERROR!

THE INSIDE STORY OF THE TERRORIST CONSPIRACY IN AMERICA

by

Yossef Bodansky

Introduction by
Congressman Duncan Hunter, (R-CA)

A division of Shapolsky Publishers, Inc.

TERROR!
The Inside Story of the Terrorist Conspiracy in America

S.P.I. BOOKS
A division of Shapolsky Publishers, Inc.

ISBN 1-56171-301-5

For any additional information, contact:

S.P.I. BOOKS/Shapolsky Publishers, Inc.
136 West 22nd Street
New York, NY 10011
212/633-2022 / FAX 212/633-2123

Printed in Canada

10 9 8 7 6 5 4 3 2 1

Contents

To Masha, with love.

Key Figures In The Book

NOTE:

The transliteration of names and terms from the Arabic alphabet into the Roman alphabet presents a number of problems. Scholars use a standard system but the accent marks and other specialized indications can be confusing to non-specialists. When journalists and other non-specialists attempt to write the names as they sound, they may come up with several spellings for the same name (Rashid, Rachid and Rasheed), which can also be confusing.

Since this book is written for the general reader, individual names that have become well-known to the public are spelled as they often appear in the press. Although this is not systematic, it is hoped that it may be helpful.

Fadil Abdelghani — Sudanese, expert terrorist already in the U.S. who was activated to assume command over the expert terrorists who planned and facilitated the operation of the second cell of the New York network.

Amir Abdelghani — Sudanese; expert terrorist activated for the operation of the second cell of the New York network; cousin of Fadil Abdelghani.

Mahmud Abouhalima — Egyptian; one of the founders of the New York terrorist network, a master terrorist and the leader of the first New York cell, which exploded a bomb under the World Trade Center on February 26, 1993.

Abu-Imamah (nom de guerre) — Egyptian; based in Iran, who runs the worldwide clandestine and terrorist operations involving Egyptian Islamists.

Ahmad Muhammad Ajaj — Palestinian; expert terrorist who arrived from Pakistan to assist Ramzi Youssuf.

Siddig Ibrahim Siddig Ali — Sudanese; the head of Turabi's National Islamic Front in the U.S., master terrorist and leader of the second New York cell, which conspired to conduct a wave of bombings all over Manhattan on July 4, 1993.

Bilal Alkaisi — Arab-American who participated in the World Trade Center bombing.

Victor Alvarez — Puerto Rican who became a devout Muslim and participated in the Fourth of July plot.

Sheikh Abd-al-Azziz Awdah — A leader of Palestinian Islamic Jihad, originally from Gaza, who was instrumental in the initial activation of the Islamist terrorist network in New York.

Nidal A. Ayyad — Palestinian from Kuwait who participated in theWorld Trade Center bombing.

Sheikh AbdAllah Azzam — Palestinian Islamist and organizer for the "Afghans" in Peshawar, Pakistan, who inspired Mustafa Shalabi's activities in Brooklyn.

General Umar al-Bashir — President of Sudan since 1989.

Ibrahim A. Elgabrowny — Egyptian; responsible for the logistics and management of the first cell of the New York network.

Tarig Elhassan — Sudanese who participated in the Fourth of July plot.

Ayatollah Muhammad Hussein Fadlallah — The spiritual leader of the HizbAllah.

Sultan Ibrahim al-Gawli — Egyptian; a rich businessman, a PLO agent, a gold smuggler and the patron of the Jersey City Islamist community in the 1980s.

Sheikh Rachid Ghannouchi — The spiritual leader of the Islamist terrorists in Western Europe, Turabi's representative in Europe, and the leader of Tunisia's Islamists.

Earl Gant — African-American Fuqra member in Philadelphia who tried to obtain high explosives for the second New York cell.

Abd-al-Rahman Haggag (a.k.a. Abdo Mohammad Haggag) — Egyptian; a key terrorist in the New York network, responsible for the plots to assassinate Egyptian President Husni Mubarak.

Clement Rodney Hampton-El — African-American member of Fuqra, one of the founders of the New York terrorist network, who played a key role in providing logistical support for the New York network.

Hojjat ol-Islam Ali Akbar Hashemi-Rafsanjani — President of Iran, former Speaker of Parliament (the *Majlis*).

Brigadier Imtiaz — A close ally of Pakistan's Prime Minister Nawaz Sharif; the former head of the Intelligence Bureau, responsible for Inter-Service Intelligence Agency's high quality training of terrorists, including Americans.

Khalid al-Istambuli — Assassinated Egyptian President Anwar Sadat in 1981.

Muhammad Shawqi al-Istambuli — Military leader of the Egyptian *al-Jama'ah al-Islamiyah*, brother of Khalid al-Istambuli.

Sheikh Mubarak Ali Shah Jilani — Pakistani Kashmiri; the leader of Fuqra in the United States and Pakistan.

Mir Amail Kansi — Pakistani; the Iranian agent who shot CIA employees at the gate of CIA headquarters in Langley, Va., in January 1993.

Fares Khallafalla — Sudanese; participated in the Fourth of July plot.

Ayatollah Ali Khamene'i — Iran's spiritual leader and former president.

Ayatollah Ruhollah Khomeyni — The founder of the Islamic Republic of Iran and its first spiritual leader.

Hojjat ol-Islam Ahmad Khomeyni — Senior Iranian politician, son of the late Ayatollah Khomeyni.

Yu Kikumura — Japanese terrorist who ran a major operation in the U.S. for Syrian intelligence in order to confirm the ability to build bombs from off-the-shelf chemicals obtained locally.

Hojjat ol-Islam Ali Akbar Mohtashemi — One of
the guardians of the Iranian system of
international terrorism. Formerly head
of the Defense and Islamic Revolutionary Guards Corps Committee in the Iranian Parliament, Minister of the Interior and ambassador to Damascus,
where he was one of the founding fathers of the HizbAllah terrorist organization.

Sayyid Abdulazziz Nossair — Egyptian; one of the
founders of the New York Islamist terrorist network, was involved in the assassination of Rabbi Meir Kahane in
1990.

Ahmad Youssuf Othman (a.k.a. Ahmed
Mohammed) — Sudanese diplomat; officially the Third Secretary responsible
for consular affairs at UN mission, in
reality the Sudanese intelligence officer
who served as Siddig Ibrahim Siddig
Ali's point of contact.

Sheikh Umar Abdel-Rahman — The spiritual
leader of the Islamist terrorists in North
America, including the New York network. Also Turabi's representative to
America and spiritual leader of Egyptian Islamists.

Muhsin Reza'i — Commander of the Iranian Revolutionary Guards Corps and a senior
figure in Iran's terrorist establishment.

Mohammed A. Salameh — Jordanian-Palestinian; drove the van-bomb into the World Trade Center.

Mohammad Saleh — Jordanian-Palestinian Islamist; participated in Fourth of July plot.

Matharawy Muhammad Said Saleh — Egyptian Islamist; participated in Fourth of July plot.

Emad Salem — Egyptian Islamist who became the FBI's informer in the ranks of the second cell of the New York network.

Mustafa Shalabi — Egyptian; founder of the Islamist support network in the U.S.; Sheikh Abdel-Rahman's first sponsor in the U.S. who was murdered by the Sheikh's followers.

Muhammad Rezah Shalchian (or Chalagian) Tabrizi-Iranian diplomat who, operating under the cover of financial comptroller of Iran's UN mission, is a senior officer of IRGC intelligence responsible for support and oversight of the Islamist terrorist infrastructure in the U.S.

Sheikh Asa'ad Bayyud al-Tamimi — Palestinian leader of the Tehran-sponsored Islamic Jihad (*Bayt al-Maqdis*, a.k.a HizbAllah-Palestine), whose son is active in supporting Islamist terrorism in the U.S.

Sheikh Hassan al-Turabi — The spiritual leader of Sudan and leader of the Sunni Islamist terrorist movement.

Abdul Rahman Yassin (a.k. a. Abboud Yassin) — U.S.-born Arab-American Islamist who participated in World Trade Center bombing.

Sarag al-Din Hamid Youssuf (a.k.a. Siraj Youssuf) — Sudanese diplomat who, while officially the Counselor of the Sudanese UN mission, is in fact Turabi's personal representative and as such the actual head of mission and responsible for supporting Islamist terrorism.

Ramzi Ahmad Youssuf — Iraqi; expert terrorist who arrived from Pakistan to take over the professional side of the New York network and was instrumental in the bombing of the World Trade Center.

INTRODUCTION
by
Congressman
Duncan Hunter

This is a book we need.

Like all other Americans, when the Cold War came to an end I was profoundly relieved, hopeful that for the first time in nearly sixty years we might now find ourselves in a world truly at peace — one in which the United States would no longer need to devote major energies to the question of defending ourselves and guarding the free world.

That was the hope just a few short years ago — but the real world has turned out to be very different.

Like all other Americans, I was shocked when the World Trade Center in New York was rocked by a bomb last February, killing six innocent people and injuring hundreds more. I was dismayed by the revelations of a plot to attack the United Nations, Federal office buildings and tunnels under the

Hudson River on the Fourth of July and angered at the thought of the carnage that would have resulted had the plot not been uncovered in time.

But as a member of Congress, I was not taken entirely by surprise. Over the past few years, reports prepared for government officials by Yossef Bodansky as Director of the Republican Task Force on Terrorism and Unconventional Warfare have made me aware that there was a very real danger that America might face a systematic campaign of terrorist attacks by an international terrorist system directed by Iran with the support and assistance of Syria, Sudan and their allies.

This book explains very clearly, and in specific, carefully documented detail, what happened at the World Trade Center and why it was probably only the beginning.

It is important for government officials, security agencies and the intelligence community to be aware of the dangers we face as a nation. But it is essential that the American people must also know what is happening. The people who were killed and injured in the World Trade Center bombing were ordinary Americans, and those who would have been slaughtered in the tunnels under the Hudson River would also have been ordinary Americans, many of them families on holiday, innocently setting out for picnics or summer vacations — and meeting instead a terrible fate.

It all seems incredible — but it has happened, and it may happen again somewhere in this country. As this book explains, the terrorist network responsible for the World Trade Center bombing reaches far beyond the handful of perpetrators who were caught in New York.

With this book, Yossef Bodansky has taken a major step toward telling the American people what they need to know — that without their knowledge they have been targeted, that we are hated by those we do not hate, that governments with whom we are willing to live peaceably have decided to be our implacable enemies, have declared a terrorist war on us and have begun to attack. It is especially important for the public to be aware of this situation because civilians are the preferred targets of terrorism.

Yossef Bodansky's extensive research, his insights and his detailed knowledge of the organizations and individuals involved in this plan to bring America to its knees enable him to trace in impressive detail the progress of these plots. This book reads almost like a thriller as he describes for the first time anywhere, in specific detail, exactly what happened in New York in February and what almost happened there in July — the meticulous preparations, the international control of the operations, who was involved and how, when, where, and why. But it is not fiction, and it is fully documented.

Bodansky makes it clear that New York is not uniquely at risk. Potentially a terrorist operation could have happened anywhere in the country — in California or Pennsylvania or Vermont — and, as he chillingly details, on a smaller scale it already has.

The American public needs to know what is going on and the threats against us. Only when we know what we face can we take wise, appropriate and proper steps to protect ourselves and our families, our communities and our country. This book provides an important, effective and highly knowledgeable warning of things to come. It is, I think, a very important book.

Duncan Hunter (R-CA)
U.S. House of Representatives
Washington, D.C.
October, 1993

Author's Introduction

The bombing of the World Trade Center in February 1993 and the plot to bomb several major targets all over Manhattan on the following Fourth of July were not the work of a small independent group of fanatic malcontents. Rather, they were watershed events in a deliberate long-term plan to wage a Holy War — a *jihad* — by means of terrorism in and against America. The Islamist* terrorist network responsible for these acts is sponsored and controlled by Iran, Sudan, and their allies. For these sponsoring governments, the terrorist operations in New York were instruments of state policy — and will not be the last ones that they will attempt.

This book is the inside story of how that holy war made its appearance on American soil in early 1993. It provides for the first time a picture of the full scope of the entire conspiracy, not only the activities of the terrorists here in America but the actions of the governments that sponsor and direct them.

* Islamists are widely — but incorrectly — referred to as "fundamentalists" in the popular press and media. It must be kept clearly in mind that not all Muslims are Islamists.

In the summer of 1993, after several months of doubt regarding the extent of the terrorist threat in America, the government of the United States finally acknowledged that the recent attacks in New York, both those that were frustrated and those that were carried out, were part of a deliberate, coherent terrorist plot. On August 26, the Islamist Sheikh Umar Abdel-Rahman and fourteen of his followers were indicted in New York for having participated in a conspiracy against the United States since at least 1989. In the words of the indictment, "They all agreed to levy a war of urban terrorism against the United States."

According to the indictment, this conspiracy resulted in the bombing of the World Trade Center on February 26, 1993, and, a few months later, an attempt to carry out a series of lethal bombings of major buildings all over Manhattan. As the conspirators' spiritual leader, Sheikh Abdel-Rahman "provided instruction regarding whether particular acts of terrorism were permissible or forbidden [under Islamic law]." Thus, the indictment asserted, Sheikh Abdel-Rahman was in effect "the leader of the organization with whom others consulted in pursuing and planning bombings, murders and other acts of terrorism."[1]

However, although the indictment did not say so, the terrorist campaign now effectively underway in the United States is more than the result of a conspiracy by a small terrorist circle of followers of a local spiritual leader. By now, it is increasingly clear that the New York conspirators did not operate alone or on their own. The campaign of which they are a part is sponsored by foreign governments and is the calculated result of more than a decade of careful longterm planning and preparation.

Several law enforcement authorities now say publicly that "a foreign government or international terror organization was behind the World Trade Center bombing and the plot to blow up New York."[2] According to one senior Egyptian official, Egyptian intelligence views the New York Islamist network as part of "an eclectic and international plot" under the centralized control of sponsoring states and involving, among others, "Iranians, Iraqis, and funding from the Muslim Brotherhood organization in Germany."[3]

Despite the FBI's success in heading off the attacks planned for July 4th in New York City, a massive terrorist threat still faces the United States. In assessing that threat, it must be kept in mind that the attacks by Islamist international terrorism are not random and not spontaneous — they are state-controlled. The terrorists conspiring in our midst — and by now there are quite a few thousands of them — are directed and controlled by, and enjoy support from, the intelligence services of several states, hiding behind a shield of deniability. This, of course, makes all the difference concerning the expertise, funds, facilities, organizational structures and specialized assistance available to them and the kind of damage they can do.

It is difficult for most Americans to comprehend the vast size and worldwide extent of the Islamist conspiracy to wage Holy War in and against America, and to do so in the name of religion (as the Islamists interpret it). To a nation for whom religious tolerance is a cherished basic principle, Islamist concepts and motives — including their insistence that America is determined to destroy Islam — seem fantastic and incomprehensible. To most Americans they may seem so incredible that they find it hard to take them seriously.

But now the American public must take them seriously. The explosion that shook the World Trade Center, and the rest of America, was only the beginning, a wakeup call. That bombing and (fortunately thwarted) plans for a series of devastating strikes in New York a few months later are but a prelude to the intended escalation of Islamist terrorism in the United States.

The declared objectives of the Islamist states and their terrorists, dumbfounding as they may be to the average American, convey the magnitude of their implacable rage, hatred and resolve. In the eyes of the Islamists, the American way of life and the very freedoms we most prize and cherish — the personal rights and freedoms of the individual, the pursuit of private happiness and betterment, the separation of church and state — make the United States "the great Satan", their chief enemy. Because our way of life stands in such stark contradiction to the repressive, constricted, authoritarian theocracy the Islamists demand for their own people, the very existence of American values is, for the Islamists, a deadly threat. They even describe it as a deliberate attack on Islam itself. *

* This brief summary is necessarily a simplification of the motives involved in a complex, tortuous,

Having concluded that the West and above all its leader, the United States, is their most deadly enemy, and that America stands between them and the fulfillment of Islam's destiny and the will of Allah, the Islamist terrorist states have embarked on a a jihad — a Holy War on behalf of Islam *as they interpret it* — against the West and especially the United States. They intend to demonstrate their supremacy over the Westernisation they so violently hate, and to bring the "enemies" that thwart them into submission. Their primary strategy is international terrorism. Their troops are the trained, controlled terrorists they have prepared and planted throughout the world in the past dozen years to await activation.

After conducting preliminary campaigns and testing their methods against Muslims who disagree with them and against America and the West in Europe, Asia, Africa and Latin America since the early 1980s — on the streets of Paris, Berlin, Beirut and Buenos Aires, over the skies of Scotland and West Africa — they signaled with the bombing of the World Trade Center in New York that they now intend to wage some of the forthcoming campaigns

vitriolic hate relationship which I have analyzed in considerable detail elsewhere, notably in my earlier book *Target America: Terrorism In The U.S. Today* (S.P.I. Books, 1993) in which I quoted many of their leaders at length. Readers who find it difficult to accept my description of their adamant irrational hatred of America and its intensity will find there a sampling of their many hundreds of official statements in addition to those cited below.

of their jihad on American soil. That was the meaning of the World Trade Center attack. It was, one might say, the terrorist states' version of Pearl Harbor, but conducted in such a way as to be apparent to those they wanted to impress — the Muslim world — while denied and concealed from those they want to lull and confuse: the United States, its law enforcement agencies, and the American people.

The Islamists' rage and determination to confront the hated West is not just the private obsession of a few individual zealots. The present leaders in Tehran, Khartoum and Damascus, who have all bought into the Islamist trend for their own reasons, are convinced that they must prevent, virtually at all cost, the emergence of a post-Cold War world order in which the United States is the sole super-power and in which Western democratic values spread and become the dominant way of life around the world. These states, which control international terrorism today, are committed to a fateful confrontation in which they determined to prevail. They have completed nearly 15 of sophisticated preparations and now they are ready. No effort, no expense is being spared. Since the escalation of the terrorist campaign is their primary weapon against the United States, this has a direct bearing on the intensity and magnitude of Islamist terrorism in America.

In sum, the governments sponsoring international terrorism — Sudan, Syria, and Pakistan, led by Iran — consider it to be an indispensible and primary instrument of state policy. They are determined to gain through the use of terrorism what they cannot possibly achieve through any conventional means of diplomacy and international relations. The plottings and operations of the New York Islamist terrorist network are a classic example of the clandestine terror campaigns through which the Islamists' Holy War is being waged.

This book tells the story of the entire system of Islamist international terrorism *as it applies to the New York case.**

The bombing of the World Trade Center was a logical step in the unfolding of the grand strategy of the leaders of the Islamist trend and their primary agencies. This strategy was formulated several years ago; its objectives have been clearly stated. The New York network that carried out that attack was organized over a period of several years and was meticulously and professionally groomed for its mission. Carrying out that mission was only a question of time.

The book aims to provide a comprehensive picture of the activities of the Islamist terrorists in the New York area, and the role they played in the state-sponsored Holy War. The focus is on the evolution of this particular network from its inception in 1989 and the relationship between its development and the waging of jihad in America. It clearly demonstrates that, committed to the Islamist message, Sheikh Umar Abdel-Rahman and his followers

---

* Other aspects of the Islamist terrorist system, the overall history of its rise and its operations are discussed and analyzed in *Target America*. A full scholarly history and analysis of the Islamist terrorist system is currently in preparation.

knowingly devoted themselves to implementing the
geopolitical strategy of the Islamist sponsoring states
— and that they were under the direct control of
those states, with all major decisions being made
not in New York or New Jersey but in Tehran and
Khartoum.

From the very beginning, the New York Islamist
cell was not merely a willing but an enthusiastic
instrument of the controlling states. In the summer of 1989, the international terrorist networks,
under tight Iranian and Syrian control, began actively preparing for a surge of operations against
America and Americans, including attacks inside
the United States. Over the next two years, intense
preparations were made for this campaign; they
were further intensified following the Gulf Crisis of
1990-91. It was during this period that the New York
network was established and began plotting its "war
of urban terrorism." Sheikh Umar Abdel-Rahman
arrived and took over the network as its spiritual
leader, a unique and specific role that is (as explained below) essential to Islamist terrorist operations.

In early 1992, there was a rapid increase in these
preparations; and in the fall of 1992, a marked escalation in Islamist terrorism, subversion and violence began all over the world. Despite the seemingly different circumstances of these incidents, they
were not isolated cases that just happened to occur
more or less simultaneously. Rather, they were the
first steps in the escalation of the Islamist jihad
against the Judeo-Christian world order. It is therefore neither by accident nor a coincidence that in

1992 Sheikh Umar Abdel-Rahman and his followers intensified their preparations for the series of bombing operations in the New York area, and that by the end of the year, they were poised to strike.

In early 1993, fully aware of the significance and gravity of the escalation it was about to order, Tehran embarked on an intense process of testing its ability to carry out attacks on American soil. The first test came in the form of the killings at the very gates of the CIA in January. Then a major terrorist conference was held in Tehran at which the jihad strategy was studied once more and the green light was given for major operations on American soil.

Within days, the World Trade Center bomb exploded, in effect signalling the beginning of the decisive phase of the Islamists' jihad — when they take on America directly, on its home territory. With the World Trade Center, the state sponsors of terrorism crossed their Rubicon. But their battle is still in its initial phase. We can expect to see a spate of terrorism unleashed throughout the West, and especially in the United States.

The magnitude of the threat should not be underestimated. The states that control terrorism, their agencies, their allies and their protegés have been preparing for this escalation for more than a decade.* Highly professional, skilled terrorist cells and networks are already in place throughout the United States, Canada and Western Europe, ready and waiting only to be activated. These, the operational

* Covered in detail in author's previous book,
  Target America: Terrorism In The U.S. Today

centers of Islamist terrorist organizations based in Lebanon, Sudan, Pakistan and Afghanistan, are being reinforced by supplies and expert terrorists arriving from Iran, Syria and many other countries. The components of Islamist terrorist system including its networks in America, now await orders from Tehran before launching their next operations.

* * *

This book portrays a conspiracy far wider and menacing than that indicated in the indictments handed down in the World Trade Center case or even in the July 4th conspiracy case, but the book is neither a conspiracy theory running wild nor an accusation of ineptitude on the part of the competent authorities of the Federal Government. The discrepancy between the conspiracy indicated in the indictments and that described in this book is a result of the profound difference between the scholarly analyst's truth and the legal truth that can be proven in the courts of the United States under the rules of evidence and other legal restrictions.

Like all defendants in American courts, Sheikh Umar Abdel-Rahman and his followers enjoy full rights to a fair trial in a court of law.

Central among these is the right of the defendant (and his lawyers) to have full access to the material used by the prosecution, including the ability to face and cross-examine the government's witnesses. In cases of national security, including terrorism, the sanctity of the defendants' rights imposes objective limitations on what the prosecution can do and what evidence it can use, and thus may limit the extent of the charges leveled against the defendants. For example, responsible government agencies may know a lot about the alleged crime from highly sensitive intelligence sources they cannot reveal or expose; it is unrealistic to expect the government to identify a highly-placed spy or informant, ending his usefulness and possibly exposing him to danger, merely in order to have him appear in court to support an enhanced or broadened indictment.

Similarly, the government would not want to reveal the extent or specifics of its ability to intercept, decipher and "read" other peoples' communications — legally — by presenting certain intercepts as evidence in the courtroom and subjecting its communications experts to cross examination. (Reportedly, the intelligence services of Israel and Egypt obtained instructions transmitted from Tehran and Khartoum to the Islamist terrorist network in New York. This information was provided to the U.S. Government.)[4]

These and similar higher considerations of national security may prevent the Government from handing such material over to the prosecution for use against the defendants in some cases. The indictments are therefore limited to those violations for which the prosecution is convinced it can present compelling evidence in a court of law. These considerations ultimately determine the extent of the legal truth that can be proven in court.

However, the fact that other matters are not dealt with in court does not mean that there is no overwhelming and compelling information about any other aspects of the issue at hand. Unlike the prosecution in a legal trial, the independent analyst can verify for himself the accuracy and strength of the evidence, drawing on sensitive sources of the kind that cannot be revealed; he can then present it to the readers in a way that will obscure, and thus protect, the sources. The ability to collect, competently analyse, and meticulously verify material is the only restraint on the analyst's truth.

In cases of terrorism, this distinction applies specifically to the vital question of the extent of involvement and responsibility by the terrorist sponsoring states. The analyst can utilize original and independent source material, including documents and written and oral communications with individuals around the world, without being required to expose his sources. He can therefore present a wider and more comprehensive picture and discuss relevant side issues and peripheral aspects of the matter, which the prosecution cannot do in a court of law.

Since Islamist international terrorism is such a dramatic and little-known subject, a note on sources and methodology may be useful. The text is thoroughly source-noted. Whenever possible, published material is identified. The newspapers in the New York metropolitan area published tremendous amounts of material, much of it excellent, about the activities of Sheikh Abdel-Rahman and his followers in the New York area. My thanks to Nathan

Adams, Roving Editor of *The Reader's Digest*, for his help.

Beyond such immediate reports, the book is based for the most part on extensive indigenous material, including a private collection of several thousand Middle Eastern, Iranian, Russian and European books, manuals and articles. In addition, the author draws on a unique private collection of primary sources developed over nearly two decades of intensive research. These include extensive interviews and communications with numerous emigrés, defectors and otherwise involved individuals from Iran, Afghanistan, Pakistan, the Middle East, several countries of sub-Saharan Africa, Latin America, many parts of the former USSR, and most of Europe (both East and West), plus original publications, documents and reports from these and other areas.

This wide range of sources constitutes a unique in-depth data base for expert analysis regarding the conduct of terrorism, subversion, intervention and other involvement, combat operations and power projection capabilities, and other aspects of this problem.

I have been studying subversion, terrorism and unconventional warfare in the Third World for some twenty years. Over such a period one has the opportunity to absorb extensive amounts of material through reading and personal discussions. Ultimately, opinions and conclusions are formulated on the basis of intensive and protracted study of the topic under consideration, plus the cumulative knowledge of related data acquired over such a long period.

Finally, the opinions expressed in this book are mine, and do not necessarily reflect the views of all the members of the House Republican Task Force on Terrorism and Unconventional Warfare, the United States Congress, or any other branch of the U.S. Government.

Washington, D.C.
October, 1993

Chapter 1

COMING TO AMERICA

The bombing of the World Trade Center on February 26, 1993, and the spate of terrorist bombings that were being prepared a few months later for the purpose of turning the Fourth of July into a day of cataclysm for New York City, the United States and the world, were the result of lengthy preparations by a terrorist network operating on behalf of an allied group of governments.

The declared objective of these sponsoring states, led by Iran, was to wage their Holy War inside America.

The alleged perpetrators were their loyal troops whose spiritual leader is a general in this Holy War.

The perpetrators and conspirators involved in the various terrorist bombings and attempted bombings that took place in New York in 1993 were members of several cells which, together with a myriad of other components around the world, constituted a single Islamist terrorist network. The establishment of this network, and its further development into an international web of cells, has been the essence of a conspiracy among the involved govern-

ments and their agents — primary among them Iran
— to wage a Holy War in and against America in
the form of international terrorism.

The origins of the specific Islamist terrorist network units that operated in New York in 1993 can
be traced back to 1989. By the time it sprang into
action four years later, this was a cohesive, veteran
network that had devoted a lot of time and effort
to operational preparations and the acquisition of
professional capabilities. The bombings — both
those carried out and those attempted but foiled —
were not the amateurish operations of a few disgruntled individuals. Like all expert terrorist networks operating in the West, the New York unit was
the agency of sponsoring governments. The activation of the key elements of this network, and the
beginning of the process that would culminate in
their bombing operations in 1993, was the result
of a decision made thousands of miles away in Iran.

BACKGROUND — IRAN SETS THE COURSE

Tehran in the summer of 1989 was a city in the
midst of a major crisis, a turning point in the history of modern Iran. The country had just emerged
from the bitter and costly war with Iraq, accepting
a ceasefire that the Ayatollah Ruhollah Khomeyni
called "worse than drinking hemlock."[1] The Iranian
economy was in ruins and the standard of living
continued to collapse. Meanwhile, the Arab world
was already going through the first phases of a

distinctive new wave of pan-Arabism that was to culminate disastrously in the Gulf War of 1991. Many conservative Arab states already recognised the importance of America and the West to their own security and survival; Tehran, however, considered American regional influence detrimental to its national security and vital interests.

The crisis in Tehran was compounded by the death of Iran's spiritual leader, the Ayatollah Ruhollah Khomeyni, on June 3, 1989. His death was hardly unexpected. He was in his nineties and his health was failing for several months during which intense power struggles over the succession were going on among his followers. Nevertheless, the shock and uncertainty that were brought to the fore by his death reinforced in the minds of the mullahs in power in Tehran the need to demonstrate their loyalty to his message. Khomeyni was the Imam, a unique religious position to which they could not lay claim. But it was imperative for the mullahs to consolidate their hold on power in Tehran by proving their legitimacy as heirs to his authority as undisputed leader of the global Islamic Revolution.

For Tehran, terrorism is a primary instrument of state policy. The mullahs consider their control over such organizations as the Lebanon-based *HizbAllah* — "The Party of God" — to be a national strategic asset. With Iran in a shambles and no improvement in sight, the spectacular resumption of its all-out jihad against the Great Satan, the United States, seemed the most effective and expedient way to restore the regime and revive the public's Islamic revolutionary spirit.

Therefore it was imperative for Tehran to begin a terrorist campaign against the U.S., preferably in America itself. Such a campaign would accomplish two major tasks:

It would demonstrate in a convincing though symbolic way the supremacy of Khomeyni's Islamist way over "Westoxication" — their term for Western influence; and it would evict American power from the Middle East, enabling Iran to assert itself as the dominant regional power Tehran is convinced it deserves to be.

The mullahs in Tehran were convinced that terrorism in America would accomplish both objectives by terrorizing Washington into disengaging from the Middle East and convincing the Arab powers in the region to submit to Iranian hegemony.

The mullahs in Tehran had reasons to be confident that they could carry out such an ambitious campaign and get away with it. After all, Tehran had just completed two major terrorist strikes against the United States: the mid-air explosion of Pan-Am flight 103 over Locherbie, Scotland, on December 21, 1988, and, in San Diego, California, on March 10, 1989, the fire-bombing of a van driven by Sharon Lee Rogers, wife of the captain of the USS*Vincennes* who had mistakenly shot down the Iranian Airbus commercial flight in July 1988.

Both terrorist strikes were highly demanding professionally, each in its own way. Moreover, both were the result of crises. Tehran was very happy with results, even though neither operation was trouble free.

Although it was a minute operation in scale, the

fire-bombing of Mrs. Rogers' van on American soil was more important for future operations inside the United States itself. Because of the identity of the intended victim, there was never any doubt that Iran was responsible for the bomb in San Diego. A pipe-bomb exploded under Mrs. Rogers's van; luckily she escaped injury but the van burned completely.[2] The clear message of this attack was that Iran was capable of locating one particular woman in the United States, clandestinely placing a bomb in her van, and completing the operation safely.

The bomb itself was a simple pipe-bomb; if expertly placed, it would have created a secondary explosion with enhanced fire. It had an intriguing fuse that was activated by the gradual heating of the van's exhaust pipe as the car was driven. However, apparently the bomb was not properly placed under the van because, although a secondary fire erupted, it did not have the desired effect and Mrs. Rogers survived.[3]

These details are important for understanding the Iranian approach to conducting terrorist strikes in the United States.

Because of its emotional commitment to revenge for the downing of the Airbus, Tehran could not avoid attacking Mrs. Rogers, but Iran's leaders had no doubt that Iranian responsibility for the attack would be clear. Therefore, Tehran decided to reduce the risk to its terrorist and intelligence networks in the United States as much as possible by conducting the operation with a simple, locally-made device that could be used by local low-quality assets. If these perpetrators were caught by the police, they were expendable. In the event, no one was caught; and while the bomb itself may have been crude, the fact that law enforcement agencies still know virtually nothing about the perpetrators testifies to the excellent quality of the Iranian network.

In any case, because of its direct link to Iranian policy, this incident crossed a threshhold of Iranian terrorism on American soil.[4] Once it was decided that Iran would have to deliver a revenge attack on Mrs. Rogers in California, there was no doubt in Tehran that such a major threshhold would be crossed and that, once crossed, there would be no way back from it. Therefore Tehran markedly accelerated its preparations for the launch of a protracted terrorist campaign in America.

During the first months of 1989, Iranian leaders thoroughly studied their terrorist policy, grappling with the challenges ahead and the entire question of a massive outbreak of international terrorism in America. By then Iran already possessed a sophisticated professional international network for political subversion and armed terror. This network, tightly controlled by President Ali Akbar Hashemi-Rafsanjani, Ali Fallahiyan (the head of Iran's intelligence service), and Muhsin Reza'i (the commander of the Islamic Revolutionary Guard Corps, the IRGC), remain at Tehran's disposal for every objective at whatever time and place it decides to act. Tehran would dictate the character of their terrorists' operations.[5]

While re-examining their policy and their options, Iranian leaders simultaneously began raising the level of their calls for the use of terrorism in, and threats to, America and Americans. President Hashemi-Rafsanjani urged the widespread killing of Americans instead of Israelis because they were more readily available: "the Americans are scattered around the world, they are everywhere."[6] Sayyid Hassan Nasrallah of the Iranian-created HizbAllah in Lebanon declared the organization's commitment to "satisfy the desire of our Imam [Khomeyni] by announcing the beginning of a real war against the United States."[7] In his first major speech after Khomeyni's death, Ayatollah Ali Khamene'i, Iran's new spiritual leader, reiterated Tehran's commitment to the use of force as a primary instrument of international politics, on the grounds that "Our enemies, including the criminal United States, do not understand [anything] but the language of power, and nothing will prevent them from continuing their plots."[8]

The mullahs in Tehran were fully aware of the crucial importance and far-reaching ramifications of their decision to expand terrorism into the United States. Therefore, between July and October 1989, they conducted a series of high-level consultations with their Syrian allies and the entire range of Islamist terrorist organizations — the HizbAllah, Islamic Jihad, and a host of Palestinian terrorist organizations. These meetings dealt with a wide array of strategic and operational matters, ranging from the situation in the Middle East (especially Lebanon) to the question of escalating terrorist activity throughout the world.[9] Sheikh Muhammad Hussein Fadlallah, the spiritual leader of the HizbAllah, hailed "the consolidation of relations between Islamic movements" because "that Islamic movement should be strong vis-á-vis the United States, Zionism, and world arrogance."[10]

One of Tehran's first decisions was to assign Hojjat ol-Islam Ali Akbar Mohtashemi, who had just been named head of the Defense and Islamic Revolutionary Guard Corps Committee in the *Majlis*, the Iranian Parliament, as the inspector of the preparations for escalating the anti-American terrorist campaign in July 1989. The choice of Mohtashemi was in itself a clear indication of how serious Tehran was: since the early 1980s, he had been instrumental in the establishment of the Iranian-controlled terrorist system and in running a series of spectacular terrorist operations all over the world.

Ali Akbar Mohtashemi was born in Tehran in 1946 to a *Sayyid* family (direct decendants of the Prophet Muhammad) that was involved in religious politics. From a very early age, he was one of the Ayatollah Khomeyni's special protegés among his students in Qum. In the early 1960s, when he was hardly into his teens, he was already serving Khomeyni as a confidential courier, delivering messages between the Ayatollah and other revolutionary conspirators. In 1966 he was finally arrested by the SAVAK, the Shah's secret police, but he escaped to join Khomeyni in Iraq. In the 1970s, Mohtashemi received training in a variety of terrorist and clandestine techniques and was actively involved in the establishment of the Shi'ite terrorist network all over the Middle East. He played an important role in the overthrow of the Shah and the seizure of the American embassy in Tehran in 1979.

Mohtashemi, who has been elevated to the rank of Hojjat-ol-Islam, has demonstrated his true capabilities since the early 1980s, backed by the powers of the Islamic Republic of Iran. First he became Iran's ambassador to Damascus, where he was instrumental in consolidating the Iranian-Syrian alliance and establishing the HizbAllah and other militant terrorist organizations. He was in charge of the series of attacks on Americans in Beirut, including the devastating 1983 suicide bombings of the American Embassy and the Marines' barracks that killed hundreds, as well as the kidnapping and assassination of individual Americans.

In February 1984 Mohtashemi was wounded when a booby-trapped Koran sent to him exploded, damaging his ear, his right hand and parts of his left hand. He was sent to Germany for a lengthy treatment. When he returned to Tehran, a grateful Khomeyni named him Minister of Interior, giving him control of the country's secret police, the SAVAMA. In that capacity, Mohtashemi played a major role in expanding the vast terrorist training infrastructure in Iran, as well as in the series of spectacular terrorist operations in the mid- and late 1980s — the hijackings of several airliners, the bombings in Paris, and the destruction of Pan Am flight 103, among others. In July 1989, Mohtashemi was named head of the Defense and Islamic Revolutionary Guard Corps Committee in the Majlis, so that he could concentrate on terrorism while retaining the semblance of deniability for the Hashemi-Rafsanjani government.[11]

In early August 1989, immediately after he

assumed responsibility for American operations, Mohtashemi indicated that Iran and its allies already had the capacity to strike the United States, emphasizing that Khomeyni "always had attacking-offensive attitude toward the U.S." and using the convoluted rhetoric of the Islamists: "Throughout the world there are many HizbAllah cells that [were] established by the Imam's holy breath and they carry the banner of death of the superpower and global arrogance." He claimed that there were thousands of volunteers for martyrdom ready for attacks on and in America.[12]

Similarly, Hojjat ol-Islam Muhammad Mussavi-Kho'iniha, another key practitioner of Iran's clandestine terrorist war and a close ally of Mohtashemi, stressed the importance of the forthcoming struggle against the United States. In a major sermon on Khomeyni's tomb on *Ashura*, for Shi'ites the holiest and most emotional day of the year, he emphasized the centrality of the struggle against America, defining it as a key element of Khomeyni's legacy and the enduring source of the legitimacy of the regime in Tehran. "There is no doubt that one of the valuable legacies of this [Khomeyni's] revolution has been the profound and extensively worldwide confrontation with the global arrogance, especially the United States." Mussavi-Kho'iniha stressed that Tehran was leading a universal Holy War, not just an Iranian one. "If an authority in contemporary history has managed to mobilize for a revolution an *ummah* [the entire Muslim community, seen as a single nation] — not the Iranian nation, but the Islamic *ummah* throughout the world

— against ... arrogance, it has been [because of] the authority of the Islamic revolution of Iran, which, thanks be to Allah, still continues today."[13]

Tehran and its allies decided that the major escalation of the terrorist campaign, especially within the United States, would be conducted in the guise of the HizbAllah and numerous Islamic Jihad organizations. Therefore, in accordance with the resolutions of the various terrorist conferences, an intense effort went into improving the professional abilities and expertise of the elite terrorists from these organizations who were being readied in the Bekaa region of Syrian-controlled Lebanon.

Once Tehran had formulated and decided on the strategy for the terrorist offensive, it was imperative to inspect the terrorist facilities and assess the organizations' abilities to carry out the planned surge. In late October 1989, Mohtashemi led an important delegation on an inspection tour of the garrisons and training of HizbAllah and Islamist terrorist forces in eastern Lebanon. Afterwards he outlined the Islamists' objectives in a speech:

"We must remove the roots of America and Israel from our countries. We must strike them in their very home because it is our legal mission," Mohtashemi declared. "Our jihad will continue until the oppressed people rule themselves all over the world." The Islamist terrorist struggle would escalate throughout the world and especially inside the United States. "The HizbAllah," he said, "now has nuclei in Islamic and non-Islamic countries, even in the heart of America, instilling fear in the ranks of the enemies of Islam, " and the highly committed and trained *Hizbollahhi* [members of HizbAllah] in Lebanon were the Islamist revolution's chief weapon. "With this weapon we can accomplish great achievements in the future," he concluded.[14]

At the same time official Tehran was proclaiming the universality of a jihad against America for the entire Mulsim world, it was also identifying jihad as a key element of Iranian policy and strategy. "In addition to the fact that the nations of the world regard the Islamic Revolution as a pattern to follow, the *HizbAllah Ummah* * of Iran has proven that in the struggle against arrogance it is able to take praiseworthy steps ... The West, and especially world-devouring America, should know that the brave Iranian nation will continue the Imam's path to annihilate arrogance from the world under the leadership of Ayatollah Khamene'i."[15] In December 1989, the Iranian-controlled HizbAllah duly issued a statement reiterating its commitment to this policy: "We are America's arch enemies. We view Washington's arrogant policy as one of self-interests, seeking to exploit peoples and intervene in their internal affairs... We confront this policy forcefully and firmly."[16]

---

* The totality of the followers of HizbAllah, so defined as to include, for example, the entire population of Iran.

THEIR ARRIVAAL IN THE U.S.

With the preparations in the Middle East essentially completed, the time arrived to notify the terrorist "sleeper" networks in the United States about the imminent escalation in activity there, and particularly about their role in it. The anticipated campaign would be a longterm professional effort, and was expected to result in numerous spectacular operations of strategic importance. It was in the context of these initial activities that three individuals who would play central roles in the New York operations, especially the 1993 bombing and attempted bombings, first surfaced together.

The crucial significance of the message from Tehran required that it be delivered in a special setting, and so it was. The terrorist masters decided to capitalise on the growing Islamist activism in the U.S. and take advantage of the gathering of thousands of Islamist activists for a conference of the Islamic Committee for Palestine held in Chicago on December 22-25, 1989, at which the important guest speakers were some twenty leaders of militant (i.e., terrorist) movements in Islam throughout the Middle East and South Asia.[17]

The vast majority of those attending the Chicago conference were devout Muslims deeply concerned about the plight of their brethren in the Middle East. Their presence and participation in the conference were entirely proper, legitimate and legal. However, concealed among them were a few hundred Islamist militants already secretly involved in terrorist-related activities. They and the numerous senior terrorist leaders who arrived as guests from the Middle East used the opportunity to meet in Chicago to discuss the decisions taken at the terrorist conferences of the previous summer and fall in Tehran, and especially go over the anticipated role of the clandestine networks in the United States.

The formal theme of the Chicago conference was "Palestine, the Intifada and the Horizons of the Islamic Renaissance." The guest speakers discussed the role of the Islamic *ummah* [nation] in the struggle "to find a light in this darkness" — that is, in the West and especially in American society — as well as emerging trends in the "Islamic strategy for confrontation" with the West.[18] The conference chairman, Sami ar-Rayan, discussed the impact of the Palestinian intifada on the Islamist community in America. "It [the intifada] should not be erroneously understood as a separate and unique event," he said. "It is part and parcel of [the] Islamic reawakening and renaissance that is fast becoming a world-wide phenomenon."[19]

Probably the most important guest at the conference was Sheikh Abd-al-Aziz Awdah (whose name is spelled "Abdul Azziz Odah" in conference literature), one of the prominent militant leaders of Islamic Jihad in the Gaza strip from 1981 until Israel deported him in 1987 for terrorist activities. Since then, he had been engaged in coordinating terrorist operations with Iran, the HizbAllah and such Palestinian terrorist leaders as Ahmad Jibril and Abu-Mussa.[20] At the Chicago conference, Awdah discussed the urgent need to destroy Israel as the starting point for a jihad against the West. Israel, he explained to his audience, is "the evil Zionist multifaceted dagger in the heart of Muslim lands. The hideous instrument of tyranny is a problem for all Muslims. This dagger serves as the frontline of confrontation between Islam and the ideological, social, political, cultural and economic aspects of the non-Islamic West." He equated the "struggle" between the West and Islam with "a confrontation between evil and falsehood and ... truth and justice."[21]

The importance of Sheikh Awdah in the Islamist terrorist movement goes beyond his role as a senior Islamic Jihad leader from Gaza, as evidenced by his theological writings about the role of Iran in the Sunni Islamist (and especially Palestinian) revolutionary armed movement. He has made a significant effort to bridge the ancient hostility between the Sunni and Shi'ite factions of Islam, at least among the Islamist and terrorist movements. As early as August 1987, Sheikh Awdah provided the most authoritative statement on the growing alienation between the established Palestinian terrorist movements — primarily the PLO — and the traditional Muslim Brotherhood (the *Ikhwan*), among themselves and with Islamic Jihad, attributing it primarily to the hostile relationship between these organizations and Iran.

"We [Islamic Jihad] do not accept the slogan that the PLO's basic faction has raised with regard to non-interference in the internal affairs of Arab nations. We regard the [non-Islamist] Arab regimes and rulers as having blessed the backwardness and defeat in the Arab world. We do not accept the truce with them. We believe that the Palestinian Revolution is the most important and most active national liberation movement in the region, and that this revolution must strengthen its alliances with the Iranian Revolution, the true ally of this revolution. Despite that, we see the Palestinian Revolution, as well as the Muslim Brotherhood, attacking the Iranian Revolution. Our political and ideological differences with the PLO do not justify the use of violence against the nationalist forces. We respect the viewpoint of the basic factions of all nationalist forces, because we believe in dialogue as the only means to reach a mutual understanding. Our main dispute is with the Israeli occupation."[22]

Concurrently, the ideology of Islamic Jihad was evolving distinctly in formulations that strikingly resembled Iranian ideology.[23] Sheikh Awdah described the Iranian Revolution as a model and precedent for Islamic Jihad to follow. "The Iranian Revolution is a serious and important attempt to achieve Islamic awakening. Iran is now trying to unify the Islamic *ummah*, that is unification between the Sunni and Shi'ite *madhhabs*.* "[24]

He was one of the first Sunni Islamists to accept and endorse the Iranian principles of international terrorism, including the disregard for human life and, especially, the legitimacy of suicide ("martyr-

---

* A *madhhab* is a school of thought, denomination, or sect. The main division within Islam is the profoundly bitter schism between the majority Sunni and minority Shi'a sects, which dates back to the 7th century and concerns the essential question of religious legitimacy.

dom") operations. Sheikh Awdah waved off fatalities among his followers by declaring them "martyrs" who "will go straight to paradise and and their sins will be forgiven as a matter of course."[25] It was at his insistence that the Palestinian Islamic Jihad adopted these principles and was fully integrated into the Iranian international terrorist system as early as 1988. On the eve of the Gulf Crisis, six months after his return from Chicago, Awdah played a major role in the preparations for the planned Iran-led terrorist campaign.

The arrangements concerning terrorism had been thoroughly thought out in Tehran. In late May — early June 1990, Tehran convened a major conference of Islamist terrorist leaders to assess their future course. Key participants included the most senior and important HizbAllah leadership from Lebanon. Several Palestinian delegations from Syrian-controlled organizations were headed by senior commanders. Key members of various Palestinian Islamic Jihad factions — notably Awdah, Sheikh Asa'ad Bayud al-Tamimi and Fathi al-Shqaqi — participated, as did representatives of Islamist terrorist organizations in Egypt, Thailand and Indian Kashmir.[26] The conference focussed on the coordination of future methods of operations among terrorist groups throughout the world.[27]

When the conference ended, a few of the Palestinian terrorist leaders most loyal to Tehran, including Tamimi, Awdah and Shqaqi, stayed on for a series of discussions with senior Iranian officials.[28] In a key strategy formulation meeting with Khamene'i, they defined "the struggles of the

Islamic republic of Iran against global arrogance, especially the Great Satan, the United States, and its illegitimate child, Israel, as a strategic posture." They once again repeated that "waging a jihad and moving along the path of Allah are the foundational elements of the Islamic revolution" and committed their respective organizations to a further escalation of their common struggle.[29] During the Gulf Crisis that erupted when Iraq invaded Kuwait three months later, Sheikh Awdah took part in several more conferences in Iran and elsewhere to formulate terrorist strategy.[30]

In the wake of the American-led defeat of Iraq, there was widespread recognition among Islamists that the only way they could realize their goals was by uniting behind Iranian leadership. The effort to achieve that unity led to the establishment of the Armed Islamist Movement [AIM] whose senior representative in the United States is Sheikh Umar Abdel-Rahman, who is now under indictment in New York.

In August 1991, Sheikh Awdah explained that "the Intifadah [is] a step on the road to a total jihad for the liberation of Palestine, but it requires support and assistance from [all] the Islamic forces — and first and foremost, Iran." He called for universal and united Islamic participation on the grounds that the Intifadah is the vanguard of "the struggle conducted between the Muslims and the Christian West and the Judeo-Christian alliance."[31] In order to further increase their political power, the Islamists of all parties established the Islamic Action Front as a single political bloc of all Islamists in

Jordan.[32] Awdah was instrumental in its formation, and since then he has been a key participant in virtually all of the Iranian-sponsored terrorist conferences and high-level consultations.[33]

On January 3, 1990, at New York's Kennedy Airport on his way home from the Chicago conference, Sheikh Abd-al-Aziz Awdah had met with three local Islamists named El Sayyid Nossair, Mahmud Abouhalima and Clement Rodney Hampton-El. He had earlier had a telephone conversation with Nossair.

At the very least, this meeting indicates that the Islamists in New York were already important enough for a senior terrorist commander like Awdah to talk to them on the phone and then meet with them. Although in August 1993 U.S. officials would still be suggesting that Sheikh Abd-al-Aziz Awdah ("Abd al-Aziz Uda" in their spelling) was not in himself an individual of overriding importance, they would acknowledge that the airport meeting in 1990 confirmed that the three local participants knew each other, and that the meeting therefore served as an indication of the possible beginning of a conspiracy that resulted in the assassination of Rabbi Meir Kahane later in 1990 and the bombings and attempted bombings in New York in 1993.[34]

In fact, however, the January 1990 meeting is of far greater importance than that for an understanding of the New York network. The meeting points to the existence of direct contacts and a relationship between key members of the New York Islamist network and the highest leadership of the Iranian-sponsored Islamic Jihad as early as late 1989.

Moreover, the timing is not insignificant.

The meeting took place just after Tehran committed itself to the launching of a terrorist campaign in the United States, to be carried out by the HizbAllah and local Islamists. The pattern of contemporary Iranian-controlled operations was already sophisticated and characteristic of modern intelligence services. Local Islamists would carry out uncomplicated attacks and would gather the intelligence required for any complicated operations, which would then be executed by professionals who would arrive from abroad especially for that purpose.[35]

Thus, Sheikh Awdah's meeting with Nossair, Abouhalima and Hampton-El after the Chicago Conference must have taken place in the context of Sheikh Awdah's overall mission to the United States, which was to promote Sunni participation in the conduct of an Islamist jihad called for by Shi'ite Iran.

The Islamists from New York were devout Sunnis and followers of radical Islam derived from the teachings of the (Sunni) Muslim Brotherhood. For them to take part in terrorist operations sponsored and controlled by Iran, they would have to be totally and completely convinced that such cooperation, including the possibility of suicide operations, would not contradict the teachings of Islam. Sheikh Awdah, one of the leading advocates of the compatibility between Khomeynist doctrine and Sunni Islamism in the context of waging jihad through terrorism, was therefore the ideal leader to convince the New York Islamists of the righteousness of cooperating with Tehran.

As further evidence, the fact that all three participants in that January 1990 meeting with Sheikh Awdah would soon emerge as prominent members of the New York area Islamist terrorist network inescapably indicates their early involvement with the Iranian-sponsored Islamic Jihad movement.

And indeed, as of early 1990, the New York Islamists, then led by Nossair, began operating in accordance with the Iranian guidelines for local cells. They began collecting general material about possible sites for sabotage in New York and Washington. By the fall of 1990, Nossair had already accumulated, just in his own apartment, 50 boxes of relevant documents in Arabic and several pictures of potential sites for sabotage. His papers included bomb formulas, diagrams of possible bomb placement sites, and design for bombs. This material provides evidence that consideration of, and preparations for, bombing of key sites in New York and Washington were being actively studied and considered as early as 1990.

It is worth noting that one of the sites being checked out was the World Trade Center. As Nossair wrote in his own notes, he and his friends wanted to "blow up their [Americans'] edifices."[36] As one law enforcement official said in the summer of 1993, the material seized from Nossair "described major conspiracies and provided a road map to the bombing of the World Trade Center and subsequent plot."[37]

INITIAL CAPABILITIES

But in 1989, Nossair, Abouhalima, and Hampton-El were not the only Islamist would-be terrorists active in the United States. In the late 1980s, Iran was already the undisputed leader of international terrorism in the United States and Canada. The Iranian commitment to conducting terrorist operations in America should not be minimized because of the prudence and patience with which the terrorism and intelligence experts in Tehran would examine, test and carefully study every aspect of this campaign.

Thus, by early 1989, the Iranian network in America was the most comprehensive, solid, secure, capable and therefore dangerous of all local terrorist networks. The desirable ratio of local Islamists and dormant expert terrorists inserted and in place had already been achieved. A comprehensive support infrastructure manned by dedicated individuals had already been functioning for several years.

Several dozen trained, expert terrorists were clandestinely deployed and ready to strike inside the United States. A few hundred of the militant Iranian students in the U.S. were organized to assist them or participate in operations: among the population of 30,000 Iranian students alone, Iran could count on some 1,000 militants to help.[38] A network of perfectly legal social service organizations, societies and foundations handled the flow of funds from, and safe commnications with, Tehran.[39]

Meanwhile, as of the late 1980s, Tehran had

established forward supervision over the Islamist networks as well as future terrorist and special operations in order to directly control and oversee the conduct of the jihad in the United States. Several key associates and disciples of Javad Mansuri, who has transformed much of Iran's diplomatic corps into trained terrorism directors, were posted to key, nominally diplomatic, posts in Iranian embassies from which they can support and expedite terrorism in North America: Muhammad Sadri is in the embassy in Havana while Sayyid Ali Mussavi is in the embassy in Ottawa.[40] Kamal Kharrazi, one of the founders of the IRGC, is Iran's permanent representative to the United Nations in New York[41], while Muhammad Rezah Shalchian (or Chalagian) Tabrizi, operating under the cover of his position as the comptroller of Iran's mission to the U.N., is in fact the senior officer of the IRGC Intelligence responsible for support of, and oversight over, the Islamist terrorist infrastructure in the U.S.[42]

The Iranian diplomatic support staff under diplomatic cover soon received reinforcement when Ali Ahmad Sahlul, a hand-picked loyalist of Sudan's Islamist spiritual leader Hassan al-Turabi, * was named Sudanese ambassador to Ottawa, from where he supervises Islamist operations in the U.S.[43] Sarag al-Din Hamid Youssuf, a.k.a. Siraj Yousif, officially the Counselor of Sudan's Permanent Mission to the United Nations, is in fact Turabi's personal representative and as such the actual head of mission.[44]

---

* Sudan's role in terrorist operations in New York is discussed in detail in Chapter 6 below.

Meanwhile, back in Tehran and Damascus, Mohtashemi and other terrorist experts closely studied the findings and impressions of the terrorist leaders back from the Chicago conference. In the spring of 1990, as the Middle East was rapidly moving toward the Gulf Crisis, Tehran had accelerated its pronouncements that, whatever its position vis-á-vis Iraq, there would be no letdown in the struggle against America, including terrorism on American soil. In March 1990, Mohtashemi, as head of the Defense and IRGC Committee in the Majlis and responsible for terrorism preparations, alluded to the growing cooperation with the American Islamists. "We have potentially big power in other countries," he said. "In the Muslim states and even in Europe and the U.S. our resources are the Muslims who are with the Islamic Revolution. Our enemies are panicked at our power abroad and at the presence of the Islamic Revolution in other lands."[45]

As the crisis in the Middle East was unfolding, Tehran reiterated that "Imam Khomeyni, may his soul be sanctified, the pioneer of the worldwide Islamic revolution, deemed the struggle against the United States the most fundamental objective of the Islamic Revolution since the inception of of the Islamic Movement." Tehran defined its relations with the Washington as "a feud between the greatest enemy of Islam, which tramples on the honor of Muslims and all the oppressed nations in bondage, on the one hand, and the Islamic Revolution, which is a manifestation of the pure Muhammadan-style Islam, on the other."[46]

Ayatollah Khamene'i defined American-Iranian

enmity as fundamental in nature and constituting the very core of Iran's policy and grand strategy. He predicted that, with the deterioration of the global situation, "all the oppressed nations of the world will stand by the Iranian nation and join their anti-U.S. struggle."[47] Mohtashemi renewed his call for action. "The only possible relationship Iran can have with the United States is to attack U.S. interests around the world," he declared. "The struggle against the United States and its illegitimate child Israel is a part of the Imam's political line and Iranian diplomacy must be based on this struggle, as well as holy war against oppression, and not compromise."[48] He stressed that if there should be any attempts to reduce tensions with the United States, "the people and HizbAllah and revolutionary forces will not allow such a thing."[49]

By then, a three-phase long-term Iranian terrorist strategy for operations in America was emerging. It was essentially a precursor of the plan that Iraq would soon attempt during the Gulf Crisis (which failed when Iran decided to withhold its support). The Iranian strategy was based on a gradual escalation of terrorist strikes that aimed at saving and securing their quality assets until the extent and effectiveness of the reaction by the American law enforcement forces were ascertained. The three phases of Iran's long-term terrorist strategy were as follows:

Phase 1: Use of local expendable assets to demonstrate action while creating problems for the local security and law enforcement agencies;

Phase 2: Quality attacks by quality assets who

are already on-site, living off of and gaining operational support from the locally-based dormant ("sleeper") networks;

Phase 3: Spectacular strikes, including suicide attacks, by specially-inserted expert terrorists, designed to demonstrate the global reach of the Iran-led Muslim block and take revenge for the despair of the Muslim world.

Additionally, in order to further reduce the risk to the terrorist infrastructure already in place in the U.S. and Canada, a separate terrorist system was to be introduced with each and every phase, further complicating the ability of the law enforcement agencies to identify a pattern. The three main components of the Iranian-controlled Islamist terrorist system already tested and proven are:

o The Iranian-HizbAllah network, predominently Shi'ite;

o The on-site elite operatives network based on various types of "Afghans";

o The predominantly Sunni Islamist network living off the Islamist community in the United States and Canada and employing local assets, most of them expendable.

At present, virtually all of the components of the system have already been tested and proven in both the first and second phases. This means that Iran's Islamist terrorist system is essentially ready for the escalation into the third phase of the terrorist struggle, that of spectacular strikes.

THE ROLE OF SPIRITUAL LEADER

Americans, accustomed to view the idea of a spiritual leader in terms of high moral principles expressed through ministers, priests and rabbis, are confused by the suggestion that a spiritual guide would, as such, play a key role in the direction of terrorist operations. But this is both feasible and necessary for Islamists.

Islamist terrorists are motivated by their religious zeal to kill both the innocent and themselves — actions which would ordinarily bar them from paradise — for what they believe to be a sacred goal. But traditional Islam forbids suicide. So it is absolutely imperative for each and every one of them that the intended action, an act of terrorism and violence, is religiously decreed to be just and religiously authorized, so that he does not risk his admittance to paradise. For the terrorist, it is absolutely crucial to have assurances from a proper religious authority that the perpetrator's own death in the course of a terrorist operation will make him a martyr, deserving direct entry into paradise.

Therefore it is impossible to overstate the importance of the spiritual leader in the Islamist terrorist system. Without him, these actions cannot be carried out.

In the late 1980s, as the Islamist terrorist system in the United States was gearing up for action, there was no authoritative spiritual leader in America. As a result, a multitude of the doubts and questions were being raised with the occasional visiting leader or during visits to the Middle East. Now, as they prepared to initiate operations in early 1990, Tehran realized that for the Islamist terrorist offensive to be truly effective, it was imperative for the American Islamists to have a spiritual leader on hand to authorize actions.

Enter Sheikh Umar Abdel-Rahman.

The blind sheikh arrived in New York in May 1990. The timing of his arrival could not have been more fortuitous. In retrospect, it is clear that the 1990-91 Gulf Crisis was a milestone in the radicalization of the American Islamist community and the most important catalyst in the Islamists' shift toward active participation in terrorism. This transformation is directly associated with the presence of Sheikh Umar Abdel-Rahman in New York.

Sheikh Umar Abdel-Rahman is uniquely qualified for the demanding task of a spiritual leader for the ambitious Islamist network in America. He was born in 1938 in a small village, al-Gamaliyah, in the Nile Delta. His father was poor, a failing merchant. Abdel-Rahman lost his eyesight to disease before he was one year old. He attended the An-Nur school for the blind in Tanta. Although he had learned Braille, he chose to learn the Koran by heart and still prefers the oral form of expression. He was recognized as brilliant and transferred in quick succession to another school for the blind in Damiat and then to the middle and high schools of the prestigious Al-Azhar University in Cairo.

After graduating from the Foundation of Islam College in Cairo, he was named a village imam by the Egyptian Ministry of Religions; but in 1969 he was fired for his fiery extremist sermons. In September 1970, preaching in one of the mosques in Fayyum, Abdel-Rahman forbade prayers for the soul of President Gamal Abdel Nasser, who had just died, on the grounds that Nasser had been an infidel. For this he was sentenced to eight months in jail.

In 1973, Abdel-Rahman began working at Al-Azhar University in Cairo and in 1977 completed higher theological studies (the equivalent of a Ph.D., hence his title of Dr.). That same year he began teaching and preaching in Saudi Arabia. In 1980 he was expelled and sent back to Egypt as part of the Saudi purge of Islamists in the aftermath of the armed takeover of the Grand Mosque in Mecca. Elevated to the title of sheikh, he was by now considered to be an Islamic authority of the highest level as well as a leading Islamist militant.[50]

Sheikh Dr. Umar Abdel-Rahman, formally the leader of the Islamic Group (*Al-Jama'ah al-Islamiyah*), was behind the growing militancy of the Islamic Jihad devotees in the 1980s. In June 1980, while he was serving on the Al-Azhar faculty in Asyut, the jihadists asked him to become their *mufti* (religious leader). Since the spring of 1981, he has issued a series of *fatwa*s (religious decrees) to the militant youth of the *Jama'at Islamiyah*, assuring them of direct entry to paradise. He also delivered fiery sermons on the importance of jihad against apostate rulers and Christians.[51] In that same spring of 1981, Abdel-Rahman also became the "*amir, mufti,* and *ulama*," a series of religious leadership titles that gave him total responsibility for and power over the *al-Jihad* group. Known for his extremist views and willingness to condone Islamist violence, he is a firm believer in the decree that jihad is a fundamental obligation of all Muslims: his first *fatwa* for the al-Jihad group stated that "it is appropriate to despoil the impious in order to finance the holy war." (This *fatwa* led to a series of extremely violent robberies of rich Coptic Christian merchants and jewelers in the Nag-Hammadi and Cairo.)[52]

Little wonder, therefore, that in October 1981, Khalid al-Istambuli, Anwar Sadat's killer, went to Sheikh Abdel-Rahman to get the spiritual assurances and blessings on the eve of the assassination of the Egyptian president. In order to avoid directly implicating the Sheikh in the murder, Istambuli asked Abdel-Rahman only general questions and Abdel-Rahman gave only general answers:

"Is it lawful to shed the blood of a ruler who does not rule according to God's ordinances?" Istambuli asked. Abdel-Rahman answered that shedding such blood was lawful and permissible. Later in the conversation, Istambuli raised the question of the Sheikh's general opinion concerning Sadat. Had the Sheikh replied that Sadat had become an infidel, that would have justified Sadat's assassination — and fully implicated Abdel-Rahman. But Abdel-Rahman, more sophisticated than in 1970, replied ambiguously, "I cannot say that he has definitely crossed the line into infidelity." The Sheikh then claimed not to know enough to form an opinion — but he went on to elaborate on the criteria according to which a ruler could be declared an infidel, thereby leaving no doubt as to his recommendation while still avoiding stating it explicitly. As Abdel-Rahman intended, this double talk convinced Istambuli that he had religious permission to kill Sadat. It also resulted in Abdel-Rahman's own acquittal in the subsequent murder trial.[53]

However, it was in 1986 that Sheikh Abdel-Rahman would finally rise to international prominence in the Islamist movement. This would come about as a result of Tehran's recognition of his importance. In February 1986, the Iranian Supreme Council held a conference in the former Intercontinental Hotel in Tehran, chaired by Hojjat-ol-Islam Mohammad Raishari, the Minister of Intelligence. One of its primary objectives was to develop "a great plan of action for Europe." The Council came up with specific plans to ship arms and explosives, activate 'dormant' networks and send emissaries responsible for indoctrinating the masses of Muslims now living there. The participants decided on an effort to give their campaign an "all-embracing nature of anti-Western terrorism" that would attract all the groups and organizations already operating in the West. (No matter who claimed them, the subsequent bombings in Europe were in fact largely a result of this conference.)[54]

The resolutions of this Tehran conference were soon translated into intense activity as Islamist leaders all over Western Europe took steps to transform these principles into actual operations. In May 1986, a critical secret four-day meeting took place in the home of Ahmed Ben Bella, the exiled former president of Algeria now living in Lausanne, Switzerland. A veteran of leftist revolutionary and terrorist campaigns, Ben-Bella "has reconverted to Shi'ite militancy since his mystic crisis," namely, his 1983 expulsion from France after a cache of Libyan weapons was found in his home there. (At first he moved into his banker's home in Switzerland, from which several Syrian and Lebanese terrorist operations were coordinated.)

The goal of the May 1986 meeting at Ben Bella's house was to further integrate the diversified activities of radical Islamist movements all over the world. Ben Bella emphasized the importance of his relations with Libya and Iran and reiterated his support for Khomeyni's revolution.[55] Special attention was paid to intensifying the revival of Islam in the Middle East and to expanding radical Islamist activities — i.e., terrorism — in the West, primarily Western Europe. The participants were such high-level figures as Yussuf Nadah, the leader of the International Muslim Brotherhood; Muhammad Shamkh'ani, one of the leaders of the Iranian Revolutionary Guards and intelligence services; Sheikh Muhammad Hassayn Fadlallah, the spiritual leader of Lebanon's HizbAllah; Ga'al Hamasah, one of the leaders of the Muslim Brotherhood in Syria; Salem Azzam, the general secretary of the London-based Islamic Conference; several representatives of Islamist subversive organizations, mainly in the Arab world — and Sheikh Umar Abdel-Rahman, amir and mufti of the Egyptian Islamic Jihad organization.[56]

The primary objective of the conference was to revitalize the Islamic world and escalate "the March of Islam" to the position of global glory and power the Islamist movement believes it deserves. In the mid-1980s radical Islam was on the rise and its leaders were more self-confident and activist than ever before. They concluded that the growing role of young militants within the movement called for the adoption of "the armed struggle" as the primary tool for the resurgence of Islam all over the world. The assembled leaders concluded that Muslims would assume the role of global leadership and domination once they overcame the current obstacles, primarily the apostates in their midst (i.e., the non-Islamist leaders in Muslim countries), and the poisonous influences of the Zionist entity and the corrupting West. The meeting therefore dealt with both problems: cleansing the Islamic world of "apostates" and conditioning the West to embrace its eventual liberation to Islam "by the sword."[57]

For Sheikh Umar Abdel-Rahman, the Lausanne conference was a turning point. For the first time he was exposed to the professional conduct of terrorism, and especially to the Iranian experts and professionals. He was convinced that even though they were Shi'ites, their perception of the jihad and the future of the Muslim world was not different from his. The lavish assistance, both professional and financial, that the Iranians offered for the Islamist revolution in Egypt appealed to him. As a result, in the summer of 1986 the initial working relationships were established between Abdel-Rahman and Iranian intelligence.

It is quite significant that Abdel-Rahman's first visit to the United States, in 1987, was organized by a Chicago-based Shi'ite organization that invited him to lecture at their conference and in their mosques. While in New York, he was introduced to Mustafa Shalabi, a Muslim Brotherhood activist actively involved in support for the Afghan jihad, especially the Islamist causes in Afghanistan and Pakistan in which the Sheikh's Egyptian followers were also involved. Shalabi and Abdel-Rahman were to meet again when the Sheikh moved to New York [58]

Meanwhile, Sheikh Umar Abdel-Rahman remained the leader of the Islamic Group (Al-Jama'a al-Islamiyah) and was thus the driving force behind the growing militancy of the Islamic Jihad devotees. During the 1980s, he concentrated on the Islamist revolt in Egypt. He issued a sweeping *fatwa* authorising and urging the assassination of Egyptian notables, both government officials and intellectuals. He revived his call for armed jihad against apostasy until finally he and more than twenty of his followers were arrested following a fire fight in April 1989.[59] Following Abdel-Rahman's arrest and again on the religious holiday of 'Id al-Idha, members of Islamic Jihad in Cairo continued to demonstrate, clashing with police[60] and demanding the Sheikh's release.[61] Meanwhile, the HizbAllah in Lebanon accused Egypt of torturing the Sheikh and his followers in prison.[62] The Egyptian Islamists accused Cairo of "a government plan in the war against the Islamic trend" and reported mass arrests and torture.[63] Sheikh Abdel-Rahman was released after some weeks, but he and about two dozen of his followers were arrested again almost immediately, after riots against places of entertainment occured in August, a clear violation of the conditions of their release.[64] A day later, Sheikh Abdel-Rahman was released into house arrest; he had served a total of slightly over four months in jail.[65]

Sheikh Umar Abdel-Rahman preached that confrontation with the Egyptian government was inevitable, flatly challenging the Islamic legitimacy and authority of the government's religious bodies, especially the Ministry of Religious Affairs; he even challenged the Muslim Brotherhood on the basis of their participation in political life. He readily admitted that he was "a terrorist and extremist in the cause of Allah and His Prophet's tradition."[66] His late deputy, Dr. Ala Muhyi-al-Din, stressed that *Al-Jihad* "will not retreat from defending honor and [that] which is holy, nor from opposing immorality and forbidden actions, regardless of the sacrifices which that will cost us."[67]

Meanwhile, the growing importance of militant Islamist activism in America and the emerging need to be able to conduct terrorist operations there made it increasingly important for the international Islamist movement to name a senior spiritual authority — that is, a supreme commander — for the American Islamists. Sheikh Umar Abdel-Rahman, the spiritual guide of the most radical branch of Islamic Jihad in Egypt[68] and a Sunni religious authority willing to work closely with Shi'ite Iran, arrived in the United States in May 1990 to fulfill that function.

Within a few months he had established an Islamist center in the Faruq Majid Mosque in Brooklyn and subsequently another one in New Jersey.[69]

Abdel-Rahman's followers in Egypt expected him to organize an anti-American Islamist revolution in Egypt from his place of exile. On the basis of the Iranian precedent, the jihadists see in his absence from Egypt a sign of an escalating revolutionary process: "Has Umar Abdel-Rahman become a new Khomeyni living in a voluntary exile and leading the revolution in Egypt through cassette tapes and the collection of contributions for the revolutionaries?"[70]

The obtaining of an American visa for Abdel-Rahman is indicative of both the importance of his presence in the United States for the Islamist terrorist campaign and the Iranian support he already enjoyed by the spring of 1990. In the late 1980s, Iranian intelligence had infiltrated its operatives into the locally-hired staffs of the visa sections of all major Western and Arab embassies throughout the Third World. One such operative was strategically placed in the consular section of the American Embassy in Khartoum. The moment the agent reported that he would be responsible for checking the consulate's microfiche list of names of those who were to be refused entry, Abdel-Rahman applied for a visa to visit the United States "to preach Ramadhan sermons."

The Sudanese consular clerk who handled Abdel-Rahman's visa request assured the American consular clerk, a CIA officer working in that capacity as an undercover assignment, that he had checked Abdel-Rahman's name against the "watch list" but he had not done so. Told that the list had been checked, the officer/clerk approved the application and Abdel-Rahman received his visa on the spot. He immediately left for America. By the time the mistake was discovered three days later, the Sheikh was already in New York; he had traveled via Pakistan instead of taking the direct flight he had stated he would take.[71]

During the Gulf Crisis, Egyptian Islamists were at the forefront of support for Saddam Hussein. On the eve of the crisis, Sheikh Umar Abdel-Rahman expressed his support for Saddam Hussein, and from his New York base he embarked on a campaign of agitation in Sudan, Pakistan and Iraq.[72] He also continued to agitate in the New York area community and to prepare for an Islamist revolution in Egypt. Several ideologists of Islamic Jihad considered the Gulf Crisis the best opportunity to implement the tenets of their all-Islamic Revolution because the Iraqis were willing to support, further and facilitate all acts of terrorism, including assassinations.[73] However, once Tehran decided against a campaign of international terrorism in support of Iraq, Abdel-Rahman dutifully restrained his followers in the United States.

By now, however, Sheikh Umar Abdel-Rahman had already begun to agitate within the Islamist community in New York, and to play a part in what would be the first major terrorist strike by his new American followers.

Chapter 2

EARLY STEPS

Soon after his arrival in the United States in May 1990, Sheikh Umar Abdel-Rahman began his association with the Masjid al-Salam (al-Salam Mosque) in Jersey City, in addition to his main center at the Abu-Bakr Mosque in Brooklyn. The subsequent, if not consequent, emergence of numerous terrorists from the ranks of his local followers there is a good example of the kind of transformation and manipulation a Muslim community undergoes in the hands of dedicated Islamist religious leadership. Jersey City thus serves as a paradigm of developments in a number of Muslim communities in the U.S. that are currently under the influence of Islamist leadership.

It should be emphasized that Sheikh Abdel-Rahman did not choose this small New Jersey Muslim community by accident. The al-Salam mosque had been established by a Libyan activist, Ibrahim Bakir. The local imam, Shaker el-Sayed, was a staunch supporter and advocate of Islamist causes. Many of the 300 members of the al-Salam community had already been involved in Islamist and Palestinian causes, including support for terrorism.[1]

Abdel Rahman's primary operational center was in Brooklyn where, in the 1980s, Mustafa Shalabi, the young Egyptian the Sheikh had met on his 1987 trip, was actively organizing an Islamist clandestine network, working with several organizations in the Brooklyn Muslim community and later with Sheikh Abdel-Rahman. As early as 1978 Shalabi was a devotee of Sheikh AbdAllah Azzam, a Palestinian Islamist and jihad organizer for the "Afghans"* in Peshawar, Pakistan. Shalabi was persuaded by Azzam to open an American support center for the Afghan jihad. In 1978 (after the communists took over in Afghanistan but before the Soviet invasion), Shalabi established a small center above the al-Faruq Mosque in Brooklyn to help Afghan causes. This soon became the Al-Kifah Center and expanded to seventeen other offices all over the U.S. (which are still active on Islamist issues such as Bosnia).

In 1987, Shalabi came under the additional influence of Sheikh Abdel-Rahman and his theories about the centrality of armed jihad in Islam.[2] As a result, in the late 1980s Shalabi and his Al-Kifah Center were transformed into more than a devoted Islamic charity organization, sending clothes and medicine to Afghan refugees. At Azzam's suggestion, they developed a clandestine side, committed to the furthering of the Islamist jihad in both Af-

---

* Foreign volunteers then in the ranks of the Afghan resistance, who would become the core of the Sunni Islamist terrorist movement.

ghanistan and America. They acquired weapons, night vision goggles, and other personal gear on behalf of Pakistan's Inter-Service Intelligence agency, the ISI. They also financed the travel of more than 200 volunteers, mostly Arabs and black American Muslims, to be trained in Pakistan and, in a few cases, also to fight in Afghanistan. Some of these volunteers would later return to the U.S. as highly trained "Afghans", ready to join the jihad advocated by Shalabi (who had become known among Islamists in America as the "Jihad Leader.")

The Al-Kifah Center provided forged travel documents for the volunteers traveling to and from Afghanistan, Pakistan, and other Islamist countries so there would be no record of their presence and training overseas. Many of these documents were recycled and used by more than one individual to further complicate the ability of any official agencies to track their users. In addition, on a farm purchased in New Jersey, Shalabi organized military training for numerous volunteers, pending their dispatch for additional training in several "Islamic countries." To finance all these activities, Shalabi and his followers were also involved in criminal activities, including the counterfeiting of U.S. dollars.[3]

Shalabi was to become Sheikh Abdel-Rahman's first patron in America.

Until the mid-1980s, the dominant figure in the Jersey City community was Egyptian-born Sultan Ibrahim Al-Gawli, a rich businessman, a PLO agent, a gold smuggler, and the patron of the community. He was the local "fixer": he loaned everybody money, arranged forged drivers' licenses for the illegal emigrants and arranged marriage licenses and certificates for those who needed them, thus buying the trust and support of everybody and especially the young Egyptians. Al-Gawli was also considered the patron of the *Ikhwan* — the Muslim Brotherhood — in New Jersey. He was arrested in December 1985 trying to smuggle weapons out of the country, including six handguns with silencers, 150 lbs. of explosives, 100 fuses, remote control detonators, and additional equipment; these arms were destined for the PLO (which planned to set off a bomb in an important public place in Israel) and the Ikhwan in Egypt (who were going use their share to assassinate President Mubarak).[4]

When he was released from jail in October 1990, al-Gawli returned to Jersey City.

FIRST SHOT

In the late 1980s, the life of the small Islamist community in Jersey City revolved around the Masjid al-Salam. Impoverished young Egyptians, some of them illegal emigrants, constituted the most vibrant element of the community. They grew hostile and bitter at the hardships of their lives and became accustomed to breaking the law just to get by; they were drawn into the fold of the mosque as a friendly haven from a hostile and alien world around them. There they were flooded with Islamist material, both written and recorded, which also served as their main contact with the Egypt they had left behind.

Under such circumstances these young men were extremely susceptible to the Islamist message and especially to its militant call for revenge against the sources of the Believers' plight and misery.[5] Given the right manipulation, they would embark on an avenging jihad of terrorist action.

Egyptian-born El-Sayyid Abdulazziz Nossair was a typical radicalized Islamist operating within, albeit on the fringes of, American Islamist communities. These individuals are pushed into extremism and radicalism that fills them with so much hate and such intense hate that they are willing to commit violence and embrace martyrdom. The growing circulation of their propaganda and agitation materials reflects their growing numbers.

El-Sayyid Abdulazziz Nossair, an emigrant from Port Said, Egypt, was a devout Muslim who could not adjust to America. He arrived in the U.S. legally in July 1981 at the age of 25, became a permanent resident through marriage, and was naturalized in September 1989. Nossair was so frustrated and stressed that he had begun to take a variety of medications. Although he had an engineering degree from an Egyptian university, he was unable to get anything better than a series of odd jobs, essentially manual labor and maintenance work. He blamed his inability to get a good job on a conspiracy against Arabs/Muslims rather than his own inadequacies.[6]

Nossair attended the New Jersey Islamic Center but was never a regular; instead he usually prayed at home and with Islamist friends. Although part of the mosque community, he was essentially a loner.

Nevertheless, Nossair was exposed to, and maintained contacts with, Islamist terrorist elements through his contacts with the New Jersey center. At least one Islamist group that maintained some contacts with other radical Islamist groups in the U.S. and abroad, including the Muslim Brotherhood and militant Islamist groups in Egypt, was associated with the Masjid al-Salam mosque in New Jersey.

Nossair is related to Sultan Ibrahim Al-Gawli, and when Al-Gawli was released from jail on October 6, 1990, he returned to Jersey City and the two spent time together. At the same time, Nossair adopted some habits of clandestine activity that he may have learned through his contacts. He obtained documents using several addresses in New Jersey and Brooklyn. One of the Brooklyn addresses he used was listed in the name of another relative of his, Ibrahim Elgabrowny, who would soon emerge as a leading figure in the New York Islamist terrorist network.[7]

Meanwhile, following his meeting with Sheikh Awdah at Kennedy Airport in January 1990, Nossair began carefully preparing to embark on violent action; specifically, he intended to assassinate a major enemy of Islam. His companions in prayer helped him buy weapons[8] and he acquired several guns, large quantities of ammunition and poison. He accumulated material about militant Islamist groups in Egypt and lists of prominent Jews, finally settling on Rabbi Meir Kahane, the militant leader of the Jewish Defense League and member of the

Israeli parliament; both the weapons and written material were stored in his home. Nossair trained on handguns and AK-47 assault rifles; as early as the summer of 1989, he had received rudimentary small arms training, primarily firing AK-47s on the High Rock Shooting Range in Naugatuck, Connecticut, as part of the program organized by Mustafa Shalabi's Al-Kifah to prepare American volunteers for the jihad in Afghanistan.[9]

Sheikh Umar Abdel-Rahman began preaching in the al-Salam mosque in Jersey City in May 1990, just about the time Nossair was entering the advanced phase of his preparations to kill Rabbi Kahane. By then, Nossair had studied Kahane for a year. He says that Shalabi sent him to see Kahane and claims to have secretly met with him twice, in November 1989 and again a few months before the assassination. Nossair insists that he met with Kahane in order "to talk with him and show that we can live with each other,"[10] but there is no independent evidence to support these claims of conversations (although there is evidence that he was where he said he was). It is more likely that Nossair was casing his intended victim and establishing contacts in order to be able to get closer to his target on the hit day.

While Nossair was influenced by Abdel-Rahman's sermons, he was already well along in his preparations for violent action when the Sheikh arrived in New York. It is not clear whether or not Abdel-Rahman gave Nossair a formal *fatwa* before his killing of Kahane; he may have only blessed him. But to be sure, upon stepping into the New Jersey mosque Sheikh Abdel-Rahman took an Islamist community that was already radicalized to the point of generating a terrorist and over the next two years transformed it into a veritable hub of Islamist militancy. Moreover, the mosques he preached in have become the centers from which his preaching has been disseminated to the rest of the Muslim world.[11]

The assassination of Rabbi Meir Kahane on November 5, 1990,[12] demonstrated dramatically that militant Islamist radicalism already existed in the America and that some believers were ready to strike. Kahane was shot from close range just as he was concluding a lecture at the Marriot East Side Hotel in Manhattan. A man who had been in the audience approached Kahane, who was surrounded and talking to other audience, pulled out a .357 pistol and shot Kahane twice in the neck. The assassin then ran out of the hall, shooting and wounding in the leg a 73-year-old Kahane supporter who tried to block him. Nossair then ran out of the hotel and jumped into a taxi, shouting "Go! Go!" But it seems that he had entered the wrong cab, missing the waiting getaway cab driven by Mahmud Abouhalima, who would later emerge as a key suspect in the World Trade Center bombing. Realizing his mistake and jumping out of the cab, Nossair than ran into, and fired at, Postal Police Officer Carlos Acosta who returned fire and shot him in the neck.[13]

In 1991 Nossair was acquitted of the murder charges but convicted on related assault and gun violations; he is presently doing time in Attica prison in upstate New York.

Irrespective of whether El-Sayyid Abdulazziz Nossair, who was caught on-site, acted alone with a little help from friends (which was the official position originally taken by the prosecution in the case) or whether, as now seems highly likely, he acted on behalf of an Islamist terrorist network,[14] the mere occurrence of assassination was itself indicative of the general circumstances in his community.

Indeed, additional evidence subsequently provided by Mahmud Abouhalima after the World Trade Center bombing more than two years later identified Nossair as being a part of a larger conspiracy in which he himself also took part.[15] (Nossair has acknowledged knowing the three key suspected participants in the World Trade Center bombing, though he has denied participating in any conspiracy leading to the bombing.)[16]

By the time of the Kahane murder, the entire Islamist community was preoccupied with the rapidly escalating crisis in the Middle East. The 1990-91 Gulf Crisis was a milestone in the radicalization of the American Islamist community. It was the most important catalyst in the Islamists' shift toward active participation in terrorism — and this transformation is directly associated with the arrival of Sheikh Umar Abdel-Rahman in New York a few months earlier. The transformation of the Islamist communities associated with Sheikh Umar Abdel-Rahman in New Jersey and Brooklyn since the autumn of 1990 has emerged as a textbook case of Islamist network building and consolidation.

Sheikh Umar Abdel-Rahman spent his first year or so in the United States consolidating his immediate position and establishing secure lines of communications with his support base overseas. He was also involved in the organization of the Khartoum-based Islamist International, in agitating among his followers in Egypt, and in arranging for the dispatch of cassettes of his sermons and other material.

Soon after the Sheikh arrived in the Jersey City mosque he began urging his followers to intensify their collection of material that might prove useful for targeting and planning future terrorist operations. They collected general data on buildings, landmarks, and other potential targets in New York, Washington, and elsewhere. A sample of this material, including instructions in Arabic on bombing criteria and identification of suitable placement points, were found in Nossair's room after he was arrested for the Kahane killing. The material clearly demonstrated that preparations for "major conspiracies" were being made as early as 1990.[17]

Accumulating problems with logistical and financial arrangements and the traffic of "Afghans" and other expert terrorists back into the United States culminated in the March 1991 killing in Brooklyn of Mustafa Shalabi, who had been Sheikh Abdel-Rahman's first patron in the New York community. Indeed, it had been Shalabi who invited Abdel-Rahman to come to the U.S. in 1990 to preach about the jihad.[18]

Mahmud Abouhalima, the taxi driver who would emerge as the Sheikh's confidante and a key player in the World Trade Center bombing, Clement Rodney Hampton-El, and Abdel-Rahman Haggag (who would soon emerge as a key terrorist) are now suspected of having conspired to assassinate Shalabi on behalf of Sheikh Umar Abdel-Rahman.[19] (It was Abouhalima who notified the police that he had discovered Shalabi's body.)[20] Shalabi had to go because he refused to permit funds collected through Al-Kifah for Islamist programs in Afghanistan to be diverted for the support of Islamist terrorism in the U.S.[21] Immediately after his murder, funds began to flow into New York through Al-Kifah, coming from Iran via Germany .[22]

Soon afterwards, a new terrorist support team in which Ibrahim A. Elgabrowny played a central role was organized. Elgabrowny (an Anglicization of his Arabic name, al Jabaruni) a 42-year-old Egyptian-born civil engineer, had worked in New York in the 1980s as a carpenter and general contractor. In late 1990, he quit his job and went on welfare in order to be able to devote himself to the defense of Nossair and other Islamist causes. Soon, however, he was in possession of large sums of money arriving from Islamists in the Arabian peninsula. In the early 1990s he made several trips to Saudi Arabia. He also became the leader of the Abu-Bakr Mosque in Brooklyn, the first center of Sheikh Abdel-Rahman's activities.[23]

Elgabrowny's new support system sustained and oversaw numerous potential recruits for terrorist roles. Several Egyptians who appear to have been veteran Islamist terrorists, both long-term "submarines" * in the U.S. and new arrivals from the Middle

---

* In intelligence jargon, a "submarine" is an agent planted long in advance and living an ordinary life until activated by the commanders.

East, made their way to New Jersey and melted into the sprawling community of young Islamists around the mosques there.[24] Meanwhile, aroused by the Sheikh's sermons and the community's dynamics, many local Islamists gravitated to his inner circle. Having been galvanized by the Gulf Crisis but prevented from acting by decisions in Tehran, the Islamist terrorists were yearning for action. Thus, by mid-1991 Sheikh Abdel-Rahman had established in the New York area a group of devotees fiercely loyal to him, who were ready to both kill and be killed in the name of the jihad he preaches, in exactly the same way he had earlier galvanized his devotees in Egypt.

THE GULF CRISIS AND ITS AFTERMATH

The threat of Islamist terrorist attacks on American soil increased markedly as the Gulf Crisis intensified. Iran and Iraq reached an agreement on launching a terrorist campaign in the context of that crisis.* In that agreement, Tehran insisted on virtual total control over the operations in the U.S. and Canada. During the fall of 1990, the HizbAllah and several other organizations sponsored and controlled by Iran and Syria were making active preparations inside the U.S. to launch a wave of terrorist strikes once the war with Iraq broke out.[25]

The international mobilization against Sunni-

* Discussed in detail in *Target America*.

ruled Iraq had jolted the Sunni Islamist movement all over the world and pushed some of its activists into action. Sheikh Rachid Ghannouchi, the leader of Tunisia's Islamists who had participated in the 1989 Chicago conference, declared that "Today the fight against America is a priority for Islam and Muslims."[26] Sheikh Asa'ad Bayyud al-Tamimi of the Palestinian Islamic Jihad stated that by sending forces to Saudi Arabia, "Bush and Thatcher have revived in the Muslims the spirit of jihad and martyrdom." He then decreed that "if war breaks out against Iraq, we will fight a comprehensive war and ruthlessly transfer the battle to the heart of America and Europe." And significantly, he warned that Islamic Jihad already had the forces to carry out such strikes "within Europe and America."[27]

A delegation of senior Islamist leaders associated with the extremist militant trend of the Muslim Brotherhood, including Sheikh Tamimi's son Yunis al-Tamimi and Muhammad Qutb, the brother of Sayyid Qutb, the Ikhwan's chief ideologue, were in New Jersey when Iraq's invasion of Kuwait occurred at the end of August. As the major speakers at the convention of the Islamic Society of North America, they exhorted their audience to adopt Islamist tenets as the only hope for Islam.[28]

New Jersey proved to be a fertile ground for the Islamists. In late November 1990, the FBI arrested a Kuwaiti-born New Jersey Islamist, Jamal Mohamad Warrayat, for making credible threats to assassinate President Bush and other senior American officials.[29] This was the only recorded act of terrorism on U.S. soil associated with the Gulf Crisis. However, in late 1990 or early 1991, Sheikh Abdel-Rahman did urge one of his followers to assassinate Egyptian President Husni Mubarak.[30] This would be only the first of repeated calls for Mubarak's assassination.

Similarly, the Muslim Brotherhood and the HAMAS organization assumed a harsh anti-U.S. rhetoric. HAMAS announced that because of Washington's general policy, aggravated by the deployment of American forces to the Arabian peninsula, "all the Arab peoples not only harbor resentment and hatred but also disgust" toward the United States: Arab hostility toward the United States, "head of the snake and the Great Satan," is so great that it was difficult to express it through any comparison and not one of the Arab leaders, no matter what they might do, "is capable of eradicating hatred toward the United States from our masses' hearts."[31] The HAMAS decreed that "America [is] the seat of evil in our world" and the struggle against America is the essence of the jihad for the very survival of Islam.[32]

Nevertheless, the Third General Conference of the HAMAS was held in Kansas City, Missouri, in late 1990, under the banner, "Palestine is Islamic from the [Mediterranean] sea to the [Jordan] river." Its declared objective was to tighten and intensify HAMAS's cooperation with the Islamist movement in America. Several senior HAMAS commanders, including Sheikh Jamil Hammami, Dr. Mahmud al-Azhar and Dr. Khalil Kawkah, arrived from the Middle East to attend.[33]

Although only one threatened action is on the

record, the fulminations of the Islamists were not idle threats. Why then did the epidemic of terror operations in America not erupt?

In early 1991, just as Operation Desert Storm was beginning, Tehran decided to disengage from the planned joint terrorist campaign and concentrate instead on furthering Iran's own interests. As a result, terrorist strikes inside the U.S. and Europe by assets controlled by Tehran and Damascus were called off, and without them Iraq was unable to carry out its threats. But in March 1991, once the immediate Gulf Crisis appeared to be over, Hashemi-Rafsanjani ordered the dispatch of several assassination teams to the West, and a few elite teams arrived in Canada.[34] They could and would be used in the United States.

In the aftermath of the Gulf Crisis, Iran resumed concentrating on the consolidation of the Islamist radical block it was leading and on the establishment of a New Islamic World Order. The primary lesson Tehran had drawn from the events in Kuwait and Iraq was that any furthering of its strategic interests would inevitably include a confrontation with the United States. It was therefore imperative to seize the initiative.

In a conference with terrorist leaders convened to formulate strategy for the Muslim world after the Gulf Crisis, Ayatollah Khamene'i explained that "America's presence in the region has brought about a long-term threat to her, which will destroy America." Clearly referring to the hundreds of deaths in the bombing of the American Embassy and the Marines' barracks in Beirut in October

1983, the holding of American hostages, and the kidnapping and murder of two American officials, he said, "The presence of the Americans in this region will cost them considerably more than their presence in Lebanon did."[35]

Sharply criticizing American policy in the Middle East and recommending that Washington had better change its policies soon, Sheikh Fadlallah of the HizbAllah alluded to his organization's ability to operate inside the United States. "We continue to ask those whom we influence not to harm America's internal security," he said, but added, "Isolation is not possible and whoever believes in the estrangement of the Arabs and Islamic world from the West is deluded and not realistic."[36]

THE BEGINNING OF THE SURGE

The period between October 1991 and March 1992 was crucial for the escalation of Islamist terrorism in the United States. During these months Tehran and its allies formulated their long term terrorist strategy in several phases, each marked by important conferences in Tehran. During the same period, the command structure of the Armed Islamist Movement (AIM), the Sunni terrorist international, was being consolidated in Khartoum, capital of the Sudan. Meanwhile, Sheikh Abdel-Rahman, who had now been named as the American-based leader, and his network of devotees began consolidating their own command and control mechanism and their support and logistics infrastructure.[37]

In the fall of 1991, as Tehran was looking ahead to the resumption of clandestine operations inside the United States and reflecting on the progress of the training and placement programs for their intelligence and terrorist operatives, the Iranians openly urged Arabs and South Asians to join the jihad. Ayatollah Abdolkarim Musavi Ardebili called on Muslim zealots to attack American targets throughout the world. "Kuwaitis, Iraqis, Pakistanis, and Iranians should set up resistance cells and endanger [American] interests wherever they are," he told a gathering of students in Tehran; it was a "religious duty" for all Muslims to deprive Americans of security just as they "stripped Muslims of security."[38]

The centrality of the uncompromising struggle against America for the future of Islam was reaffirmed at a Tehran terrorist conference on October 18-22, 1991, where over 400 delegates from between 45 and 60 countries deliberated the strategy characterized by international terrorism for the global jihad against "Pax Americana".[39] Ayatollah Khomeyni's son Ahmad clearly identified the ultimate strategic target of Tehran and its allies — America. He insisted on the inevitability of the battle between Islam and America: "We should realize that the world is hostile toward us only for [our commitment to] Islam. After the fall of Marxism, Islam replaced it; and as long as Islam exists, U.S. hostility exists; and as long as U.S.hostility exists, the struggle exists."[40] Muhsin Reza'i, head of the IRGC, summed up the expectations and intentions of conference participants, predicting, "The Muslims' fury and hatred will burn the heart of Washington some day and America will be responsible for its repercussions."[41]

Two delegations from the United States took part in that conference in Tehran.

One was headed by Muhammad al-Asi, the Sunni Friday prayer leader of the Washington Mosque. He compared the differences between the conferences in Tehran and Madrid (where the American-sponsored "peace process" negotiations between Israel and the Arab states were just beginning) to the difference "between justice [Tehran] and injustice [Madrid]."[42] He vowed to do everything possible to make "American statesmen come to their senses."[43]

The second delegation was headed by 'Abd-ul-'Alim Mussa, the Shi'ite Friday prayer leader of the Mustazafeen [Oppressed] Mosque in Washington, which is associated with Tehran. In an oblique reference to activities in the United States, he urged "the funnelling of all possible support for the intifada in Palestine."[44]

The resolutions of the Tehran conference were soon reported to the American Islamists, using as cover another major conference. The chief recipients of the message would be the militant branches of the Muslim Brotherhood and Islamic Jihad, who were active in the United States. On December 21-26, 1991, a major conference was held in Phoenix, Arizona, under the auspices of the Muslim Youth League and The Islamic Committee for Palestine. Egyptian sources pointed out that Phoenix "was chosen as the venue because it is out of the way and would not attract attention." Some 4,000 concerned young people attended the conference, legally and legitimately. However, the conference was also attended by key leaders of the Islamist terrorist organizations who had come from abroad and at least one hundred domestic Islamist militants, including members of Islamic Jihad. In fact, the conference served as a cover for consultations between the international Islamist terrorist leaders and their commanders in the U.S. The leaders encouraged their militant followers to endure their trials and tribulations in the U.S. patiently and await the order to strike.[45]

TEST IN ARGENTINA

In the winter of 1991-92, Tehran decided that the time was ripe to revive the terrorist assault on America. However, the ever-prudent terrorist masters in Tehran and Damascus were apprehensive about the tight security measures implemented in the United States and throughout the entire West during the Gulf Crisis, when an Iraqi terrorist offensive was expected. They therefore decided to conduct a major test run that would enable them to better read Washington's reaction to what one knowledgeable Iranian called "the jihad crossing the Atlantic."[46] Argentina was selected as the site of the test run in the Western Hemisphere. The Israeli Embassy in Buenos Aires would be the target.

The choice was not random. Argentina has long been a favorite entry point into the Western Hemisphere for both Syria and Iran. Members of the large Lebanese-Syrian emigrant community there have relatives in the Middle East and maintain close direct contact with their homelands. The community includes many followers of the Lebanese Shi'ite leadership, who are available to support the HizbAllah.[47]

The existing supporters in the community were reinforced in the early 1980s by the insertion of numerous operatives prepared for long-term penetration and the consolidation of local Islamist networks. Among them were "Muslims from Argentina" as well as "refugees" from many Muslim countries — Iran, Lebanon, Turkey, Iraq, Pakistan, Syria, and Egypt — who either stayed in Argentina or used it as a transit stop en route to their ultimate destinations in the United States and Canada.[48]

One of these "refugees" was Muhsin Rabbani, a Shi'ite from Tehran who arrived in Buenos Aires in 1983 as a 29-year-old "refugee" but now admits that he was sent to convert Argentines to Islam. Rabbani runs the al-Tawhid mosque and leads a small but fiercely dedicated Islamist network in Buenos Aires which is called the Muslim Brotherhood of Argentina and is loyal to Khomeyni's message. Its members include ten Argentine converts to Islam, one of whom has identified himself as "one of the members of the group who had taken upon himself the goal of destroying the State of Israel."

The group is virtually underground, maintaining what is technically known as virtual clandes-

tine routine. Its first major public action was the
al-Quds [Jerusalem] Day march in March 1992,
which ended in front of the Iranian Embassy. In
his speech, the Iranian cultural attache praised
Anwar Sadat's assassin "as a symbol" for the Argentine group.[49]

Aside from such groups, the very top levels of
the Argentine political establishment are filled with
Syrian emigrés who maintain very close contacts
with their homeland. Many of them exploit their
close relations with the Middle East for "private
ventures." Of importance in this connection is the
"Yoma ring" which, in a major scandal in 1991,
was implicated in widespread drug trafficking and
money-laundering operations.

The ring was led by Amira Yoma, whose older
sister, Zulema, was then married to Carlos Menem,
the President of Argentina. Amira Yoma's husband,
Ibrahim al-Ibrahim, a former colonel in the Syrian
military, played a crucial role in bringing the drugs
and laundered money into Argentina. President
Menem put his brother-in-law al-Ibrahim in charge
of customs at the Ezeiza international airport.
Menem also appointed his wife's younger brother
Karim Yoma, a former low-level Syrian diplomat,
to the post of Undersecretary of Foreign Affairs. In
his official diplomatic capacity Karim used to trans-
port large quantities of cash into Argentina.[50]

A friend and business partner of the Yoma ring
was a Syrian drug and arms smuggler called Monzer
(Mundhir) al-Kassar. He supplied the Lebanese
drugs that the ring was smuggling into Argentina
from Europe (primarily from Spain). The Yomas

arranged for Monzer al-Kassar to receive first an Argentine residency permit and then an Argentine passport.[51]

But Monzer al-Kassar and his brother Ghasam had other important friends besides the Yomas. The brothers are friends and "business" associates of Rifat Assad, dealing with drugs from Lebanon. In the mid-1980s Monzer al-Kassar built his palace in Marbala, Spain, near Rifat's palace. By then the al-Kassar brothers were also deeply involved in providing weapons for Iran and supporting terrorist operations on behalf of Syria. From the 1980s on, Monzer al-Kassar has been believed to be one of the major arms suppliers for Syrian-sponsored Palestinian terrorists in Western Europe. In the fall of 1990, when both of them (but primarily Monzer) were reactivated to support the terrorist effort, the al-Kassar brothers were exposed as the primary traffickers in weapons and explosives from Eastern Europe to Spain for the PLF and the PFLP-SC.[52] (Monzer insists that he is innocent of all the allegations.[53])

In the winter of 1991-92, when Tehran and Damascus decided to proceed with the Israeli Embassy test operation in Buenos Aires, they activated a contingency plan prepared a year earlier for use during the Gulf Crisis. At that time, explosives and specialized equipment like fuses and detonators were smuggled into Argentina by the al-Kassar network, using their easy access through the Ezeiza airport. Additional equipment, especially the new electronic remote control detonators just introduced into operational use by the

HizbAllah, were smuggled into Buenos Aires in early 1992.[54]

Argentine security sources believe that two others were also involved: a Brazilian of Arab descent and a former Argentine military man who had travelled repeatedly to the Middle East since 1990 and had been involved in Gulf War-related terrorist preparations and incidents.[55] These sources would later conclude that the operation "must have been planned abroad with the aid of local planners who provided logistical support."[56] Israeli experts concluded that the operation had been carried out "by HizbAllah terrorists who were assisted by the Iranian Embassy."[57] A German Red Army Faction explosives expert, Andrea Martina Klump, may have assisted in the construction of the car bomb. She arrived in Uruguay only a few days before the explosion, and thus she could have provided the expertise needed by the local Islamic Jihad cell.[58]

The final preparations for the operation began in mid-March 1992. By now an intelligence-gathering and advanced-preparations operation was already well under way. These services were provided by four Pakistanis using the names Muhammad Azam, Muhammad Nawaz, Muhammad Nawaz Chadhary, and Azhar Igbal. They bought an apartment overlooking the Israeli Embassy on 916 Arojjo Street from which they studied the embassy building — and from which the remote-controlled detonator would later be activated. They also purchased at above-price the Ford Fairlane used for the bomb. One of the Pakistanis rode a motorcycle past the embassy at high speed for a last minute check of the operation site a few minutes before the car bomb was blown up .[59]

The car bomb itself was built in accordance with the proven principles of shaped charges used by the Iranian- and Syrian-controlled terrorists since the bombings of the American and French installations in Beirut in 1983. The bomb contained over 100 kilograms of high explosives, made up of a 55-60 kg. charge of hexogene reinforced by other solid plastique elements to enhance blast and fragmentation, as well as fats or wax to ensure the contours of the shaped charge. The charge was so formed as to make the explosion "unencased and directed." It was activated by a remote-controlled electronic detonator; possibly a back-up timer was also installed.[60]

In the early afternoon of March 17, 1992, a Ford Fairlane driven by a white male parked just in front of the Israeli Embassy. Witnesses remembered that the driver stayed in the car, a fact that reduced the alertness of the embassy guards and policemen. Later, nobody remembered seeing him leave the car. Then, shortly after 2:30 p.m. local time, a huge explosion shook central Buenos Aires, causing the collapse of the four-story building and spewing shrapnel and debris across a radius of 500 yards. A cloud of smoke hung over the city.[61] The explosion left thirty people dead and 252 injured.[62]

The driver may have had to stay in the car until the last minute in order to disarm the suspicions of the embassy guards, leading to confusion in the ranks of the terrorists as to whether he survived the operation. Indeed, the first Islamic Jihad communique claiming responsibility for the operation referred to a suicide driver, identifying him as one Abu-Yassir and as an Argentine convert.[63] However, searches at the explosion site showed no evidence of a suicide driver. In all likelihood he was able to escape and simply melted into anonymity in Buenos Aires. The bomb had been activated by remote control from the apartment across the street.[64]

In Buenos Aires, Islamic Jihad claimed responsibility for the bombing, which it called an act of vengeance for Israel's recent killing of HizbAllah leaders in Lebanon.[65] Islamic Jihad in Beirut, however, denied involvement.[66] In Tehran, Ayatollah Ali Akbar Meshkini hailed the success of the terrorists as "a source of pride to an entire nation" and announced that "there will be more" operations of the same kind.[67] In Lebanon, leaders of HizbAllah-affiliated terrorist organizations denied direct involvement but endorsed the operation. Sheikh Hussein al-Mussawi of Lebanon's Islamic Amal, while denying HizbAllah involvement, said,"the Islamic Jihad Organization ... carried out the operation, [and] might have had its own justifiable reasons for doing it."[68] Sheikh Nasrallah, secretary-general of the HizbAllah, also denied the HizbAllah's involvement and any HizbAllah connection with Islamic Jihad.[69] Even though evidence gathered at the explosion site proved that Iran was involved in the Buenos Aires bombing,[70] Tehran consistently denied any involvement and rejected accusations that the Iranian Embassy in Buenos Aires was involved.[71]

EXPEDITING THE TERRORIST EFFORT

Meanwhile, in February 1992, as the preparations for the test run in Buenos Aires were already well under way, Tehran was beginning to feel a sense of urgency in connection with the need to markedly escalate the struggle against the United States. Tehran repeated its assertion that America constituted the greatest threat to the revival of Islam and to Iran. Delivering a Friday sermon in Tehran, Ayatollah Fadlallah of the HizbAllah thundered that "world arrogance, especially America, continues to confront the Islamic revolution and pan-Islamism/all-Islamism in the world, because it considers this movement to be against its interests."[72]

Tehran's views were confirmed and reinforced by Secretary of State James Baker's visit to the newly independent states of former Soviet Central Asia, where he warned the local governments against establishing close ties with Iran. Tehran considered Baker's remarks to be "a declaration of war against [Islam], a blatant effort to interfere in the Islamic countries' internal affairs and one which should be answered with a strong slap in the face by the Islamic nations. How each nation solves its problems and deals with its enemies is something which concerns the nations and their cultures. And this is a terrifying thought for the United States and its henchmen."[73] The Iranian statement contained a less-than-veiled threat to use international terrorism.

Following the killing of a key HizbAllah commander, Sheikh Abbas Mussawi, by Israel on February 16, 1992, the HizbAllah increased its pressure on Tehran to embark on a major campaign of revenge. Indeed, the date of the of the long-planned operation in Buenos Aires may have been changed to meet the need for an act of symbolic revenge.[74] But it was not until early March that Tehran discussed a future terrorist campaign with Sheikh Hassan Nasrallah, the newly-elected Secretary General of the HizbAllah.

In Tehran, Nasrallah stressed the importance of "armed jihad" as the only realistic form of struggle.[75] On March 2, he held lengthy meetings with Maj.Gen. Vahidi, the commander of Iran's al-Quds Forces; senior *Pasdaran* [IRGC] officers, and several senior officals. "To us, the United States is always the Great Satan, for whose destruction we will strive," he told them.[76] The next day, March 3, Nasrallah met with both Hashemi-Rafsanjani, Khamene'i and other Iranian leaders to discuss upgrading the HizbAllah's fight.[77] He was shown "a new plan for the escalation of the armed struggle, not just against Israel, but also against the United States" and was urged by the followers of the Imam's line, most particularly Ahmad Khomeyni and Mohtashemi, to "turn the world into hell for the U.S., Israel and the West."[78]

Apparently what he was shown was a version of the long-term jihad strategy that had been agreed upon in the fall of 1991.

Preparations for the escalation began immediately.

Despite the success of the test run in Buenos

Aires, there remained the lingering question of the real capability of Iran's own operatives and terrorists to operate and survive in the United States itself. The assassination teams sent to Canada back in March 1991[79] were still there or in the U.S., safely concealed. One of these teams would be activated to demonstrate the ability of Iranian assets to operate in the U.S. and provide an example that Tehran and its associates could study.

The Iranians struck around 8:45 or 9:00 on the evening of March 26, 1992, in Franklin Lake, New Jersey. A professional killer approached an Iranian emigré, Mrs. Parivash Rafizadeh, near her suburban home and shot her twice in the abdomen from close range (5-6 feet). The hit was professional. A "cleaned"* .45-semiautomatic was used twice and discarded near the getaway car and the killers disappeared without a trace.

Before 1979, Mrs. Rafizadeh's husband and his brother had been senior officers in SAVAK, the Iranian secret police in the time of the Shah.[80] Tehran did not claim credit for her assassination. It had no need to. It was abundantly clear to all that Iran's long hand had struck with impunity in the very heart of the United States. The safe insertion and escape of the hit men was the confirmation of the effectiveness and professionalism of its American-based networks that Tehran so urgently needed.

Mrs. Rafizadeh's murder took place on the eve of the greatest public demonstrations of the strength

* In police parlance, a "cleaned" weapon is one from which all identification marks have been removed.

and self-confidence of the supporters of the Imam's
Line that had ever been held in the United States
and Canada. March 27, 1992, was declared by
Tehran to be the International Day of *al-Quds* (the
Muslim name for Jerusalem) and the Believers were
urged to publicly demonstrate their commitment
to the Islamic Cause.[81] Demonstrations and marches
were organized by a variety of organizations: the
Muslim Student Association in U.S.& Canada—MSA
(PSG); the Tawhid Association; the Islamic Educa-
tional Development League; and the Malaysian Islamic Society of North America (MISNA). Conferences were held in St. Louis, Washington and several Michigan cities. The most important of these
events were the public demonstrations held in Washington, Ann Arbor and Dearborn, Michigan, and
Montreal and Toronto.

Hundreds of demonstrators paraded through the
center of Washington, shouting Koranic verses and
Islamic HizbAllah slogans in Arabic, carrying
HizbAllah banners and Islamist slogans and pictures of Ayatollah Khomeyni, Sheikh Abbas
Mussawi, and other Iranian and HizbAllah leaders.[82]

Tehran could not, and did not, miss the significance of this show of force right in the center of the
American capital. The preparations for implementing the anti-U.S. struggle strategy were accelerated.
Indeed, in late May 1992, Sheikh Nasrallah of the
HizbAllah anticipated an imminent escalation in
the HizbAllah's struggle to win the soul of Islam.
He vowed that, despite a conspiracy against Islam
controlled and directed by the United States, the

struggle against America and Israel would continue and even escalate .[83]

Now the time was ripe to activate the primary components of the vast and comprehensive Islamist terrorist network. They would soon be tested in action.

Chapter 3

THE FORMATIVE PHASE

The period between October 1991 and March 1992 was crucial for the escalation of Islamist terrorism in America. During these months Tehran and its allies formulated their long-term terrorist strategy in several stages, each starting and concluding with conferences in Tehran.

During the same period, the command structure of the Armed Islamist Movement (AIM), the Sunni terrorist international, was being consolidated in Khartoum, Sudan.

In the United States, Sheikh Abdel-Rahman, who had been appointed as the American-based leader, and his network of devotees began consolidating their own command and control mechanism as well as a widespread support and logistics infrastructure.[1] The New York network resumed its active study of prospective terrorist strikes. In November 1991, Elgabrowny, Emad Salem, and "others" began discussing plans to bomb several buildings and other key sites in the New York area; some of these were the targets that would be earmarked in the summer 1993.[2]

Sheikh Abdel-Rahman did not remain aloof. In late November or early December 1991, he tried again to get one of his followers to assassinate Egypt's President Mubarak, who was scheduled to visit Washington and New York.[3] This would not be the last time Abdel-Rahman would try to have Mubarak assassinated.

Meanwhile, Abdel-Rahman's importance continued to grow with the evolution of Hassan al-Turabi's Popular International Organization [PIO], an umbrella organization of Sunni Islamist organizations worldwide. In late 1991 Turabi, the spiritual leader of Sudan, established a supreme council for the PIO. The movement's top leaders, in addition to Turabi in the Sudan, were Sheikh Umar Abdel-Rahman (for Egypt), Sheikh Rachid Ghannouchi (for Tunisia), and Sheikh Abbas Madani (for Algeria, though he was in jail there). Ghannouchi, living in exile in London, and Umar Abdel-Rahman in New York were appointed as the senior members of the leadership entrusted to act as its representatives abroad, authorised to assign their networks and cells to commit specific terrorist attacks in accordance with a master plan of jihad and agreed-upon priorities and strategy.[4]

Indeed, Abdel-Rahman, Turabi and Ghannouchi were the three Islamist leaders who "personally selected" candidates for extensive training in terrorism and clandestine operations, which includes psychological and Islamic tempering to make them capable of sustaining clandestine operations under conditions of "materialistic Western slavery" without losing their identity and Islamist zeal. Once fully prepared, they would serve as the new commanders of the Islamist jihad in the West.[5]

Between March and December 1992, the now fairly solid Islamist terrorist network in the New York area made its actual preparations for major strikes at the heart of the Great Satan. Initially — at least until the late summer of 1992 — the bulk of the work was done clandestinely by the expert terrorists both in New York and overseas who conducted a survey of potential objectives for the purpose of selecting the targets. Detailed planning such as bomb design followed.

The specific plans were completed in Tehran by experts. It is highly likely that some experts were even sent to New York during the summer and fall to personally inspect the potential targets in order to better design and calculate the type and size of the bombs needed.

They acted in accordance with the main lesson they had learned in a probing operation conducted four years earlier by an operative from the Japanese Red Army: in 1988 Yu Kikumura had demonstrated to Tehran's satisfaction that they could get everything they needed for a major sabotage operation in the United States. There was no need for their operatives to take the risks involved in smuggling in tremendous amounts of explosives, especially the telltale plastique.

THE KIKUMURA CASE

One of the most challenging aspects of any major sabotage operation is the acquisition of large quantities of high explosives, usually hundreds and thousands of pounds, without the knowledge of security and law enforcement agencies.

One way to get them is to steal them. Although commercial explosives such as dynamite of the type used for civil engineering projects can sometimes be stolen in quantity, the acquisition of military-type high explosives is far more difficult. Moreover, since terrorist networks usually plan an extended series of bombing operations, it is imperative for them to secure a continuous supply of explosives; for such networks, an ability to steal some explosives here and there is no substitute for a regular source of supply.

Another standard option available to terrorist networks is to smuggle the required high explosives into the country. The terrorists have no problem obtaining virtually unlimited quantities of the best high explosives from their sponsoring states. However, because of the large volumes of explosives required, it is virtually impossible to smuggle them via the diplomatic mail of those governments (which are often the avenues used for other types of weapons). Explosives are therefore smuggled via criminal networks such as drug traffickers who are accustomed to handling large-volume items.

But there is an objective limit to the volume of cargo that any network, huge as it might be, can smuggle into the United States; and since the drug traffickers are more interested in getting their lucrative drugs into the country, the quantities of explosives that the terrorists can count on having safely smuggled into the U.S. is not large. The availability of a sophisticated smuggling network like the Yoma ring in Argentina is a rarity.

All of these facts were well known to the terrorist experts in Damascus and Tehran back in the mid-1980s when they first undertook a serious professional examination of the potential for a major escalation of terrorism inside the United States. In the fall of 1987, Iran was actively preparing suicide attacks in America and France, to be conducted in the name of Islamic Jihad. The Iranian embassy in Beirut brought several IRGC recruiters to Lebanon to select the most suitable candidates for these operations from among HizbAllah volunteers.[6]

Starting in the summer of 1987, there had also been a marked increase in the activities of the Syrian-Iranian support system in Lebanon. These active preparations were presented as part of Iran's support for the Palestinian armed struggle, which, Tehran now argued, must include the escalation of the terrorist struggle against America: "The interests of Zionists and the Americans must come under attack throughout the world. The United States, which is a supporter of the occupiers of Palestine, and the Zionists themselves must lose their sense of security throughout the world. The world must become a graveyard for the Americans and the Israelis."[7]

A precondition for any sophisticated and spectacular terrorist operation on American soil was the regular availability of sufficient quantities of high explosives. The Iranians and the Syrians therefore decided to find out whether they could obtain explosives in the U.S. itself before they committed their high-quality operatives to action in the heart of America. These exploratory operations would have to be deniable, so Iranian and Syrian intelligence started by inserting international terrorist detachments which, if exposed through capture or terrorist action, would not be associated with the Islamist networks.

Iranian and Syrian intelligence first tried to ascertain the potential for smuggling large bombs or quantities of high explosives. One such attempt by the Syrian Socialist National Party (SSNP) to insert a major bomb in October was accidentally spoiled.

The SSNP is an arm of Syrian intelligence and the KGB for international terrorism. Its members were trained for terrorism in Western Europe through George Habbash's PFLP and Wadi Haddad's PFLP-SOG, which employed the notorious Carlos as a senior trainer.[8] The SSNP cooperated with foreign international terrorist organizations such as the Japanese Red Army (JRA)[9] and provided cover for the Syrian-controlled program for suicide terrorists.[10]

The test operation took place on the night of October 23, 1987, in Richford, Vermont, on the Canadian border. Walid Kabbani, a Lebanese based in Canada, brought a backpack across the border, filled with the components of a bomb powerful enough to blowup a small building. Two "locally respected" merchants from Burlington, Vermont, Georges Younan and Walid Mourad, were waiting to pick up the backpack (and, in all likelihood, pass it on to other members of the network). The operation was accidentally exposed only because the van in which the two Burlington businessmen were waiting was illegally parked. When the local police chief approached them, the two men aroused his suspicion, panicked and gave away the operation.[11] But although a specific act of sabotage was prevented, no other members of the sleeper network were exposed.

Moreover, it is clear that the foiled smuggling operation in Vermont was not the only test run by the Syrians and the Iranians. At least a few efforts to smuggle bombs across the Mexican border succeeded,[12] but the quantities of high explosives brought into the U.S. in these test runs were relatively small, limited to what could either be carried on a man's back or safely concealed in a passenger car. Building the required stockpiles would require a very large number of cross-border smuggling runs, and that would tremendously increase the risk of early discovery.

It became clear to the experts in Damascus and Tehran that an alternative source of explosives must be found. Soviet and East German intelligence experts had long been arguing that any network should be self-sufficient, including a capacity to produce explosives from off-the-shelf chemicals. In Western Europe, the easy availability of high-quality high explosives routinely smuggled from the East Bloc and the Middle East made such a requirement for terrorist self-sufficiency superfluous. However, in view of the challenges encountered in the smuggling tests across American borders, the experts of the Iranian and Syrian intelligence decided to reexamine the possibility of local production. They decided on an audacious test run in which an expert terrorist would build bombs from off-the-shelf components and then explode them.

In order to increase the likelihood of success and maintain deniability, Damascus and Tehran decided to use specially-inserted foreign experts.

Thus in early 1988 the PFLP (Popular Front for the Liberation of Palestine) arranged for a Japanese Red Army expert terrorist to be slipped into the United States. Since the early 1980s, the JRA has had a "suicide corps" in Lebanon, "fighting together with the PFLP" all over the world.[13] One of this group, 36-year-old Yu Kikumura (who used the nom de guerre "Abu-Shams" during his training in the Bekaa), was dispatched for this mission. Although the planned operation was ostensibly on behalf of Libya, it was actually an operation of the new system of international terrorism dominated by Iran and Syria; a simultaneous JRA bombing in Naples, Italy, which was similarly attributed to Qaddafi, was claimed by the Organization of Jihad Brigades, an Islamist organization affiliated with the HizbAllah.[14]

Kikumura started his trip on February 23, 1988, in Western Europe. For the rest of the month he travelled through several European countries, changing passports and sending money to the U.S.

from several banks. Using a false Japanese passport, he finally received an American entry visa in
Paris on February 29th.

Kikumura flew into New York on March 8. He
rented a small apartment in Manhattan; bought a
second hand car, a 1980 Mazda, in the Bronx, paying cash; and left all the obvious indications of an
intention to stay in the New York area.

Then he began his mission. He concealed a wad
of cash and an automatic pistol under the driver's
seat of his car. On March 14, he embarked on an a
trip of more than 7,000 miles across seventeen states
during which he collected components for his
bombs. He stopped frequently along the way to buy
small quantities of various items, each of which, by
itself, seemed innocent: for example, he bought a
number of ordinary thermometers. But in fact these
purchases provided him with the key components
which, in combination, would be transformed into
lethal bombs by the end of his trip: Hercules gun-
powder, aluminium powder, ammonium nitrate,
and mercury. (The mercury came from those innocent thermometers.)

Kikumura's test run was not entirely trouble-free
— in Nashville, he broke a muffler and froze with
terror when the garage mechanic used a blowtorch
under his car, warming up the concealed explosives.
But by the end of March he had completed the purchase of all the necessary ingredients. He then began mixing various explosives, testing the suitabil-
ity of the materials he had purchased. He successfully mixed the main explosive incendiary charge,
made of aluminium powder and ammonium nitrate.

He then planned to work on the very sensitive mercury fulminate detonators.

On April 5, Kikumura stopped at a motel in Pennsylvania and began working on the detonators. He intended to mix nitric acid, mercury and methyl alcohol. Something went wrong. Apparently, Kikumura used the wrong type of alcohol — isopropyl instead of methyl alcohol; the result was a small explosion and a flash fire. Kikumura was burned, especially on his arms. Despite his injuries, however, within a few days he had converted three ordinary red cylinder fire extinguishers into extremely lethal anti-personnel bombs with time-delay fuses.

It was only by sheer chance that his plans were foiled. On April 12, on his way back to New York, Kikumura was arrested by accident on the New Jersey Turnpike when — for no concrete reason the trooper could later specify — something about his car or his driving aroused the suspicion of a New Jersey state trooper. The trooper pulled him over, inspected his car closely, and found the sophisticated bombs disguised as fire extinguishers Kikumura had made from the off-the-shelf parts and supplies he had collected in his travels. (As a result, Kikumura was tried and sentenced to thirty years in prison.)

He had planned to detonate those bombs in mid-Manhattan, targeting the main Armed Forces recruiting station, on or around April 15, the second anniversary of the American bombing of Libya.[15] Had he been successful, the murderous explosion would have been blamed on Qaddafi — though in fact it was in effect controlled by Syria and Iran.

Kikumura's was a highly professional operation optimized to deal with, and take advantage of the realities, the circumstances of life in the United States. It demonstrated the terrorists' extensive knowledge of American life and ways of doing things. Kikumura, who had not previously visited the United States, had been accurately provided with full details on where and how to purchase all the components needed for his bombs in a manner that would not attract attention of law enforcement agencies. He almost accomplished his mission successfully: the New Jersey state trooper had approached him "more on intuition than anything else."[16]

Moreover, the close relationship and cooperation between the JRA and the SSNP suggests that the two failed operations (in Vermont in 1987 and Kikumura in April 1988) may have been merely components in a larger effort by Syria and Iran to conduct terrorism and sabotage in America. Possibly Kikumura was dispatched as a fallback plan after the capture of the SSNP couriers in Vermont. In either case, it points to the network's organizational flexibility and suggests that as early as the late 1980s, the network already had a redundency of assets inside the United States.

Although Kikumura was captured before he was able to detonate his bombs, Damascus and Tehran were very satisfied with the results of his operation. He had proved that it was indeed possible to obtain all the necessary components for sophisticated explosives and bombs off-the-shelf locally and without arousing the suspicion of the American law enforcement authorities — and that, rather than the actual bombing, was the primary purpose of his operation. He had also proved that the component lists they had provided to him were essentially correct, which meant that their information sources were reliable.

The Syrian and Iranian experts therefore concluded that in the future, major terrorist strikes on American soil could and would rely on home-made explosives made from locally-available components, eliminating the need for risky smuggling operations. Thus the Kikumura episode provided the terrorist controlling states with valuable lessons that will be applied in future operations — and indeed, already have been applied, most notably in New York City.

BEGINNING THE PREPARATIONS

Although the principals of the terrorist conspiracy had been discussing potential terrorist plans for America since November 1991, and had in effect been collecting target data since January 1990, the specific conspiracy to blow up the World Trade Center began in April 1992.[17] It was then that the relatively unfocussed discussions about optional terrorist and bombing plans and desires for vengeance began to be transformed into practical preparations for a professional terrorist operation.

The network's professionals were now taking care of several seemingly mundane logistical matters, like the safe transfer of funds from overseas. They also planned and prepared getaway plans, obtaining foreign passports which were provided by loyal Nicaraguan Sandinistas (who are still in Nicaraguan government service). Ibrahim Elgabrowny was one of the senior professionals in the network's support system. As early as 1991, he had arranged Islamic supporters, transportation and bodyguards for the defense during Nossair's trial for the Kahane murder. Now he was the president of the executive board of Abdel-Rahman's mosque in Brooklyn, responsible for the sheikh's earthly needs.[18] Elgabrowny was also the contact man between the elusive and shadowy professionals and the expendables. American authorities would eventually find in his apartment five Nicaraguan passports (including one for Nossair), a 9 mm. pistol, 150 rounds of ammunition and two stun guns.[19] In June 1992, other members of the network became involved in preparations for Nossair's possible escape. Among them was Emad Salem, who would become the government informer; in June 1992 Salem visited Nossair in Attica prison and discussed "bombings, securing of safe houses and a plan for Nossair's escape from Attica."[20]

Most important was the identification, recruitment, and manipulation of the expendables, the local zealots who would actually carry out the operation and be sacrificed in the process. The preparation of expendables is a lengthy process, because it requires thorough psychological tempering and conditioning. The primary candidates are desperate drifters within the Islamist community who are yearning for revenge and overcommitted to the cause as a matter of principle. They must be susceptible to the influence of spiritual leaders such as Sheikh Abdel-Rahman. Their loyalty must be unquestionable, preferably reinforced through blood ties. In addition, the recruiters search for people with useful skills who will be manipulated into roles in which they will provide a shield and cover for the real experts. The search for the candidates began in the spring of 1992, most likely around March, and was essentially completed within a few months.

In fact, most of the initial stage of preparations were complete in the summer of 1992 when Abdel-Rahman held discussions with Turabi of the Sudan, who was then visiting the U.S. The two men met in New York to further coordinate Islamist activities in America, including the possible launching of terrorist operations. Soon afterwards, Abdel-Rahman intensified his fundraising for Islamist causes in the U.S. and Canada, smuggling the money back to Egypt via the Faysal Islamic Bank.[21] In the fall of 1992, Turabi decided to further escalate operations in the America. Of the some $100 million allocated by Tehran as the initial budget for Turabi's Islamic Popular Arab Congress (*Al-Mu'tamar al-Arabi al-Shabi al-Islami*), a major portion is earmarked as an "investment" in the United States to consolidate networks and establish a center for publications and communication with groups everywhere through faxes and phones.[22] These activities are to be conducted through the establishment of a world-wide education and proselytization network under the cover of the Washington-based World Institute of Islamic Thought.[23]

The most important and secret purpose of Turabi's 1992 visit was to enable Turabi and his escorts to thoroughly study and inspect the terrorist plans of the New York network. In their meetings, Turabi and Abdel-Rahman studied closely the strength of the American Muslim community, examining its ability to withstand a massive anti-Islamic assault.[24] In essence, the two senior leaders were assessing the ability of the American Islamist community to withstand the consequences of a major terrorist operation conducted by its members.

Meanwhile, terrorism experts travelling with Turabi were meeting with their local counterparts. The visiting experts told several of their American-based counterparts to begin "credible" (i.e. concrete and specific) preparations to escalate the jihad. At a few key sessions, Turabi and Abd-al-Rahaman were present as well as the experts in Turabi's entourage. Among these attending these key sessions were Mahmud Abouhalima and Siddig Ibrahim Siddig Ali, who would soon command the Islamist terrorist cells activated in the New York area.[25]

Meanwhile, there were also Iranian operatives directing the accelerated preparations for major action.[26] Expert terrorists and instructors of the HizbAllah and the *Tawhid*, the HizbAllah's Sunni sister organization in Lebanon, arrived in America from Lebanon to train American and Palestinian terrorists.[27]

Upon his return to Sudan shortly thereafter, Turabi's impressions of the situation of the Islamist community in the U.S. and its ability to wage a jihad were closely studied by the AIM's recently established Higher Liaison Committee in Khartoum. The main task of the Higher Liaison Committee is to supervise Islamist groups and organizations and to coordinate and support their operations. The Committee concluded that the American network was essentially ready and decided to urge Tehran to launch a jihad on or around Al-Quds Day — March 19, 1993.[28]

Meanwhile, there was a major development in the overall posture of the New York Islamist terrorist network. In mid-1992, as result of the move to consolidate the PIO and AIM, Sheikh Umar Abdel-Rahman was made a senior member of the Supreme Leadership, entrusted to act as the Islamists' senior representative in North America. He was now authorized to assign the local Islamist cells to commit specific terrorist attacks, though they had to be in accordance with the master plan and agreed-upon strategy which were still determined only in Khartoum and Tehran.[29] Most importantly, Sheikh Abdel-Rahman was now also authorized to issue *fatwa*s permitting suicide operations in North America, making the Islamists' ability to conduct terrorism in the United States significantly easier.

Indeed, as of mid-1992, Sheikh Abdel-Rahman had joined Sheikh al-Turabi as one of the two "most prominent" leaders of the Islamist international — Abdel-Rahman because of his control of American operations.[30] This development would significantly enhance the ability of the New York Islamist terrorists to embark on a spectacular and ambitious terrorist campaign.

PREPARATIONS BEGIN IN EARNEST

Actual preparations for Islamist terrorist operations in New York began gradually between June and August 1992. Several contingency plans for anticipated operations, ranging from assassinations to major sabotage, were studied and prepared for. Among the possible operations studied in great detail at the time were the assassination of the United Nations Secretary General Boutros Boutros-Ghali, a Copt (an Egyptian Christian) and a declared enemy of Sheikh Abdel-Rahman, and the bombing of the World Trade Center, the UN building, and other major structures in New York.

The seriousness of this planning was indicated by the activation of a few senior expert terrorists already living in America as long-term plants. Mahmud Abouhalima, an Egyptian, was activated in August to assume command over the preparations of one cell.[31] Siddig Ibrahim Siddig Ali, a Sudanese, was activated for subsequent operations by a second back-up cell.[32] It is worth noting that both had attended meetings with Abdel-Rahman and Turabi during the summer.[33]

At least two dozen Egyptians and several Sudanese and American black Muslims were also involved to some degree in these early activities and preparations.[34]

Mahmud Abouhalima [Abu-Halima], 33, the major operative activated in August 1992, is an Egyptian electrician who worked as a cab driver in Jersey City and Brooklyn. He first arrived in America in 1982, after two years in Germany. He left the U.S. around 1985 and returned again in October 1986 from Munich, married to a German woman through whom he gained German citizenship. He continued to travel between Germany and America quite frequently — travel that was beyond his apparent means.[35]

Abouhalima's presence in, and trips to, Germany were important to the consolidation of the Islamist network in the New York area. By the 1980s, Germany had become the center of the Islamist radical trend and was riddled with Islamist terrorist networks. Part of this system is a center in Aachen from which Syrian Intelligence works both to entrap followers of the Syrian Muslim Brotherhood (staunch enemies of the Assad regime) and to run Islamist terrorist operations in the West. The Egyptian Muslim Brotherhood manages an important international Islamist cell in Munich, where Abouhalima used to live. On his frequent trips to Germany, he repeatedly visited both the Ikhwan in Munich and the Syrian center in Aachen;[36] and he maintained close links with the Islamist groups in Germany.

Funds for the New York network were channelled via the Brotherhood's contacts in Germany, as well as Iranian businesses and expatriates in Europe, especially Germany.[37] It is therefore safe to assume that Abouhalima received instructions while in Germany and that his points of contact and shelter in Europe were there. Within a few months, the existence of working contacts in Germany would prove crucial to the success of the New York terrorists' plans.

In the mid-1980s, Abouhalima had been trained in Pakistan and even fought in Afghanistan with the Afghan mujahideen for a few months in their war against the Soviet occupation.[38] Returning to the U.S., he increased his involvement in terrorism. He attended the al-Salam mosque in Jersey City, was active in Afghan causes, and was a friend of Mohammed A. Salameh, the primary expendable of the World Trade Center cell. Abouhalima was involved in the November 1990 assassination of Rabbi Meir Kahane as the driver of the getaway taxi and in 1991 was reported to have had blasting caps and other sabotage equipment in his Brooklyn apartment.[39] In the fall of 1992, anticipating an imminent terrorist strike that would attract attention to himself, Abouhalima sent his wife and four children back to Egypt.[40]

Abouhalima was also a close confidant of Sheikh Abdel-Rahman, serving as his driver and escort.[41] For the impending terrorist strike, Abouhalima was more than the leader of the New York-based network[42] and, in his own words, "the leader of *al-Jama'ah al-Islamiyah*" in the U.S.[43] He was the representative of Sheikh Abdel-Rahman, ensuring that all the religious decrees and professional instructions were carried out and making progress reports to the Sheikh while at the same time creating an essential shield of deniability between the spiritual leader and his terrorist disciples.[44]

Siddig [Siddiq] Ibrahim Siddig Ali, 32, is a Sudanese immigrant who arrived in the United States in 1986, and again, legally, in 1988.[45] In the early 1980s, Siddig travelled to Afghanistan, where he fought with the mujahideen for about two years. While in Afghanistan or Pakistan, he was identified by Iranian recruiters and sent to Iran for several months of intense advanced training in terrorism and clandestine work. He was then dispatched to the United States via Sudan.[46]

Arriving in America, Siddig claimed to have a degree in economics from a Sudanese university; but he worked in New York as a security guard and cab driver, jobs that would later prove to be of great significance. He also trained with Muslim militants in self-defense techniques in Harrisburg, Pennsylvania, on weekends. Siddig was very active in Islamist politics as well as in publicized campaigns like the one in support of Nossair[47] on which he worked together with Ibrahim Elgabrowny.[48]

In reality, Siddig was the head of the New Jersey and New York branch of Turabi's National Islamic Front.[49] He was instrumental in organizing the recruitment of future terrorists from among Americans and Sudanese. He travelled frequently to Sudan, organizing training and support. More recently, he "wanted to help oppressed Muslims" worldwide and expressed interest in joining the "jihad" in Bosnia.[50]

From early 1993 on, Siddig was the interpreter for Sheikh Umar Abdel-Rahman.[51] Very much like Abouhalima, Siddig was operationally more than just the leader of a terrorist cell. He too served as the representative of Sheikh Abdel-Rahman, ensuring that all the religious decrees and professional instructions were carried out and reporting progress to the Sheikh while at the same time creating a shield of deniability.[52] In the summer of 1993, Siddig would emerge as the ringleader who was clearly in charge for the July 4th operations, selecting targets, making decisions and responsible for "building bombs, getting timing devices," and other aspects of the conspiracy.[53]

In the fall of 1992, the terrorists suddenly learned that the FBI was investigating Abouhalima and other Egyptians in connection with the conspiracy to assassinate Boutros Boutros-Ghali.[54] As a result, what was then the back-up cell led by Siddig Ibrahim Siddig Ali, which was made up primarily of Sudanese,[55] was immediately separated from the main network to ensure its security and the terrorists in Jersey City were provided with "a primer on how to handle the FBI."[56]

The brush with the FBI did not diminish the network's determination to assassinate major enemies of Egypt's Islamists. On the contrary, in late 1992 they embarked on a conspiracy to assassinate Egypt's President Husni Mubarak. In order to ensure the safety and security of this conspiracy, it too was separated from the main sabotage operation. Abdel-Rahman Haggag (a.k.a. Abdo Mohammed Haggag), age 26, was put in charge of the assassination plans. Haggag, who worked for a telephone company, was an Egyptian-borne aide and translator for Sheikh Umar Abdel-Rahman. He lived in the the same apartment building as the sheikh and worshipped in his mosque. Haggag would be arrested in mid-July 1993.[57]

The plan to assassinate President Mubarak reflects the extent of the assets available to the New

York Islamists. Most important is the realization that the conspirators had access to material that was obviously provided by a well-placed spy either in the Egyptian Mission to the UN or the Egyptian Embassy in Washington, a follower of Sheikh Umar Abdel-Rahman who had managed to hold onto a job in the Egyptian government despite repeated purges of Islamists.

This spy had access to the planned itinerary of Mubarak's visit to the United States in March 1993. The conspirators in New York were able to identify the hotel where Mubarak was expected to stay while he was in New York. They studied the hotel closely, looking for ways to reach Mubarak. They obtained hotel uniforms that would enable them to gain access to his immediate vicinity. In early 1993, Haggag's network was ready for action.

By then, the assassination cell had been integrated into the sprawling Islamist terrorist network in the area. Haggag, Siddig, Hampton-El, and possibly ten other support personnel were involved in the assassination plot. But at the last minute Mubarak cancelled his planned stop in New York and returned to Cairo directly from Washington.[58]

Months later, Siddig Ibrahim Siddig Ali would claim that the reason that Mubarak was not assassinated at the time was that U.S. intelligence agents had visited Sheikh Abdel-Rahman, told him that Washington was aware of the assassination plans, and warned him not to go ahead.[59]

ENTER THE EXPERTS

In the preparations of the New York network for the conduct of a terrorist strike, a major milestone was the arrival of several outside senior expert terrorists to take over and run the final phase of the operation. First, two Iranians, probably intelligence officers, arrived in New York some months before the World Trade Center bombing. They met with some of the main leaders of the Islamist network.[60]

In early 1993, Egyptian security authorities warned that several groups of Islamist expert terrorists who specialized "in blowing up sensitive locations using booby-trapped cars" had already been dispatched abroad. At least one, a group of seventeen terrorists, was known to be operating in Egypt.[61] It is noteworthy that the expert terrorists known or believed to have entered the United States in connection with the impending operation included Sunni Arabs, Lebanese and several Iranians.[62]The decision to draw on such a diverse pool of expert terrorists, and the ability to do so, clearly demonstrates the importance given to the operation by the sponsoring states.

One of these experts was a 25-year-old Iraqi named Ramzi Ahmad Youssuf who arrived without a visa on September 1, 1992, on PIA Flight 703 from Karachi, Pakistan. According to his passport, he had lived in Kuwait, Jordan, Iraq, and Pakistan. Not mentioned on his passport, of course, was the fact that he had also received terrorist training in Pakistan and Iran.

Claiming to be seeking political asylum, Youssuf was allowed into the United States pending a hearing. He moved in with Mohammed Salameh (who would become the network's main expendable), attended the al-Salam Mosque, and became a cab driver in New York City. Before long, Youssuf would be involved in virtually all aspects of the preparations for, and the conduct of, the World Trade Center bombing, from the organization of the overseas finances to the purchase of the chemicals to being seen in the bomb-van a day before and on the day of the explosion.[64]

Another expert terrorist arrived on the same flight as Youssuf. A 27-year-old Palestinian name Ahmad Muhammad Ajaj, he carried a forged Swedish passport in the name of "Khurram Khan." He was detained by the Immigration and Naturalization Service [INS], even though he claimed political asylum on the grounds that he had suffered torture in Israel. Ajaj is from the Hebron area and was a member of the PLO; his brother is still an assistant of Faisal al-Husseini, one of the PLO's most senior leaders. After accepting voluntary exile from Israel for five years, Ajaj travelled from Jordan to Iraq, Iran, and Pakistan.

Ajaj had been in America before. He first arrived in January 1991, asking for political asylum. Admitted pending a hearing, he headed for Houston and Mesquite, a suburb of Dallas, both known centers of Islamist Palestinian activities. Soon after, he left the United States for Peshawar and stayed there and in Afghanistan, receiving sabotage training that would later be used in New York.

When Ajaj returned to New York on September 1, 1992, with Youssuf, he was carrying a suitcase packed with twelve manuals for sabotage techniques, including detailed instructions for mixing explosives from conventional off-the-shelf materials and the construction of bombs from "improvised explosive devices using urea and nitric acid." Other manuals covered the use of poisons, mines, concealed weapons, etc. Youssuf's fingerprints were subsequently found on two of the manuals and the bomb-makers for the World Trade Center would essentially follow the instructions in the sabotage manuals.

Ajaj was released by the INS on February 28, 1993, and immediately went back to Houston and Mesquite again; but he was rearrested on March 9, 1993.[64]

Both Youssuf and Ajaj had received instructions in Pakistan, reportedly from the Pakistani ISI, on the best approaches to use with the INS in order to gain entry into the United States as political refugees.[65] While in the U.S., and apparently also while abroad, Youssuf and Ajaj used the same documents interchangeably, including identical aliases such as "Khurram Khan," "Azam Muhammad," and "Rashid," in order to further confuse law enforcement authorities.[66] (Abouhalima knew Youssuf only as Rashid.)[67]

The arrival of these experts was also the result of another major achievement of the leaders of Iran and Sudan — the integration of the Egyptian Islamist terrorist experts, especially those based in Pakistan, into the Iranian-controlled international Islamist terrorist system.

It is necessary to take a brief look at the situation in Pakistan:

Back in 1980, soon after the Soviet invasion of Afghanistan, a few Islamist Egyptians, some of them former officers in the Egyptian army, began arriving in Pakistan and Afghanistan to share their military knowledge with the Afghan mujahideen.[68] Many of these first arrivals were led by Ahmad Shawqi al-Istambuli (the brother of Khalid al-Istambuli, Sadat's assassin) and were fugitives from the purges in Egypt that followed Sadat's murder.

In 1983, Ahmad Istambuli organized a network in Karachi for smuggling people and weapons to and from Egypt,[69] and since the late 1980s, the Egyptian jihad movements have had their supreme military headquarters, training facilities and stockpiles of weapons in the Peshawar area of Pakistan's Northwest Frontier Province, near the border of Afghanistan.

The Islamic Group's office there is led by Talat Fuad Qassim, who answers to Sheikh Dr. Umar Abdel-Rahman. Qassim spent seven years in jail for participation in Sadat's assassination and then escaped to Peshawar in 1989.

The Islamic Jihad Movement is led by Ahmad Shawqi al-Istambuli and Dr. Ayman al-Zawahiri, both of whom are in Peshawar. Key terrorist operations in Egypt, including assassinations, are planned in the Peshawar headquarters and some of the key operatives receive specialized training in Afghanistan and Pakistan before travelling to Egypt. Efforts are being made in Peshawar to unify the two movements in Egypt in order to better prepare for the challenges ahead. Several members of the Islamic Jihad Group "joined" the Islamic Group as the initial step in the anticipated "full merger between the two groups."[70]

The Egyptian Islamists also maintain a major center in Kabul, the Afghan capital, where two sons of Sheikh Umar Abdel-Rahman wait with another expert terrorist detachment for their return to Egypt, where an advance party of some thirty "Afghans" has already been infiltrated.[71]

Sheikh Umar Abdel-Rahman maintains special relations with Ahmad Shawqi al-Istambuli. In 1990, Abdel-Rahman spent some six months in Peshawar as Istambuli's guest.[72] According to Ahmad Zaidan, an Egyptian journalist, Abdel-Rahman and his followers used Istambuli's Peshawar headquarters facility to make cassettes and prepare other propaganda and agitation materials to be smuggled into Egypt and other Arab countries.[73]

In September 1991, Turabi visited Pakistan and Afghanistan to coordinate terrorist support activities. (As will be discussed in detail below, by 1991 Turabi was already involved in the effort to train and deploy American terrorists from Pakistan.) Several local and regional Islamist organizations became members of the Turabi-led Popular International Organization, and, in this capacity, they now provide assistance to, and closely cooperate with, Islamists from Egypt, the HizbAllah from Lebanon, and Islamists in other parts of the world. PIO members exchange experts and cooperate in joint support and training activities.[74]

At the same time Turabi was also working to

expand the international relations and mutual co-operation of the terrorist infrastructure in Sudan. In late November 1991, he consolidated arrangements for the exchange and dispatch of trainees to Islamist, mainly Muslim Brotherhood, sites in Peshawar.[75]

In the spring of 1992, Tehran was making special efforts to align the leading Sunni organizations, primarily those with ideological standing and popular support, with the Tehran-led terrorist establishment. A major breakthrough took place in July 1992 when, after mediation by Turabi, Dr. Ayman al-Zawahiri, one of the leaders of Egyptian Islamic Jihad based in Peshawar, arrived in Tehran. Tehran agreed to provide comprehensive assistance to the Egyptian "Afghans". About 800 of their people then in Pakistan and Afghanistan would be provided with advanced terrorist training in Iran, mainly in the northwestern city of Mashhad, by the Quds Forces. In addition, 473 young Egyptian sheikhs were to be sent to special spiritual training in Qum, south of Tehran, and Mashhad to be prepared for their role as spiritual leaders of the anticipated Islamist surge.

Iran would also take care of transportation to Sudan for Egyptians to be trained by the HizbAllah and the Pasdaran (IRGC) in the Shandi and Omdurman camps. And Iran would also provide very lavish financing and weapons for the plans to escalate the jihad against Cairo.

For all this, Tehran made only one condition: the Islamic Jihad would have to join the Arab Liberation Battalions of the IRGC Intelligence.[76] The Egyptians accepted.

In the late summer, at Tehran's invitation, Muhammad Shawqi al-Istambuli travelled to the Bekaa in eastern Lebanon, to inspect the HizbAllah facilities and discuss HizbAllah assistance in training Egyptian mujahideen already in Sudan, who would constitute the first Egyptian Liberation Battalion. In addition to the Egyptians sent to Iran, another 500 terrorists were sent to Sudan where they too joined the HizbAllah training program. Thus, by the fall of 1992 the main Egyptian Islamist groups were being integrated into the Iranian-HizbAllah terrorist system.[77] It is therefore no accident that the Egyptian Islamic Jihad began issuing communiques from Tehran in December 1992.[78]

Moreover, the terrorist headquarters of the Egyptian Islamists was established in Tehran and Qum under the command of the mysterious, yet very effective, Abu-Imamah. This is the nom de guerre of an Egyptian lawyer about thirty years old who emigrated to Denmark in 1987 after years of underground work in Egypt. He opened a restaurant in Copenhagen that served as a center for clandestine Islamist activities. Yearning for more action, Abu-Imamah soon sold the restaurant and went to Pakistan and Afghanistan, where he underwent comprehensive training and then fought with the mujahideen.

In 1989, he moved to Qum at the invitation of the Iranians. After undergoing higher Islamic studies, he established an Egyptian command center in Iran which, with extensive supervision and sponsorship from Iranian intelligence, runs the worldwide terrorist networks of the Egyptian "Afghans" and other Egyptian jihadist groups. Through Abu-Imamah, Tehran runs the actual clandestine activities during the high quality terrorist operations of the Egyptian Islamists, including those in New York and the United States as a whole.[79]

Meanwhile, with the establishment of AIM in 1992, the Peshawar-based Tal'at Fuad Qasim of Egypt's Islamic Group and Ahmad Shawqi al-Istambuli and Dr. Ayman al-Zawahiri of Egypt's Islamic Jihad Movement became the emissaries of the PIO's supreme military headquarters, in charge of coordination with Islamabad, the training facilities and the stockpiles of weapons.[80]

It was here in Peshawar that terrorist experts began to plan and calculate the professional specifics of the various sabotage plans for New York. And it was in Peshawar, Pakistan, that Iran's direct involvement in, and control over, the entire operation was clearly demonstrated.

According to Egyptian Intelligence, some of the planning for the World Trade Center and other sabotage targets took place in Istambuli's Peshawar headquarters.[81] The conspirators received professional help from foreign experts. According to Abouhalima, the World Trade Center bombing plan was worked on in Peshawar and was approved there by officers of Iranian Intelligence before being submitted for the general approval of Sheikh Abdel-Rahman.[82]

Thus, by the time the terrorist experts like Youssuf and Ajaj began arriving in New York, they had already studied specific operational plans with many of the details and calculations already ironed out. They were carrying instruction books optimized for the tasks ahead. And all of this material, as well as their own training, had been checked and approved by Iranian Intelligence, the true masters of the operation.

THE RECRUITMENT OF THE EXPENDABLES

Meanwhile, in New York in the fall of 1992 the search for the expendables narrowed and their recruitment was completed. This was reflected in emerging financial arrangements. Ultimately, at least some ten individuals were recruited and involved in providing some form of support, usually marginal, to the terrorists.[83] Numerous new bank accounts were opened, some jointly with the the expendables for their immediate use. Money was wired to New Jersey from Iran and the Middle East via Germany, a classic Iranian transfer point. Some $100,000 was transferred to the terrorists' accounts from Iran alone.

The accounts remained relatively small, totalling between $50,000 and $100,000 at any given time. At least $8,000 was deposited in a joint account held in the names of Salameh, Ayyad, and others; the money arrived from Germany in the last months before the operation in two deposits of about $5,500 and $2,500 that were wired in late 1992 and were withdrawn by Salameh a month later.[84] As usual, funds from various sources were routed through the Ikhwan's German and Iranian expatriate contacts in Europe, especially Germany.[85] Muhammad Rezah Shalchian (Chalagian) Tabrizi, operating under his cover as the comptroller of Iran's mission to the UN, oversaw the distribution of the Iranian funds to Sheikh Abdel-Rahman and the terrorists.[86]

Twenty-six-year-old Mohammed A. Salameh of Jersey City was the classic expendable. He is the son of a Jordanian military officer who escaped in 1967 from Biddya on the West Bank to Zarka, Jordan, when Salameh was only three months old.[87] He grew up amid the intense hatred of the West prevailing in the Islamist Palestinian community of northern Jordan after Black September in 1970 (when the Jordanian forces slaughtered Palestinians, suppressing the PLO's state-within-a-state). Many of the area's young men were recruited for Islamic Jihad in 1986-87 by Khalil al-Wazir (nom de guerre Abu-Jihad) with the help of the Jordanian Muslim Brotherhood; some were even sent for training in Afghanistan.[88] Salameh may have been identified and recruited at that time: by then he was studying the *Shari'ah* (Muslim law) at an Islamic college.[89] Salameh arrived in America on February 17, 1988 with a Jordanian passport, a six-month visitor's visa and an intention to remain indefinitely. Since then he had lived as an illegal alien.[90]

When he arrived here in 1988, Salameh contacted his distant cousin, Ibrahim Elgabrowny. Elgabrowny helped him get documents, including a driver's license, giving his own apartment as Salameh's address. He also brought Salameh to the al-Salam mosque in New Jersey, where he was eventually exposed to Abdel-Rahman. Elgabrowny also introduced Salameh to another mutual relative, Al-Sayyid Abdulazziz Nossair.

Salameh settled into the life of illegal alien, living in a small apartment with three roommates (two women, other men and, after September 1992, Ramzi Ahmad Youssuf). He remained devoutly religious, isolated and remote from the American society around him. His only social life centered around the Masjid al-Salam. He became very close to Nossair, religiously attended his trial and visited him in jail. It is thus very likely that Salameh was strongly influenced by Nossair's beliefs and commitment to the Islamist jihad. Moreover, Salameh became a devoted and active follower of Sheikh Abdel-Rahman.[91]

By the fall of 1992, Salameh was completely trapped in the Islamist web, wholly captivated by the call to jihad, hostile to American society. His trustworthiness and commitment were demonstrated repeatedly. Moreover, as a relative of Elgabrowny, Salameh could be trusted to shield his associates. In short, he was ripe for recruitment for a glorious act of jihad. In the early summer of 1992, after the leadership of the New York network decided to consider the use of a carbomb, Salameh was sent to learn to drive, but from July 23 on, he failed four driving tests in New Jersey. With time running out, he applied for a license in New York, using Elgabrowny's address to qualify in New York State, and passed the test on September 8.[92]

The terrorist leaders now needed a "bomb

maker," another expendable who would shield the real experts by diverting law enforcement investigators away in the aftermath of the terrorist strike. Nidal A. Ayyad was a young chemical engineer in Maplewood, N. J., recently married; his wife was expecting their first child. Born in Kuwait of Palestinian descent, he was unable to go back because of the repression of Palestinians in Kuwait. At twenty-five, Ayyad was the main provider for an extended family he had brought to America once he was naturalized. He was frustrated and in need of money, and thus was an ideal "professional expendable."

Moreover, Ayyad was a devout Islamist who had attended the New Jersey mosques since the early 1990s. Ayyad had known Salameh for about a year, had befriended him and was eager to help. Their friendship may not have been spontaneous; it is possible that Salameh may have entrapped Ayyad. In any case, by the end of 1992, Ayyad was committed. He had joint bank accounts with Salameh. A few weeks later he went with him to lease the van to be used in the bombing of the World Trade Center.

As a chemical engineer, Ayyad could appear to have provided the know-how to mix the chemicals to make the explosives.[93] Just to ensure that Ayyad was incriminated, Salameh repeatedly called him from the storage company site where the chemicals used in making the bomb were stored.[94]

Two Arab American brothers, Mousab Yassin and Abdul Rahman Yassin (a.k.a. Abboud), were also implicated in the plot. Both regularly attended the mosque in Jersey City. Rahman Yassin helped teach Salameh to drive both a car and a van of the type that would be used for the bomb; the driving lessons for the van took place only a few days before the bombing. Rahman also helped mix the explosives in January 1993.

Mousab Yassin, a professor of electrical engineering, stayed at Salameh's apartment and later claimed ownership of the electrical equipment found there. Mousab also invented the fictional figure "Josie Hadas" and a story of an imagined Israeli provocation that was spread throughout the Arab world as proof of Israel's complicity in the World Trade Center bombing.

Abdul Rahman Yassin's involvement in the terrorist preparations may have gone beyond driving lessons and mixing explosives, since he was able to escape to Iraq where he still remains. His brother Mousab is still in the U.S.[95]

At least ten other local Islamists were recruited to provide indirect support of one kind or another. In the wake of the bombing, the discovery of their involvement would help complicate the work of the law enforcement agencies as, one after another, they were implicated in aiding and abetting the terrorist network. For example, Bilal Alkaisi (Al-Kaisi) was implicated because his American Express card was found in Salameh's pocket.[96] He knew Ayyad and had used his address when he arrived America in 1987,[97] and he also had a connection to the joint bank accounts held by Salameh and Ayyad.[98] Indeed, in the investigation of the World Trade Center bombing, the FBI recovered fingerprints of as many as eighteen people believed to have been involved, thus suggesting an even greater number of participants.[99]

By October 1992 the entire network was in place, other preparations were complete and the Islamist terrorist network in the New York area seemed to be ready to escalate the Holy War on American soil.

Chapter 4

TRIALS AND ACHIEVEMENTS

GHOSTS FROM THE PAST

In mid-October 1992, just as everything seemed to be going very well for the New York terrorist networks, Tehran was suddenly faced with a major security crisis with the potential to bring about the collapse of the entire operation. The direct cause of the crisis was the sudden reappearance of old ghosts from the days of the Beirut hostage crisis and the U.S.-Iranian deals that came to be known as Irangate.

The catalyst for the sudden crisis was the publication of the book *Terry Waite and Ollie North* by BBC correspondent Gavin Hewitt, about the representative of the Archbishop of Canterbury who was trying to arrange the release of hostages in Beirut and the Marine officer who became embroiled in the Irangate scandal. The book exposed one Ian Spiro as having been part of Lt. Col. Oliver North's inner circle at the time. Passing as a Greek, Spiro had business in Lebanon and his wife was a nurse in the American University hospital in Beirut. He was on very familiar terms with the influential and the elite in Lebanon, including the pillars of the Shi'ite community.

In reality, Spiro was working for both American and British intelligence, carrying out "deep covert operations" for them during the period of the hostage crises. In the aftermath of the 1984 kidnapping of William Buckley, the CIA chief of station in Beirut, Spiro was considered one of the CIA's most valuable assets in Lebanon. He was able to acquire a copy of Buckley's confessions, extracted under torture by his captors. At North's behest, Spiro used his extensive connections throughout Lebanon to help Terry Waite establish contacts with the appropriate Lebanese in Beirut. On November 18, 1985, Waite met Spiro, who then helped to set up security and the schedule of meetings for Waite's first visit to Beirut.

In his youth Spiro had attended private school along with members of the Kuwaiti royal family, and at the request of North and Waite, he tried to help find a solution to problem of the Kuwait 17 * through private contacts and channels. He also used his skills and connections to mollify HizbAllah notables when contacts with the American government were going nowhere.

---

* Seventeen Islamist terrorists jailed in Kuwait, whose release was one of the demands of hostage-takers in Beirut.

Even after the exposure of the Iran-Contra scandal, Spiro continued to assist Washington in its efforts to resolve the hostage crisis. In early January 1987, he warned Terry Waite, who was about to return to Beirut, that Imad Mughaniyah was convinced that he had been shortchanged in the Iran-Contra deal and was likely to try to settle scores by kidnapping Waite. When Waite persisted in returning to Beirut and was indeed kidnapped, Spiro pulled every string possible in Lebanon to try and locate him; and in the next few years he handled several offers for ransom and deals on behalf of governments and individuals trying to bring about the release of Western hostages.[1]

A good deal of this was in Hewitt's book.

However, the cause of the crisis in Tehran was not so much the disclosures in Hewitt's book as Spiro's reaction to the book's publication.

By the fall of 1992, Ian Spiro was having severe personal financial problems, perhaps even a financial crisis[2], which he decided he could solve by selling his story. Spiro told his brothers-in-law that he was going to expose some new, detailed, incriminating material about the entire hostage crisis and the deals with Iran[3] and headed for Hollywood to discuss movie deals, apparently with some success. James W. Street, one of his neighbors in California, later remarked that although Spiro was having financial problems, he was about to sign a very big deal with Hollywood for a movie about himself.[4]

At some point between early and mid-October, soon after Hewitt's book came out, Ian Spiro called Con Coughlin, another British correspondent then in London writing a book about the hostage crisis, and arranged to meet with him when he arrived in London "soon." Over the phone, Spiro provided Coughlin with additional new details about his involvement in the hostage crisis, which[5] Coughlin disclosed in his book *Hostage* — that North had originally introduced Waite to Spiro because the latter had contacts with Islamic Jihad and Spiro then introduced Waite to Dr. Adnan Mroueh, his conduit to the Shi'ite leadership in Beirut. Ominously, Coughlin also wrote that Spiro "was later given a new identity by the CIA and now lives in California."[6] Coughlin had learned all these details from Spiro himself in their transatlantic telephone conversation — a call that must have been intercepted.

Now, in mid-October 1992, with the active preparations for the escalation in the terrorist campaign in a very advanced stage, Tehran had reason to fear for the security of the operation. Iranian intelligence and terrorist officials were apprehensive that Ian Spiro could identify some of the key Iranian and HizbAllah operatives who were then already clandestinely in the United States in connection with the impending escalation. This had important ramifications: failure to launch the terrorist campaign in the United States would have a direct and dire impact on Tehran's ability to implement its grand strategy in the Muslim world.

Therefore, Spiro had to be silenced, which, for Tehran, meant that he had to be killed. Moreover, since Spiro was identified as a CIA and SIS [British intelligence] agent, it was not only imperative to kill him immediately before he had a chance to betray Iran's operatives and terrorists but it was necessary to carry out the 'silencing' in such a horrible way that anybody else who might have learned something from Spiro would be frightened out of betraying what they knew to the U.S. government.

It did not take the Iranians long to locate Ian Spiro and his family at their Rancho Santa Fe home near San Diego. Immediately after the publication of Hewitt's book, Spiro began receiving threatening phone calls.[7] Ken Quarton, Spiro's brother-in-law, claimed that in the last two weeks of October 1992, Ian Spiro "feared for his life" because he had been identified as having worked for U.S. intelligence. Spiro told Quarton that he was getting "very disturbing phone calls" as a result of his exposure in the book.[8] Quarton further stated that later in the fall Spiro believed he was "in mortal danger" because of "something that had come to haunt him from the past."[9]

Other friends and neighbors agree that in October Spiro had "ominous concerns" as a result of a series of telephone calls.[10] At the time, Spiro did not have a gun. On October 22 he borrowed a .38-calibre handgun from his neighbor James Street. Street later said that Spiro "appeared to be quite concerned about his personal safety" when he borrowed the handgun[11] but stressed that Spiro had borrowed the gun "to insure his family's safety." He was distressed because the publication of his identity put his entire family in jeopardy.[12]

Spiro's fears were warranted, leading to what law enforcement authorities call a "confusing" case.[13]

The Spiro family was last seen by their neighbors on November 1, 1992.[14] From October 30 to November 1, the whole family, including Ian, spent a happy Halloween weekend, displaying no sign of an impending crisis or catastrophe.[15]

When Spiros' housekeeper arrived on Monday morning, November 2 , she saw Ian Spiro in a bathrobe. Spiro was surprised to see the maid. He quickly got dressed and before she could begin cleaning the house, drove her back to the migrant camp where she lived, telling her that the family was not there and that he was having "problems."[16] On Wednesday, November 4, a mysterious man stopped in front of Spiro's house to take pictures, then vanished.[17]

On November 5, the bodies of Gail Spiro and the three young Spiro children were found by neighbors at their Rancho Santa Fe home. They had been shot in the head from close range while they were asleep. Investigators believe the Spiro family was killed on November 1 or 2 . According to the local police, there were no signs of forced entry and nothing was missing from the house. However, British pathologists who examined her body insist that Gail Spiro struggled, and was severely bruised on her face, lips and knuckles, before she was subdued and shot. The gun used for the murder was not found. Ian Spiro had disappeared. After the bodies of his wife and children were found, attention immediately was focused on him as the prime suspect.[18]

Ian Stuart Spiro was last seen alive in the next day or two while making a call from a pay phone. According to an eyewitness, his eyes were strange, as if he was crying or drugged.[19] On November 8,

Ian Spiro's body was found in his Ford Explorer in an isolated spot in California's Anza-Borrego Desert State Park. He had been dead for several days, putting the time of his death close to the time of his family's murder. Since he was suspected in their killings, his death was assumed to be suicide.[20]

Spiro was found slumped over the steering wheel of his Explorer. No weapon was found in the vehicle. Police found sodium cyanide granules in a plastic bag in the Ford, as well as a cup and two water bags. Other traces of cyanide were found in the car, leading investigators to conclude that Spiro had died as a result of cyanide poisoning. However, an autopsy failed to reveal any specific cause of death.[21]

Two suitcases and Ian's briefcase were found in a deep ravine in the desert some three miles away from where his body was found. They were filled with family bills and other documents. The papers were organized inside. There were no clothes or other items in the bags. Law enforcement investigators concluded that the bags were tossed down the ravine by someone who did not want the papers destroyed but wanted them to be very hard to find. Investigators believe that Spiro threw the bags from his Explorer.[22]

Among the records recovered was an audiotape with a monologue of a very rambling Ian Spiro. The tape shows him as being very distressed over financial disasters and suggests that Gail had threatened to leave before her death. Alrogether the Spiro tape strongly suggests that Ian Spiro was in a personal crisis so desperate as to explain his committing the murder-suicide.[23]

However, immediately after the bodies were found, there were early indications that Ian Spiro and his family "may have been killed by international terrorists," although the local sheriff in Rancho Santa Fe insisted that there was no evidence to support such a hypothesis.

Ian's brother-in-law Ken Quarton stated emphatically that it was "totally inconceivable" that Spiro would kill his family and commit suicide. Although Spiro might have been in financial difficulties, Quarton insisted, he would not have committed murders and suicide over money issues.[24] Other relatives of Gail Spiro similarly insist that Ian was not capable of killing his beloved wife and children.[25]

Ken Quarton speculated that the Spiros "might have been victims of a terrorist hit squad."[26] British investigators suggest that by murdering the entire Spiro family, the killers sent a clear message to all others involved in the Iran-related affair not to dare to speak out. The people who were involved with Spiro know who they are; and therefore merely reading or hearing about the gruesome killings of the Spiros would suffice to convince them not to speak out for fear of bringing a similar fate upon themselves and, especially, their families. California law enforcement authorities remain convinced that it is a case of a murder-suicide fueled or motivated by an economic collapse leading to a mental break down.[27]

But there is a strong evidence that the death of Ian Spiro, the Jewish operative who helped both the CIA and the SIS/MI6 during the Iran and Lebanese hostages crises, was not a suicide.[28]

In Lebanon, Spiro had continued to be involved in clandestine affairs other than the hostage crisis at its height. In May 1987, he was involved in establishing high level contacts with Iran for the U.S. via his contacts in Lebanon.[29] In 1988, he tried to revive a humanitarian program in southern Lebanon which aimed at expediting the release of hostages and was derived from an audacious earlier British plan.[30]

Both projects had brought Spiro into close contact with some key members of the Iranian terrorist and intelligence elite. Among them were senior operatives who would be clandestinely deployed in the early 1990s for operations in the West.[31] Perhaps unwittingly, Ian Spiro was in a unique position to identify these individuals as Iranian or HizbAllah operatives by recognizing their faces.

Middle East sources have provided additional evidence that makes it possible to reconstruct Spiro's last days.[32] The Iranian agents who made the threatening phone calls to Ian must have concluded that while he was appropriately worried for the safety of his family, he was at the same time defiant enough to justify Iranian intelligence's concern that he might report them to the American security authorities. Therefore not only was it necessary to silence Spiro and set a horrifying example for others, but it was also imperative for Tehran to discover whether Spiro had already betrayed anyone.

According to several sources in the Middle East, Tehran decided to bring in a special team in order to insure the clandestine character of the Spiro

project. Gulam Hussein Shurazeh, a highly experienced senior Iranian intelligence officer and a
veteran of sensitive overseas hits such as the assassination of former prime minister Shapur
Bakhtiar in Paris, was sent to California to organize and oversee the silencing of Spiro. Shurazeh
has a valid U.S. Green Card — an official residence
permit for legal aliens living permanently in the
United States — identifying his place of residence
as a location on the West Coast. This simplified
his task.[33]

At least some of the other members of this hit
team were former East German and/or Soviet intelligence expert operatives who were brought to the
United States especially for this operation. On the
night of November 1/2 they took the entire Spiro
family hostage. On the morning of November 2, the
family was still alive, held hostage. This explains
why Ian Spiro refused to let the maid into the house
but instead hastily took her home, then returned to
his house. In order to extract information from Ian,
the operatives may have abused the Spiro family;
this would explain the bruises and struggle marks
on Gail Spiro.

For some reason, the operatives decided to remove Ian Spiro for further interrogation elsewhere.
He may have mentioned something that warranted
a knowledgeable interrogator, or perhaps he simply would not break and the interrogation therefore required drugs the operatives did not have on
hand. On the night of November 2, the operatives
methodically eliminated the Spiro family (except
for Ian) by shooting them in the head at close range

as they slept. They must have used a silencer, for no noise was heard in the neighborhood.

The operatives then left clandestinely in Spiro's Ford Explorer, taking Ian and large quantities of his papers with them. The mysterious man who arrived two days later to take pictures must have been an Iranian intelligence operative checking the house for external signs and any other evidence left behind by the hit team.

After his family was killed, Ian himself must have been further tortured and drugged for some time in order to find out exactly what he knew and had reported. This interrogation took place in the Anza-Borrego Desert State Park area. In the process, Spiro was forced to make the audio tape about financial and marital crises that would presumably indicate a motive for murder-suicide. Apparently he succeeded in escaping in his car, got rid of the bags with his papers, and even tried to make a phone call in a vain effort to get help. But he was recaptured soon after. The operatives must have concluded that there was no point in keeping him around any longer. His suicide was then "induced" and "assisted."

It is worth noting that all the procedures and approaches described here are identical to these repeatedly used by both the Soviet and Iranian intelligence services in the Middle East and Western Europe. Moreover, as demonstrated after of the March 1989 fire bomb attack on Mrs. Rogers discussed in Chapter 2 above, in which the perpetrator(s) made a perfect escape, and the similarly smooth handling of the Spiro operation, Iran has a very efficient and superbly tight network in the San Diego area — so much so that "the elimination" of Ian Spiro and his family in San Diego went without a hitch and in November 1992, Iran was free to resume the execution of its plans for the bombing in New York .

The HizbAllah version of the Spiro story, although self-serving, is telling. According to them, Ian Spiro was a "double agent" who had mediated between Tehran and Washington and London, and he and his family were eliminated by the CIA in order to silence him before he could publish what he knew about the hostage crisis and other American deals with Iran. The HizbAllah insists that the SAVAMA was eager to strike immediately in America in November 1992 in order to avenge Spiro's blood but was constrained by logistical problems.

This Tehran-inspired version of the Spiro affair, though convoluted, essentially confirms two key points: that Spiro was killed in order to silence him permanently, and that in November 1992 Iranian terrorist assets were already in a position to strike.[34] Thus, the terrorist mission in New York had to be delayed until after Ian Spiro was eliminated and the safety of the networks was confirmed.

REACHING A MILESTONE

At this point, the imminent terrorist campaign in America had already become a crucial component of Iran's grand strategy. In early November 1992,

President Hashemi-Rafsanjani elucidated the Iranian strategic vision, alluding to the role of international terrorism on American soil. He attributed Tehran's inability to unify the Muslim world, establish Iranian hegemony over the region, and destroy Israel to the American presence and influence in the Middle East.

Hashemi-Rafsanjani stressed that in the wake of the American elections the time was uniquely appropriate for the Islamists to revive their Holy War against America and Israel. "If the United States becomes entangled in domestic problems, as we are seeing now, the people here will settle accounts with them," he added.[35] One way to insure Washington's preoccupation with internal problems is, of course, through a terrorist campaign at home.

With the Spiro threat taken care of, it was time to present the plans for the New York operations to the terrorist masters from Tehran and Khartoum for their approval. By mid-November 1992, the terrorist leaders in America were confident that they were capable of launching a major terrorist strike in the middle of New York. On November 30, using the name "Kamal Ibraham", Ramzi Ahmad Youssuf purchased several chemicals of the type that would later be used to build the bomb for the World Trade Center, including urea and nitric acid. He ordered the materials delivered to a storage locker in Jersey City that had been rented earlier that day by Salameh, who also used the same alias, "Kamal Ibraham".[36]

A major challenge facing the expert terrorists was selecting the proper detonator. It is highly likely that it was a combination of a remote control device[37] with a simple timer as a back-up system.[38] The main problem with a building the size of the World Trade Center is the immense steel structure that masks virtually any radio communication, including signals, within enclosed spaces such as the underground parking garages. (This same phenomenon causes your car radio to stop playing when you drive under bridges or in underground parking lots.) Major exceptions are the frequencies used for cellular telephones and pagers.

The expert terrorists capitalised on this in selecting the primary remote-control detonator for the World Trade Center bombing. The detonator seems to have been a modification of a Swiss-made telephone pager — a beeper. Such a detonator could be activated by a simple phone call, even from a pay phone, a carphone, or a hand-held mobile phone. In late 1992, Vienna-based Palestinian operatives, formerly associated with Abu-Nidal and currently associated with Iranian-controlled Islamists, ordered 150 of these pagers from a Swiss company. The pagers were soon delivered. The Vienna bank account used for the payment had been used by Abu-Nidal terrorists for some four years.[39]

The possibility that one of these pagers was used in New York should also be assessed on the basis of the extensive evidence connecting Vienna with the network involved in the World Trade Center explosion.[40] Another business account in the same bank was a front for a Beirut-based Islamist terrorist organization and was used to transfer funds to Ayyad's bank accounts.[41]

Furthermore, a group of Sheikh Abdel-Rahman's activist followers operate within the Islamic Center in Vienna, from which they distribute Islamist leaflets and literature warning of an escalating global jihad.[42] During his frequent trips between Germany and the United States, Abouhalima passed through Vienna several times and could have coordinated operations with the local followers of Sheikh Abdel-Rahman. Abouhalima also maintained close relations with the Muslim Brotherhood network in Munich, who could pick up the telephone pagers in Vienna if necessary. It is therefore likely that Vienna was used by the expert terrorists later involved in the New York operation as a source for their remote control device — a beeper.

The World Trade Center was selected as the first objective primarily because it was a low- risk target. Siddig Ibrahim Siddig Ali, the leader of the back-up cell, had worked in the World Trade Center as a security guard for the Federal Home Loan Bank between August 1988 and December 1991. In this capacity he received training and acquired experience on the electronic surveillance systems installed in the building and the parking areas.[43] Such knowledge would greatly assist in planning for the placement of the car-bomb, and indeed, Siddig did help plan the bombing.[44]

On May 18, 1993, when the FBI informant Salem tried to probe Siddig for a motive for the World Trade Center bombing, he could not get a straight answer.[45] In another conversation, Siddig acknowledged that the United Nations building was the conspirators' primary target and that the World

Trade Center was a secondary alternative choice. This time Siddig provided an explanation for that choice: "The operation is to make them lose millions and that is what happened. This is a message. We want to tell them that you are not far from us, we can get you any time."[46]

Abouhalima would later confide to his cellmate, Theodore Williams, that the secondary or follow-up target of *his* cell was the Statue of Liberty: with their capabilities proven in the World Trade Center, the Islamists would then proceed to bomb the very symbol of America.[47] This logic, again, suggests that the World Trade Center was to be a low-risk operation in which a successful powerful explosion was an achievement in its own right.

Nevertheless, Tehran continued to urge caution and asked for a thorough evaluation of the network's actual professional and security capabilities.[48] In early December 1992, there were indications of impending major events in Islamist international terrorism. Abdel-Rahman summoned two of his closest aides from Egypt for urgent consultations in New York, ostensibly in connection with his forthcoming deportation hearings. In reality, they met to discuss and coordinate terrorist strikes in the Middle East and the West and charted the transfer of "talent" from Sudan, Afghanistan, and Lebanon to their ultimate objectives.

(In retrospect, it is worth noting that about that time, Egyptian police discovered "an explosives factory and explosives and incendiary charges" in a house of one of Abdel-Rahman's followers. The instructions for making explosives and building bombs had come from abroad.)[49] In addition to overall strategic discussions concerning Islamist terrorism, the Sheikh's aides who came to New York had both the knowledge and authority that enabled them to inspect the proposed plans and carry an authoritative detailed report back to Tehran and Khartoum.

In connection with his possible deportation for Green Card violations, Abdel-Rahman was notified that fall-back headquarters had already been set up for him in London and Khartoum.[50] Nevertheless, he applied for political asylum in America, citing as justification the fear of retribution from Egypt if he was deported.[51] His followers were making plans for him to settle in either Syria or Iran if he was deported from the United States.[52] (But after the World Trade Center bombing Tehran told the Islamists that it will refuse to accept the Sheikh: Tehran is convinced that giving shelter to Abdel-Rahman would serve as a legal excuse to implicate it in the New York terrorism and serve as an excuse for Israeli and American strikes against Iran.[53] His request for asylum in the United States has since been denied.)

Meanwhile, the command structure of the Islamist terrorist network that was committed to a spectacular operation in New York was consolidated toward the end of 1992. Abouhalima, one of its senior commanders, later acknowledged that it was "financially backed and spiritually guided by Iran."[54] He added that his own cell was "part of a nationwide organization funded from overseas," stressing that it was only a small component of a larger terrorist network. "It's not just us, it's 300 men across the country who would do anything to hurt the U.S. Government," he told his cellmate Williams.[55]

Like all major Iranian-controlled networks, the New York network was headed by four key commanders, each with a different background and distinct responsibility:

1. Muhammad Rezah Shalchian (or Chalagian) Tabrizi was the senior Iranian intelligence commander. As noted above, Shalchian, a senior IRGC Intelligence officer, works under the cover of his diplomatic position as comptroller for Iran's mission at the UN.

2. Ramzi Ahmad Youssuf was the senior terrorist expert, the professional commander who arrived from the center especially to conduct the operation and departed safely immediately after its completion. He was in command of the several expert terrorists like Ajaj who planned and facilitated the operation. He was in charge of the professional aspects of the operations, from building and rigging the bomb so that it inflicted the anticipated damage, to its correct placement and activation, to the timely, safe and secure escape of all the expert terrorists.

3. Mahmud Abouhalima was the leader of the New York-based network in his capacity as the representative of Sheikh Umar Abdel-Rahman. He ensured that all the religious decrees and professional instructions were carried out and made progress reports to the Sheikh while creating a shield of deniability between the spiritual leader and his ter-

rorist disciples. He was one of the on-site professional leaders activated for the operation and provided direct support services to the expert terrorists who arrived from overseas.

4. Ibrahim A. Elgabrowny (al-Jabaruni) was in charge of the support team, providing logistics for the quality operatives and terrorists while controlling and maintaining discipline among the expendable "martyrs." He was the stay-behind commander, intentionally left in place to go to jail, where he make insure that the captured expendables continue to perform their preassigned roles, i.e., to attract attention to themselves (thereby diverting it from others) and transform their trial into a show of Islamist defiance.

THE FUQRA FACTOR

As they were planning and preparing for the major sabotage operation, the expert terrorists needed specialised materials and components for the bomb, ranging from plastique high explosives to blasting caps, as well as weapons for possible assassinations. Meeting these requirements resulted in the activation of the Pakistan-sponsored Fuqra organization, thereby serving as a further demonstration of the comprehensiveness of the Iranian-controlled terrorist system in the United States and Canada.

An American black Muslim involved with Fuqra, Clement Rodney Hampton-El, soon emerged as the key to a separate logistical system. (Hampton-El was one of the original activists in the conspiracy, one of the three who met with Sheikh Awdah at Kennedy Airport in January 1990.)

Clement Rodney Hampton-El, age 55, a.k.a. Rashid Hampton, Abdul Rashid Abdullah and Dr. Rashid, is an American-born black Muslim activist.[56] According to one of his neighbors, Hampton-El "was devoted to Louis Farrakhan" and praised him repeatedly.[57] In 1984 Hampton-El spent a year or more as a combat medic in Afghanistan, serving with the Islamist forces of Gulbaddin Hekmatyar until he was wounded and evacuated home to the United States.[58] Soon after, Hampton-El became connected with the Fuqra organization in New York and was soon working closely with it.

Fuqra had used Hampton-El as a source for weapons and explosives for their criminal and terrorist activities in recent years.[59] By the late 1980s, Hampton-El was believed to be a leader of a violent Islamist faction in Brooklyn, already planning assassinations and implicated in murders.[60] He was also directly involved in the Islamist network's bomb-making effort. In June 1993, police would find in his apartment manuals for bomb-making that originated in Pakistan and were identical to these recovered from Ajaj and Youssuf in connection with the World Trade Center bombing.[61]

The recruitment and activation of black American Muslims like Hampton-El under the banner of Fuqra is the culmination of a lengthy process on which Tehran embarked in the mid-1980s. The Iranian-Afghan mujahideen connection has been instrumental in Tehran's concentrated effort to recruit, train and sustain an indigenous cadre of operatives and terrorists in the United States. Iran concentrated its efforts on the American Black Muslim community for two reasons: the strong influence of Daoud Salahuddin (born David Belfield), who committed Khomeyni's first assassination in the U.S. in July 1980 and then escaped to Tehran to become the Ayatollah Khomeyni's's protegé, and Qaddafi's claims of success in building terrorist cadres among black Muslims in America. As a result of a long-term Iranian program, there is already a sizeable cadre of highly-motivated American terrorists in Pakistan. In the mid-1980s, under Khomeyni's supervision, Tehran decided on a specific recruitment drive among black Americans.

The popularity of the Afghan cause in the West and the great success of Iranian intelligence's initial cooperation with the ISI-*Mujahideen*, convinced Tehran that it would be most expedient to capitalize on this connection in order to implement Salahuddin's program for terrorist recruitment in America. In 1985, Iran established within the foreign ministry's "Export of the Revolution" section a department headed by a Pakistani mullah to provide clandestine assistance to hard-to-reach Islamist communities — and especially American blacks. The funds would come from the Martyrs' Foundation and be distributed via legal charities.[62]

Daoud Salahuddin remained personally involved in the recruitment of Black Muslims in the United States for the Iranian terrorist network as well as in training terrorists in Iran for operations in America.[63] In the 1980s he was also an instructor in hand-to-hand combat and assassination techniques in an IRGC school near Tehran.[64]

Initial recruitment came from among the veteran Muslim radicals of the 1960s and 1970s and their younger followers who were inspired by the romanticization of the Iranian revolution and/or the jihad in Afghanistan. Special attention was paid to disgruntled but highly experienced Vietnam veterans.

Some of these Americans even converted to Shi'ism. Most of them were trained in Pakistan and Iran. From the mid-1980s on, many fought in Afghanistan — and in Beirut, where some of them were formally associated with the HizbAllah. The organized reinsertion of a select few of these American *Hizbollahhi* and mujahideen into the United States began around 1987-1988, once Tehran and Damascus were convinced that their infrastructure of support networks was capable of sustaining the required operations. [65] For example, the New York house where Tarig Elhassan — a Sudanese who was arrested for involvement in the terrorist plans of summer 1993 — lived, had served in the mid-1980s as a safe house and transit point for American volunteers on their way to and from Afghanistan. Most of them were black Muslims and veterans of military service who frequently identified themselves as "demolition experts."[66]

When the novelty, zeal and hope of the Iranian Revolution began to subside, Tehran shifted to recruiting among blacks in American prisons, converting them to fundamentalist Islam and, when possible, Shi'ism specifically. Because of the operation's missionary aspects — i.e., conversion to Shi'ite Islam — it began under Khomeyni's supervision. In early 1986, Iran began approaching and ultimately recruiting prisoners while they were still incarcerated. Iranian-supported front organizations made contact with disgruntled black Muslim prisoners in all the major prisons in America.

Shi'ite charities established small communes in various cities, ostensibly for the rehabilitation of former prisoners, where recruitment is finalized. After brain-washing, selected ex-prisoners swore allegiance to the Ayatollah Khomeyni and volunteered for jihad.They were then sent to Pakistan for training with the Islamist mujahideen and the ISI. The more promising among them were identified and kept for additional specialized training. Although several such ex-prisoner recruits finished terrorist training in Pakistan in 1988-1989, they were kept there, and apparently only a few have as yet been infiltrated back into the United States.[67] The black Muslim candidates for terrorism in the U.S. are now drawn from those who have returned.

Another drive to recruit American black Muslims for the "jihad worldwide" was started in 1986 by Sudanese Islamists. The Bedford-Stuyvesant district in Brooklyn was one of the primary areas of recruitment activity.[68] Siddig Ibrahim Siddig Ali, who arrived in America when these recruitment efforts were beginning, soon emerged as their leader. Some of the Americans and Sudanese immigrants in Brooklyn were trained, supposedly to join the mujahideen in Afghanistan. Many of the American Muslims then left for Pakistan and Afghanistan; but the Sudanese are not known to have left the United States.

The "spiritual leader" of the Islamist Sudanese in America is Imam Siraj Wahhaj, an African-American preaching at the al-Taqwa mosque in Brooklyn who shuttles between the U.S. and Sudan.[69] In recent years the recruitment drive among American black Muslims was stepped up by Siddig who "wanted to help oppressed Muslims" and expressed interest in joining the jihad in Bosnia.[70]

Years earlier, back in the mid-1980s when American recruitment was picking up, a need emerged for an institutionalized selection, training, and vetting program that would screen a large number of volunteers, identify the most promising, and then recruit them and provide them with extensive terrorist training. Such a process had to take place outside the United States, and Pakistan was identified as the most suitable location. Ostensibly an ally of the U.S., Pakistan was the gateway to the war in Afghanistan, a war that was supported by the American government and the public. A constant stream of Western journalists, relief and humanitarian aid personnel and officials came and went regularly. Americans travelling to Pakistan would therefore not raise suspicion. In any case, the ISI and Islamist organizations like Shalabi's Al-Kifah Center in Brooklyn provided many of the volunteers with forged papers enabling them to travel without any record.

By then there was a rapidly expanding training infrastructure in Pakistan for the Afghan mujahideen which provided a perfect cover for the handling of the American Muslims. The American black Muslim recruits were sent to Pakistan for training with the Islamist mujahideen and the ISI. The more promising were identified and received additional training in Pakistan, Lebanon and Iran.[71]

In sum, in the mid 1980s, Pakistan's ISI was completing a vast training infrastructure for the Afghan resistance that could be used just as well for the training and support of other regional groups. And although this training infrastructure was being financed largely by the United States to help the Afghan struggle against the Soviet occupiers, the vast majority of the Afghan resistance organizations supported by it were anti-American.

In a 1983 decree, for example, the leader of the Jamiat-i Islami Afghan Islamist organization, Burhanuddin Rabbani, (currently the President of Afghanistan) equated the United States and the Soviet Union as the infidel enemies of Islam: "In point of us conquerist America and bloodthirsty USSR are both enemy of the great revolution of Iran and Afghanistan. And the intrigues that America design against the revolution of Iran, criminal Russian confirmed it. And the flood of blood that circulate by the executioner Russia in Afghanistan is confirmed with America. [signed] Rabbani."[72]

Nevertheless, via the ISI the mujahideen of Jamiat-i Islami received tremendous amounts of training, weapons and supplies, financed by the United States .

Little wonder, therefore, that Islamabad went to great lengths to insure that the CIA was isolated by the ISI from the training infrastructure it financed.

Brigadier Mohammad Yousaf, the head of the Inter-Service Intelligence's Afghan Bureau, complained that General Abdul Rahman Akhtar Khan, Chief of ISI from 1980 to 1987, "faced many problems with the Americans and the CIA." Akhtar adamantly refused American requests to train the mujahideen or even to have direct access to them. "Akhtar never allowed Americans to become directly involved in the jihad," Yousaf recalled. Akhtar and the ISI high command strongly insisted on "keeping Americans out" of the entire training and supply system they were sponsoring.[73]

Yousaf emphasized that the ISI was the sole provider of training in Pakistan and Afghanistan, and that "no American or Chinese instructor was ever involved in giving training on any kind of weapon or equipment to the mujahideen ... This was a deliberate, carefully considered policy that we steadfastly refused to change despite mounting pressure from the CIA, and later from the U.S. Defense Department, to allow them to take over." Yousaf points out that "from the start" the ISI leadership "successfully resisted" all American efforts to be directly involved in the support for the Afghan mujahideen, noting to the ISI's ability to impose limitations on CIA visits to training camps even though the CIA was financing them. "General Akhtar was initially adamant that no visitor should be allowed to any camp; however, the clamor from the CIA and the U.S. was so persistent that eventually he conceded that CIA officials could be admitted."[74]

Islamabad's critical need to shield and conceal the American-financed training infrastructure from American officials was based on much more than the disagreement between the ISI and Washington over the Islamist character of the favored recipients of military assistance. The ISI was adamantly opposed to supporting the resistance organizations associated with the predominantly tribal/traditional Pushtun population, the dominant ethnic group in Afghanistan before the war, who were essentially pro-Western. Instead the ISI insisted on diverting some 70% of the foreign aid to the Islamist parties, who were inherently and virulently anti-American.

But the most important reason for the ISI's insistence on keeping the CIA and other American officials out of the camps was the extent of the training and supporting of "volunteers" and others in these camps.

The most numerous of these were the thousands of Islamist trainees from Indian Kashmir, and, to a lesser extent, Sikhs from the India's Punjab province, both of which were centers of violent insurrection against the Indian government. In addition, hundreds of Islamists from all over the Arab and Muslim world were routinely trained in the camps originally set up to train Afghan mujahideen. From the mid-1980s on, Pakistan's ISI was training an average of 100 Arab mujahideen a month. They received military training in Peshawar and, after their return from Afghanistan, refresher courses and advanced training special camps in Sudan and Yemen.[75]

The work of AbdAllah Azzam was most important in establishing a cadre of "Afghan" terrorists in America. A Palestinian from Jordan, Azzam — who inspired Shalabi to start his Islamist center in Brooklyn — was among the founding fathers of what is today the International Legion of Islam. He started his work in Peshawar by establishing a center to channel the Arab volunteers to the Islamist resistance organizations. Within a few years, Azzam's work was transformed into organizing bodies of volunteers that would be of use back in their home countries.

As one example, some of the 3,000 Algerians who fought in Afghanistan established their own "Algerian Legion" which fought under Ahmad Shah Massoud, the commander in Afghanistan's Panjsher Valley and nominally part of Rabbani's Jamiat (who has benefited from a great deal of attention in the Western press). Azzam was instrumental in cementing relations between Massoud and the Algerian mujahideen and brought to Massoud the leading Algerian commander known as "Hajj Bunua." Indeed, Azzam's own children are with Massoud.[76]

Azzam devoted a lot of time and attention to the Islamist cause in America because he recognized that America offered a tremendous potential for numbers of educated Believers capable of providing high-quality human resources for the jihad. Toward this end he encouraged Shalabi to expand his efforts to support the jihad from America.

Most important, however, was Azzam's influence over the American volunteers in Peshawar. He spent a lot of time with them, instilling in them the spirit of jihad. Many were persuaded of the importance of this "opportunity" to fullfill the Holy Duty of jihad. Abu Mahmud Hammoody, now living in Chicago, was so influenced by Azzam that he spent the next eight years fighting in several jihad causes from Afghanistan to Bosnia. "Sheikh AbdAllah knew when and where he had to implement his political and religious beliefs," explained Hammoody. As Azzam hoped, many of his committed followers returned to America, establishing cadres of "Afghans".[77]

AbdAllah Azzam was assassinated by a car bomb in Peshawar on November 24, 1989.[78]

Meanwhile, as mentioned above, the organized infiltration of a select few of these American Hizbollahhi and mujahideen back into the United States began around 1987-1988 when Tehran and Damascus were sure that their support infrastructure there could take care of them.

Capitalizing on a 1984 agreement between Iran and Gulbaddin Hekmatyar, an Afghan resistance figure (now prime minister of Afghanistan) who was fronting for the ISI , the Iranian, HizbAllah and Pakistani terrorist experts who were needed to expand the Fuqra networks in the United States could travel to America via Pakistan using the make-shift travel documents standardly given to the Afghan refugees and resistance fighters. The ISI routinely vouched for these travelers as being Afghan mujahideen or refugees, thus significantly expediting their receiving American entry visas.[79]

Iranian intelligence began infiltrating operatives and terrorists into many predominantly Sunni Islamist movements considered pro-Western, like the

Afghan resistance and several Arab organizations, and through them deployed their assets in the United States, where these terrorists and operatives now wait, ready to be activated as needed.[80]

Meanwhile, although several of the American ex-convict recruits finished terrorist training in Pakistan in 1988-1989, they were kept there. At that time, apparently, only a few had been infiltrated back into the United States, but the black Muslim candidates for terrorism in the U.S. now are drawn from these cadres.[81]

In the 1990s, the Armed Islamic Movement [AIM] began to play an increasingly major role in the consolidation of Pakistan's terrorist capabilities. In the spring of 1991, eighteen Kashmiri Islamists were accepted for about six months of highly specialized terrorist training in Sudan personally supervised by Turabi and Mustafa Uthman, Turabi's deputy for intelligence.[82] In September 1991 Turabi visited Pakistan and went into Afghanistan to coordinate terrorist support activities; the local Islamist movements became members of Turabi's Popular International Organization [PIO]. In this capacity they now provide assistance to, and closely cooperate with, Egyptian Islamists, Lebanon's HizbAllah, Algeria's FIS, and the Sudan's NIF. PIO members exchange experts and cooperate in joint support and training activities.[83]

Meanwhile, Turabi continued his efforts to expand international ties and cooperation among the elements of the terrorist infrastructure in Sudan. In late November 1991, he consolidated arrangements to exchange and dispatch trainees to Islamist (mainly Muslim Brotherhood) sites in Peshawar.[84]

In 1992, AIM began preparations in Pakistan to upgrade terrorist operations in the United States and Canada as part of Tehran's master plan. These preparations are conducted under the cover of *Jamaat-ul-Fuqra*, ostensibly an organization led by Sheikh Mubarak Ali Shah Jilani, a Pakistani Kashmiri living in Lahore. But in Pakistan Jamaat-ul-Fuqra is really controlled by the ISI. Specifically, since mid-1992, the ISI's Brigadier Imtiaz has been responsible for "training Black Muslims from the USA and Canada through the Jamaat-ul-Fuqra for terrorist operations in North America and West Europe."

Sheikh Jilani himself is directly involved in recruitment of American Black Muslims in Pakistan and their indoctrination. For actual preparing them, "Jilani, with the help of the ISI and the Pakistan IB [Intelligence Bureau], runs a training center near Lahore where Sudanese instructors carry out their task." But Jilani and Imtiaz have no operational responsibility in North America,[85] for that rests with Sheikh Umar Abdel-Rahman in New York.

The direct involvement of Imtiaz in the Fuqra program is a reflection of the extent of the Pakistani support for the export of terrorism to the United States. Brigadier Imtiaz is a former director of the ISI Internal Security Wing, and a protegé of General Akhtar Abdul Rahman Khan, ISI's powerful chief.

After the death of Pakistan's President Zia in a plane crash in 1989, Imtiaz was instrumental in the establishment of the IJI party as a countervailing political force to Benazir Bhutto's PPP. This gave Imtiaz tremendous and lasting influence on the key politicians. He was soon rewarded. When Nawaz Sharif of the IJI party took office as prime minister in late 1990 Imtiaz was named Chief of the Directorate of Intelligence Bureau (DIB). Sharif and Imtiaz are fiercely loyal to each other and one rarely if ever makes any political move without the other. The restoration of Sharif as prime minister in the summer of 1993 signalled the return of Imtiaz.[86]

In the United States, the Fuqra is essentially an organization within an organization. On the outside, there is a veteran quasi-criminal organization involving some 3,000 members, mainly black Muslims, which has been in existence for fifteen or twenty years. Some members of the Fuqra "Islamic fundamentalist sect" come from, and continue to maintain ties with, Pakistan. Their Pakistani leader, Sheikh Jilani, is committed to the "plight of African-Americans."[87]

But most important is the inner core of Fuqra, only a few hundred strong, for which the larger visible Fuqra serves as a cover and front. The inner group are highly trained terrorists. They are predominantly American black Muslims recruited in the 1980s to fight for Afghanistan and shipped to Pakistan for lengthy training in the Lahore area. They have been prepared for terrorism in America and since the 1990s, a growing number of them are being infiltrated back home.

When he was in America, Rodney Hampton-El sustained operations under the cover of Fuqra. The quasi-criminal character of the larger, more visible Fuqra provides an explanation for the weapons and explosives, which appear to be for the purposes of the organization's criminal activities and attacks on popular Indian-style cults. But in fact some of these weapons and explosives are actually stockpiles for the Islamist terrorists — and an increasing number of highly-trained black American terrorists receive shelter and support in the Fuqra's inner core as they wait to be activated.

Meanwhile, the more ordinary criminal/quasi-terrorist activities associated with Fuqra increase. A characteristic example occurred in the Colorado Springs area, where some local members of Fuqra come from, and maintain ties with, Pakistan. In 1989 and 1992, police discovered explosives, bombs, pagers modified as fuses, guns (including automatic rifles), military manuals, and pictures of Sheikh Abdel-Rahman in the Fuqra compound. In 1992, two members were accused of stealing money from the state Workmen's Compensation fund in order to finance their operations.[88] Altogether, seven Fuqra members in Colorado are accused of bilking the government out of some $355,000 and using it to finance terrorist training camps in Pakistan.[89]

In recent years Fuqra activities have become increasingly ideological: 5-6 members from the Brooklyn area were arrested in October 1991 on the Canadian border, on their way to Toronto to blow up a Hindu temple and a theater in Toronto.[90]

Another recent example of criminal activities pointed to association with Sheikh Umar Abdel-Rahman and indicated that the Fuqra members are aware of relations with Islamist terrorists. In early August 1993, agents of the Bureau of Alcohol, Tobacco and Firearms arrested nine black Muslims for selling explosives (including four home-made explosive devices) and 180 "cleaned" submachine-guns, automatic pistols, and revolvers from which all serial numbers and other identifying marks had been professionally erased. One of these guns had already been used in a drug-related slaying in Brooklyn.

Members of the arrested gang of gun and explosive dealers considered Sheikh Umar Abdel-Rahman to be their spiritual leader. Earlier that summer, on June 15, the group leader, 43-year-old Lamont Holder (a.k.a. Massoud Shaheed) from Staten Island, had invited Federal agents to meet Sheikh Umar in his mosque in order to prove his own importance and his access to the top. Holder identified one "Rasheed," the source of their pipebombs, as the main supplier of the New York plotters.

"Rasheed" was a name used by Rodney Hampton-El, and indeed, after Hampton-El's arrest Holder told the undercover agents that explosives were "too hot" and that because "Rasheed has been arrested" he "can't do it", i.e. provide explosives. Holder refused to provide a pipe bomb because of the arrests of Sheikh Umar Abdel-Rahman and his followers, expressing apprehension about getting implicated through the Fuqra connection with the Islamist terrorists. Another key member of Holder's Fuqra network, 45-year-old Leon Holland (a.k.a. Abdoul Malik Shabazz) from Brooklyn, was also involved in crack trafficking and weapons violations.[91]

To date Hampton-El is the only member of the Fuqra's inner core who has been exposed, but ultimately, the high-quality inner-core Fuqra operatives and terrorists will provide quality-edge capabilities to the larger and more comprehensive Islamist network in the United States and Canada, the one based on the Muslim emigré communties. The bombing of the World Trade Center and the operations planned for July 4th, 1993, were among the first such operations involving a contribution by Fuqra elite terrorists.

But the training and preparation of such Fuqra terrorists continues to be carried on in Pakistan under Imtiaz. In view of the intimate relations Imtiaz enjoys with Sharif, it is inconceivable that the latter knows nothing about the Fuqra project. Since he is Prime Minister, Nawaz Sharif's knowledge and inaction as an individual can be interpreted as the acquiescence in, if not outright support for, the conduct of Islamist terrorism in the United States by the Government of Pakistan as a state.

OTHER CRIMINAL ACTIVITIES

The Fuqra members are not the only Islamist terrorists involved in ordinary criminal activities in addition to their participation in preparations for terrorist strikes. Some of the defendants involved in the New York bombing plots were also involved in drug trafficking and sales, supposedly in order to finance operations.[92] One of them, Matharawy Muhammad Said Saleh, was convicted as a heroin dealer in Detroit in 1988.[93] However, a major scheme to finance the New York network brought up by Siddig Ibrahim Siddig Ali strongly points to yet another form of contact and cooperation with Iranian intelligence.

On May 18, Siddig told Salem that he could lay his hands on "millions" in counterfeit American dollars to be laundered via contacts in the Persian Gulf. Siddig offered to sell a million dollars for $150,000, well below market value. The source of the money was identified as "a good Muslim."[94] Quantities of counterfeit $100 bills were later found at the apartment of Sheikh Umar Abdel-Rahman, indicating that the network has already received some of the money.

The network's access to counterfeit U.S. dollars is extremely important.

Since 1991, the governments of Iran and Syria have been actively engaged in economic warfare against the United States through the production and distribution of very large quantities — estimated at billions of dollars — of high-quality counterfeit U.S. currency, primarily $100 bills. The actual smuggling of the counterfeit bills and their distribution in the U.S. and elsewhere are carried out by the international terrorist networks controlled by both states. These operations exploit existing terrorist and drug-smuggling networks already in place.

Iran and its allies produce and distribute the counterfeit U.S. notes in three qualities: extremely high quality, medium quality and a low quality that nevertheless is actually quite good. The high-quality $100 notes are used directly against the American banking system. The notes are printed in the official Iranian mint in Tehran, using equipment and expertise purchased from the United States in the days of the Shah. Israeli officials have stated that these dollars are being printed on "high-tech, state-owned presses with paper acquired only by governments." The plates used for all the counterfeit $100 bills are virtually perfect and the specialized ink is almost always of extremely high quality, mixed in the laboratories of the national mint in Tehran by chemists who studied in the U.S.[95]

The HizbAllah is responsible for the distribution of the counterfeit $100 bills in the United States and Canada on behalf of Iranian Intelligence. Large quantities of counterfeit money are smuggled into both countries along the proven routes that the HizbAllah and other terrorist organizations controlled by Syria and Iran have long been using to insert weapons, explosives, drugs and operatives. Roundabout routes via Persian Gulf states have been in use since early 1992.

The chiefs of the IRGC Intelligence and the VEVAK (the Ministry of Intelligence and Security) are convinced that the modes and avenues of entry into the United States they are using are safe and solid, and thus can sustain a greater volume of shipments.[96] The "millions" of counterfeit U.S. dollars claimed by the New York Islamist terrorist network could not have come from any source other than Iranian intelligence and their HizbAllah distribution networks in the United States. The availability of these counterfeits reflects the existence of comprehensive relations between the New York Islamist terrorist network and Iranian intelligence.

Chapter 5

FIRST STRIKE

Fully aware of the significance and implications of the impending strike in New York, Tehran decided in December 1992 on last-minute political maneuvers to provide Iran with a political alibi.

All of the preparations for the terrorist assault on America had been made during the period of Republican administrations, which were perceived to be implacably anti-Iranian. The Iranians were surprised when the Democrats won the 1992 presidential election. They considered the possibility that the new Clinton administration might alter the situation, and decided to undertake a major last-minute test to see if there was any new American political posture.

This rather hectic effort to find out exactly where Washington, and especially the new Democratic administration, stands vis-á-vis Iran, the Islamic bloc it controls, and the Islamist campaign it leads, makes absolutely clear the extent of Iranian control over Islamist terrorist operations in the U.S., and just how fully integrated they are as an element of Iranian-Islamist policies.

Last Minute Test, First Strike

In order to minimise the possibility of misunderstandings in this last minute probe, Tehran decided to capitalize on personal relations that its own diplomats had established with American officials of the Carter era, particularly during the negotiations for the release of the American embassy hostages in Tehran in 1979-80. Many of those American officials were now expected to assume senior positions in the new Clinton administration.

Ibrahim Yazdi, a former Iranian foreign minister, had taken part in hostage negotiations with Warren Christopher, who was slated to become the new Secretary of State. In early December 1992, Yazdi was sent to the United States, ostensibly to visit his family in California. In fact, he immediately began meeting secretly with former Carter administration officials who had been involved in negotiations with Iran more than a decade earlier. Through them, Yazdi reached high levels of the prospective Clinton administration. Reportedly, he even met with Christopher himself.

Yazdi claimed to be speaking for former Prime Minister Mehdi Bazargan, but this kind of initiative could not have taken place without the personal approval of Hashemi-Rafsanjani.[1] Yazdi urged his American contacts to improve economic and political relations and open negotiations with Tehran in order to preserve what he and others describe as the "moderate" and "pragmatist" regime of Hashemi-Rafsanjani.

But Washington "turned a deaf ear" to the Iranian request that money that the former Shah had paid for weapons be returned to Iran following secret negotiations.[2]

While Yazdi was making his approaches, Tehran warned the U.S. government indirectly — via Arab intermediaries, primarily the intelligence services of the Arab States of the Persian Gulf — that if its political overtures were rejected, there would be a "war between the CIA and the Iranian SAVAMA."[3] When Tehran learned of the negative American reaction to Yazdi's diplomatic initiative, they decided it was high time to demonstrate the SAVAMA's ability to strike at the CIA.

On the morning of January 25, 1993, a lone gunman carrying an AK-47 assault rifle calmly walked along a line of cars jammed up on the highway turnoff outside the entrance to CIA headquarters in Langley, Virginia, and methodically shot several CIA employees, killing two and wounding three others. He then got into a brown van and vanished.[4]

What was initially interpreted as the irrational action of an individual, perhaps a disgruntled CIA employee, in fact turned out to be an operation of Iran's "Afghan" network.

The killer was soon identified as Mir Amail Kansi, a 28-year-old Pakistani.[5] Kansi was an Iranian long-term plant, an illegal agent who had been infiltrated into the United States for operations in the Washington area. There he waited until he was activated to carry out the CIA killings. His background points to a clear pattern of identification, recruitment and training by Iranian intelligence.

Mir Amail Kansi is a member of the Kansi Pushtun tribe, which lives in Pakistan's Baluchistan Province near the Afghan border. Since the mid-1980s the Kansi Pushtuns have been involved in moving weapons and goods in and out of central Afghanistan. Although initially it was predominantly an ISI operation, it also brought the Kansi Pushtuns into close cooperation with Iranian intelligence and Shi'ite mujahideen organizations. [6]

Since the late 1980s, and especially in the eighteen to twenty-four months before the CIA murders, the balance of operations has shifted in favor of Iran. The Kansi lines of communications are now increasingly used to ship weapons and heroin from southern Afghanistan to Quetta, the capital of Baluchistan, and Karachi, from where they are smuggled to the West as part of the support system for the new Sunni Islamist International. [7] These activities have created an excellent manpower pool for audacious sabotage and terrorist operations. By late 1992, some 1,200 "Afghans" in Pakistan were involved in smuggling drugs from Pakistan to Europe and the United States to help finance the Islamist networks in those countries. [8]

Mir Aimal Kansi probably came to the attention of SAVAMA when he was studying in Quetta College between 1983 and 1986. By then he already had impeccable credentials. [9] Small changes in his life during this period suggest that he had already been approached and recruited by a Baluchi cut-out. * While in Quetta College, he was initially, and

* In intelligence jargon, a "cut-out" is an agent who has no apparent connection with an intelligence agency

appropriately, a member of the Pushtun Student Association.[10] Then he suddenly switched to the Baluchi Student Association.[11] For Kansi, who was a member of a noble Pushtun family of public distinction, this was a highly irregular move, a step downward socially.[12]

By 1987, Mir Aimal Kansi began studying for his M.A. in English literature in Baluchistan University, Quetta. English studies are considered the most expeditious way to gain admission and even scholarships for graduate studies in American colleges. By now, Kansi was openly involved in Baluchi politics, participating in several well-publicized protests against the persecution of Baluchis by the Government of Pakistan. With hindsight, it appears that this activism may have been designed to pave the way for him to obtain American residence: when he asked for asylum in the U.S. on March 3, 1991, he cited as his reason a fear of persecution in Pakistan because of his activities on behalf of the Baluchi cause.[13]

Mir Aimal Kansi must have been recruited by Iran's SAVAMA while he was at Baluchistan University in 1987-88. By then, he was increasingly involved in the Kansis' convoluted dealings with the ISI, the Shi'ite mujahideen and Iranian intelligence. The actual approach by the SAVAMA and the ensuing recruitment were probably conducted by Iranian intelligence operatives who regularly travelled secretly with Afghan mujahideen from the Hazarajat region in central Afghanistan. Iranian

and can be used for initial recruitment and communication while concealing the agency's involvement.

and HizbAllah officials frequented the Quetta-Hazarajat route and probably came to know Kansi. It would have been very easy for the Iranians to approach him on one of their trips.[14]

In 1988, the circumstances of Mir Aimal Kansi's life made him an ideal candidate for placement as an illegal, a long-term agent who lives in the target country without any contact with any overt representative of the sponsoring country. He was 18 or 19 years old. His mother had died in 1982, and in 1988 his father was dying of cancer. By tribal tradition, he was the family member primarily responsible for carrying out the blood revenge for the 1984 assassination of his uncle Malik Gul Hasan Kansi, which in Quetta was widely attributed to the CIA because of Gul Hasan's involvement with the Iranians. A rather artificial tension arose between Aimal and his half-brothers, which may possibly have been a cover for a lengthy disengagement from his family in Quetta, a step that would otherwise be very unusual in the clannishly close Kansi tribe.[15]

In February 1989, Mir Aimal Kansi was a key member of a strong-arm squad sent by an Iranian-connected Baluchi cell to intimidate American guest faculty at Quetta University into leaving town; it is HizbAllah doctrine that the most dangerous and subversive American intelligence presence exists in the guise of teaching because such activities contaminate young minds. Kansi's group burst into the university shouting "Death to America! Death to the CIA!" and attacked the American instructors. Kansi was the squad member responsible for drawing weapons and shooting into the air or, should the need arise, at the Americans who refused to flee. As it turned out, he only fired in the air.[16]

The incident involved direct contact with Iranian and HizbAllah operatives, and only the most trusted local terrorists were fully initiated into this type of operation. The fact that Mir Aimal Kansi played a central role in the incident in itself indicates that by February 1989 the Iranians fully trusted him.[17]

Later that year he made an unusual trip to Germany: he was gone from Pakistan for a long time but he stayed in Germany for only a month.[18] This suggests that the German trip may have been a cover for a classic backdoor infiltration to Iran, used in highly sensitive cases: from 1985 on, numerous Iranian agents and terrorists used this route. They would enter West Germany legally, and then, without any need for travel documents, go to West Berlin, cross into East Berlin by subway, board a flight to Damascus and go on to Tehran. They would return to the West the same way. Islamic cultural institutions in West Germany provided bogus alibis for some of the more important agents/terrorists. Mir Aimal Kansi could have travelled to Syria and Iran that way, possibly in order to receive advanced training in preparation for operations in America. Indeed, soon after his return to from Germany to Pakistan, Kansi announced for the first time his intention to emigrate to the United States.[19]

Kansi's behavior after he arrived in America strongly suggests preparations for clandestine and terrorist activities. Despite his university degrees, he sought employment as a messenger with a courier company that serviced the CIA.[20] He gradually accumulated weapons. He also prepared a getaway plan — which he executed perfectly at the end of January 1993 after the CIA killings. He reached Quetta safely, spent a week with his family and then disappeared.[21]

Taken together, the background of the Kansi tribe's close association and cooperation with Iranian intelligence coupled with the specifics of Mir Aimal Kansi's biography strongly suggest that he was an Iranian agent and, therefore, that the Langley killing was an act of Iranian state-sponsored terrorism — and probably not unrelated to the threat of a "war" between SAVAMA and the CIA.

Concurrent developments in Iran testify to the importance of the CIA massacre for Tehran. During the mid and late 1980s, Brigadier General Qaani was the commander of the Eighth [Imam] Corps of the IRGC and in this capacity responsible for intelligence and sabotage operations in Pakistan through the Shi'ite mujahideen of Afghanistan. The IRGC was responsible for recruiting and training Afghans and Pakistanis in Iran and organizing them into networks. With the militarization of the IRGC and the increase in Iranian terrorist operations in and via South Asia, Tehran decided to establish a separate organization exclusively for the support of subversion and terrorism. The result was the Fourth Partisan Corps, established in 1992.

It was detached from, but still remained connected with, the Eighth [Imam] Corps. Both Corps are under the command of Qaani. The main bases of the Fourth Partisan Corps are in Tayebad,

Islamist Terrorist Network

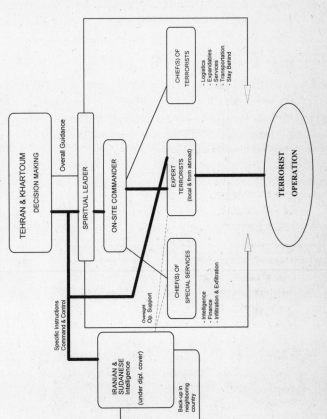

THE STRUCTURE OF THE NEW YORK ISLAMIST TERRORIST NETWO

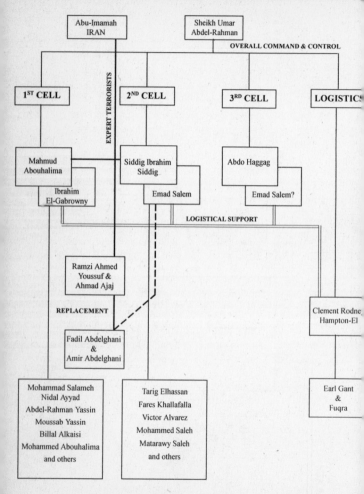

NEW ISLAMIST TERRORIST COMMAND STRUCTURE
(as of 1993)

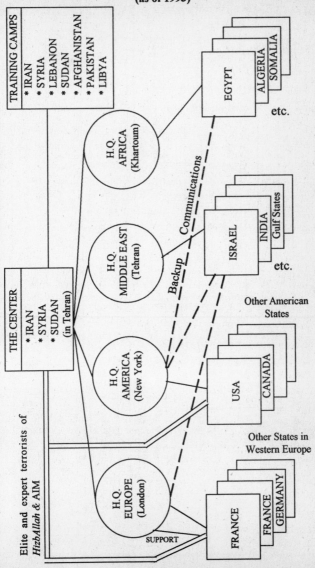

COMMAND STRUCTURE OF THE *HIZBALLAH* IN LEBANON

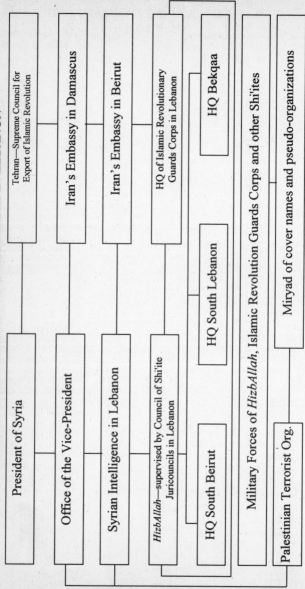

الإسلام طريق في فلسطين

بسم الله الرحمن الرحيم

So when the second of the warnings came to pass, (We permitted your enemies) to disfigure your faces, and to enter the Masjid as they had entered it before, and to visit with destruction all that fell into their power. (17:7)

Islamic Committee for Palestine

Second Annual Conference

Palestine, Intifada and the Horizons of the Islamic Renaissance

Friday-Monday, December 22-25, 1989

McCormick Center Hotel
Chicago, Illinois

Invited Speakers

Sheikh Muhammad Al-Ghazali (Egypt)
Dr. Ahmad Sodki Dajani (Palestine)
Dr. Abdalla El-Nafisi (Kuwait)
Dr. Fathi Abdulaziz (Palestine)
Sheikh Maher Hammoud (Lebanon)
Mr. Fahmy Howaldy (Egypt)
Mr. Salah Jourachi (Tunisia)
Mr. Azad Garmiani (Kurdistan)

Sheikh Abdulaziz Odah (Palestine)
Sheikh Rashid Ghanoushi (Tunisia)
Mr. Adel-Hussein (Egypt)
Dr. Taha Jabir (USA)
Dr. Muhammad Sakr (Palestine)
Mr. M. Abulgasim Hag Hamad (Sudan)
Sheikh Abdulhadi Awang (Malaysia)
Mr. Hussein Ashur (Egypt)

And many other speakers from the USA and abroad

For More Information Please Call: 1-813-980-AKSA, in Chicago call 404-AKSA

TOPICS

● Intifada and Jihad: Concepts and Principles ● The Contemporary Islamic Movement and the Renaissance ● Intifada and Current Affairs ● The Ummah, the Islamic Movement and the Challenges of the Palestinian Issue ● Muslims in America & The Palestinian Issue ● The Quranic Dimension of the Palestinian Issue ● The Linkage between the Liberation Strategy and the Revival of the Ummah ● Towards an Islamic Strategy for Confrontation ● The Renaissance and the Challenges of Unity ● Political Initiatives and Social Changes in Palestine ● Islamic Causes: Kurdistan and Africa

Invitation Flyer of the Islamist conference in Chicago, 1989.
Invited guests included such terrorist leaders as Fathi Abdulaziz (Shqaqi) of the Islamic *Jihad*; Ghanoushi from Tunisia; and Odah (Awdah) of the Islamic *Jihad* in Gaza. Also note the preoccupation with the *Jihad* issue.

THE FIRST CELL OF THE NEW YORK NETWORK

Sheikh Umar Abd-al-Rahman:
The spiritual leader of the American Islamist community, and the senior leader of the Armed Islamist Movement in the US.

Muhammad A. Salameh:
The expendable martyr of the Islamist network. He performed these tasks, such as renting the bomb-carrying van and the storage site for the chemicals — services that would ultimately expose him as a participant in the network.

Mahmud Abdouhalima:
An 'Afghan', who was one of the principles of the Islamist network, the on-site professional leader activated for the operation against the World Trade Center.

Nidal A. Ayyad:
A chemical engineer and another expendable martyr of the Islamist network. He was implicated to appear as the network's bomb-maker.

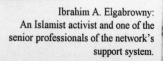

Ibrahim A. Elgabrowny:
An Islamist activist and one of the senior professionals of the network's support system.

Amir Abdelghani —
Sudanese; expert terrorist activated for the operation of the second cell of the New York network; cousin of Fadil Abdelghani.

Fadil Abdelghani —
Sudanese, activated to assume command over second cell of the New York terrorist network.

Clement Rodney Hampton-El — African-American member of Fuqra, one of the founders of the New York terrorist network, who played a key role in providing logistical support for the New York network.

Ramzi Ahmad Youssuf
— Iraqi; expert terrorist
who arrived from Paki-
stan, was instrumental
in the bombing of the
World Trade Center.

Abdul Rahman Yassin
(a.k.a. Abboud Yassin) —
U.S.-born Arab-American
Islamist who participated
in World Trade Center
bombing.

Ahmad Muhammad Ajaj
— Palestinian; arrived
from Pakistan to assist
Ramzi Youssuf.

Continued
THE SECOND CELL

Siddig Ibrahim Siddig Ali
— Sudanese; the head of
Turabi's National
Islamic Front in the U.S.,
conspired to conduct a wave
of bombings all over Man-
hattan on July 4, 1993.

KEY MEMBERS OF THE NEW YORK NETWORK

Abd-al-Rahman Haggag (a.k.a. Abdo Mohammad Haggag) — Egyptian; a key terrorist in the New York network, responsible for the plots to assassinate Egyptian President Husni Mubarak.

Sayyid Abdulazziz Nossair — Egyptian; one of the founders of the New York Islamist terrorist network, was involved in the assassination of Rabbi Meir Kahane in 1990.

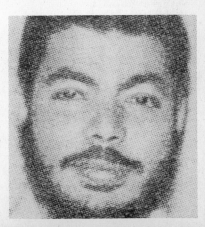

Sheikh Umar Abdel-Rahman — The spiritual leader of
the Islamist terrorists in North America, including the
New York network. Also Turabi's representative to
America and spiritual leader of Egyptian Islamists.

Ali Akbar
Hashemi-
Rafsanjani,
the President
of Iran.

HizbAllah fighters marching over U.S. flags lying on the ground
in Lebanon, in 1992/93.

Sheikh
Muhammad
Hussein
Fadlallah,
the spiritual
leader
of the
HizbAllah.

Symbol of *HizbAllah* — includes:
(at center) the writing
"HizbAllah" integrated into a
combination of a hand holding an
assault rifle (the symbol of the
armed movement); the Holy Quran
(symbol of Islamic association);
the branch (symbol of renewal);
and the globe (symbol of the
universality of the movement).
Underneath the *HizbAllah* name:
"The Islamic Movement in
Lebanon".

Sheikh Hassan Nasrallah the Secretary General of the *HizbAllah*.

Sheikh Hassan al-Turabi, the spiritual leader of Sudan.

JANIN/AFP

Emblem to the right:
The Armed Islamist Movement — in the center, the crossed Swords of Islam; above, the Holy Quran; writing in the center ''The Muslim Brothers''; at the bottom ''The Call [of Islam]''.

جيش التحرير
الفرقة الخامسة
العزيز لمركن أبوبكر المكي

New York Times
229 West 43rd Street
New York, NY 10036

The following letter from the *LIBERATION ARMY* regarding the operation conducted against the W.T.C.

We are, the fifth battalion in the *LIBERATION ARMY*, declare our responsibility for the explosion on the mentioned building. This action was done in response for the American political, economical, and military support to Israel the state of terrorism and to the rest of the dictator countries in the region.

OUR DEMANDS ARE:

1- Stop all military, economical, and political aids to Israel.
2- All diplomatic relations with Israel must stop.
3- Not to interfere with any of the Middle East countries interior affairs.

IF our demands are not met, all of our functional groups in the army will continue to execute our missions against military and civilians targets in and out the United States. This also will include some potential Nuclear targets. For your own information, our army has more than hundred and fifty suicidal soldiers ready to go ahead. The terrorism that Israel practices (Which is supported by America) must be faced with a similar one. The dictatorship and terrorism (also supported by America) that some countries are practicing against their own people must also be faced with terrorism.

The American people must know, that their civilians who got killed are not better than those who are getting killed by the American weapons and support.

The American people are responsible for the actions of their government and they must question all of the crimes that their government is committing against other people. Or they -Americans- will be the targets of our operations that could diminish them.

We invite all of the people from all countries and all of the revolutionaries in the world to participate in this action with us to accomplish our just goals.

". . . IF THEN ANYONE TRANSGRESSES THE PROHIBITION AGAINST YOU TRANSGRESS YE LIKEWISE AGAINST HIM . . ."

LIBERATION ARMY
FIFTH BATTALION

AL-FAREEK AL-ROHH, Abu Bakr Al-Makee.

Zahedan, Zabol, and Birjand, near Iran's border with Afghanistan and Pakistan. Qaani is now responsible for command and support of the Islamist terrorist infrastructure in Afganistan, Pakistan, Kashmir, and India. He is also responsible for extending Iranian operations into Central Asia via Afghanistan.[22]

In the late autumn of 1992 the four bases of the Fourth Partisan Corps were put into a higher state of readiness and local units were reinforced. These forces could have been used a few months later to assist Kansi in evading Pakistani authorities; according to ISI, Tehran notified Islamabad that it would assist in the search for Kansi provided that Tehran was convinced that he had committed a crime.[23]

Mir Aimal Kansi was not the only Iranian agent being prepared in Pakistan in the late 1980s to be inserted as a long-term illegal in the United States. An Iranian called Ali Reza was detained in Karachi on September 25, 1989 on suspicion of trying to hijack a Saudi airliner, possibly in connection with Iran's Hajj wars.* Ali Reza was a long-term illegal plant being prepared by Iranian intelligence to be infiltrated into the U.S., perhaps as an Afghan or Iranian political refugee. He had arrived in Karachi from Iran in February 1989 and had since been studying English in schools operated by the UN High Commissioner for Refugees while preparing

---

* The series of Iranian terrorist operations against Saudi Arabia, primarily in the holy cities of Mecca and Medina.

to emigrate to the United States.[24] Apparently he was activated ahead of schedule by the SAVAMA and sent to hijack the Saudi airliner in revenge for the execution of sixteen Kuwaiti Islamists in Saudi Arabia.[25]

It is still not clear why Tehran decided to sacrifice an agent of a major intelligence operation then in successful preparation in order to make a hasty, unprofessional hijacking attempt. It was the opinion of the Pakistani security authorities at the time that the SAVAMA already had so many agents in preparation or already in place that they could afford to sacrifice Ali Reza.

Meanwhile, without a word being said in Tehran, the Kansi episode sent shivers throughout the Middle East, and especially Egypt and the Persian Gulf states. In Middle Eastern countries, the intelligence service — the *mukhabarat* — is not an organization preoccupied primarily with the collection and analysis of material, as is the case with the CIA. In the Middle East a *mukhabarat* is a super-secret police, the guardians and saviors of the regimes, and it is universally believed in the region that the CIA is really an American *mukhabarat*. It is a common belief in the pro-Western Arab states that America is safeguarding its allied regimes by warning about, preventing and protecting against conspiracies and coups.

Having transmitted the warning about SAVAMA's threatened war against the CIA to Washington, the intelligence services of the Gulf States had no doubt about what happened at the entrance to CIA headquarters in Langley, Virginia, or what it meant. The fact that an Iranian agent was able to carry out such an audacious (though symbolic) act and get away with it sent a chill of fear throughout the Middle East. "If the U.S., having been forewarned, still could not protect the headquarters of its own *mukhabarat*, how can we trust them to protect us?" wondered officials of several security and intelligence services in the Arab world.

FINAL PREPARATIONS

Tehran waited with trepidation for an American response to its audacious strike at the CIA, interpreting the media's description of the event as a crime (rather than a political action) as a disinformation cover masking an American counterstrike. Anticipating Washington's possible retribution, the terrorist masters in Tehran decided to reexamine yet again the specifics of the impending operation in New York. Having given up hope of retrieving its frozen assets from the U.S., as well as the possibility of a rapprochement with the new administration in Washington, Tehran decided by the end of January to go ahead and implement its plan for revenge by striking a key symbol of American economic might — a skyscraper in New York.[26]

(The revenge issue would resurface in the Iranian analysis of the bombing.[27]) It should be remembered that Siddig Ibrahim Siddig Ali later explained that the bombing in the World Trade Center had been aimed at causing America to "lose millions" as well as to demonstrate that the Islamists "are not far" and "can get you any time."[28] He was essentially giving voice to Tehran's logic.

By now Tehran had reached the conclusion that "an Iran-U.S. clash" was likely because "Islam [is] at its most sensitive and that heightens our responsibilities more than ever."[29] In Iranian eyes the West is bent on containing the spread of Islamism, knowing full well that Iran is the fountainhead and bastion of the worldwide spread of the Islamic Revolution.[30] Therefore, Tehran believes, Washington has no alternative but to confront Iran and Islam in order to solve its own problems. As an editorial in the offical Iranian government newspaper put it, "No matter how we look at it, the solution would be linked with the defeat of Iran as an important and potential regional and world power ... Iran is a repository of a very deep form of Islamism, which makes it an indicator of the future world order." It is therefore imperative that "the wave of Islamism [be] boosted abroad as one of the main pillars of our national security."[31]

Tehran concluded that since confrontation with the American-led West is inevitable, preemption is preferable to any other form of struggle. Iran's top leadership decided "to move the confrontation to the West in order to destabilise them [Western governments]." This made it necessary for Tehran to activate and launch its pre-set plan for a terrorist campaign in America and Europe, a terrorist surge that would involve spectacular operations, including the widespread use of car-bombs.[32] In an address to the IRGC, Khamene'i stressed that "Islam

has proposed jihad against infidels and hypocrites*
as a solution and a defense against internal and
external calamity."[33]

In late January, the New York network was ordered to proceed with its preparations and, when
given the order, strike. Meanwhile, Iranian intelligence operatives in eastern Canada began preparing a back-up escape system for the key agents and
expert terrorists. The escape route chosen led from
the New York area to Toronto, from Toronto to Swe-
den, and then on to the Middle East.[34] Monsour
Mahani, a 29-year-old Iranian "sleeper" agent operating in the Toronto area, was responsible for
preparing safe houses, new identification papers
and escape routes.[35] Mahani, a veteran of several
terrorist operations overseas, had arrived in Canada
as a "political refugee" from Sudan in October
1991.[36] Another operative, a Sudanese national,
purchased fifteen Toronto-Stockholm airline tickets, some of them in the names of terrorists who
ultimately surfaced in New York.[37] (Both Mahani
and the Sudanese were arrested in mid-June.)

The last pre-strike checks took place in late January, just before and after the Kansi strike. On January 22, the American Embassy in Algeria received
a call. Speaking in the name of the PFLP, the caller
threatened a bombing in New York City within 48
hours unless the Palestinians whom Israel had deported to Lebanon were immediately returned to
Israel. A second call came on January 24, extend-

---

* Islamists use the term "hypocrite" to refer to Western-
ized Muslims.

ing the deadline to January 26.[38] (The PFLP would later deny any connection with the bombing.)[39]

The actual motive behind these calls was to create a provocation that would enable the terrorist masters to see what kind of precautions and defensive measures the American authorities might take if they knew that a skyscraper was going to be hit. Moreover, on the principle of crying wolf, the fact that two warnings proved false was likely to influence law enforcement authorities not to take any subsequent warning seriously — so that, if any leak about the forthcoming operation occurred, the response of security agencies would probably be minimal.

Between February 2 - 9, 1993, Tehran conducted a final last-minute study of the challenge. The entire issue of conducting terrorist operations in the United States and Canada was re-examined during a major Islamist international terrorist conference in Tehran at which guidelines for future operations were issued.

The conference itself was a milestone in achieving worldwide coordination among diverse Islamist movements, both Shi'ite and Sunni, for the purpose of establishing joint "Islamic revolutionary action." Some 400 Islamists from fifty countries participated. Among them were senior representatives of Sheikh Abdel-Rahman, including those responsible for maintaining connections with the Iranian interest section in Pakistan's embassy in Washington, which handles Iran's affairs in the United States.

Hashemi-Rafsanjani and other Iranian and

HizbAllah leaders told the assembly that Iran's policy of "moderation" had failed to attract economic assistance and investment from the West, and that instead, the West, and especially the United States, was paying increasing attention to Iran's growing power and to the spread of Islam. Therefore, Tehran had decided that there was no alternative to the resumption of an uncompromising terrorist struggle against the West — and *in* the West — and especially the United States, including "using new means of violence and returning to a policy of hostage taking."

Significantly, the conference decided that the struggle against the United States would include among its priorities "targeting buildings for bomb spectaculars."

Senior Iranian leaders — specifically Ayatollah Khamene'i, Shamsoddin Wahhabi, and Asfar AliZadeh — emerged as the leaders of the new terrorist surge, which is to be tightly controlled by the VEVAK/SAVAMA.[40] It is therefore highly likely that the very small select group of senior Iranian, HizbAllah, and Islamist terrorist commanders present, who are known to have held separate discussions concerning future terrorist operations in the United States, studied and re-examined the impending operation in New York; such last minute oversight is characteristic of the ever-prudent and professional Tehran.

MOVING AHEAD

Meanwhile, in New York in January and February the actual preparations for and by the expendables had accelerated. Safe storage was organized. The explosives were easy to make from readily available chemicals, primarily nitric acid and sulfuric acid (used in nitroglycerin) and urea, which is a common ingredient in fertilizers.

Hundreds of pounds of industrial chemicals that could be used to make explosives, including nitric and sulphuric acid were puchased and stored in a rented space at "A Space Station", a storage company in New Jersey, where police would later find some that could have made explosives that would have left the nitrate traces found in the debris at World Trade Center.[41] The one thousand pounds or so of chemicals used for the actual bomb cost about $400.

Simple blasting caps were provided by Hampton-El.[42] Several items that could be used for a timer and detonator were also purchased, among them small metal alarm clocks that may have been used as timers. Three such clocks were later found by investigators in New Jersey.[43] Moreover, according to a police expert, tools and parts found at an apartment Salameh used constituted evidence of a "bomb maker."[44]

As the date of the operation drew near, the terrorists left nothing to chance.

In February, Mahmud Abouhalima, Ramzi Ahmad Youssuf, Siddig Ibrahim Siddig Ali, Clement Rodney Hampton-El, Salameh and possibly others took part in a test run with the home-mixed explosives and the detonating devices near New Bloomfield, Pennsylvania, not far from Harrisburg. The explosion was a success; the mixture would soon be used operationally.[45] By this time, Siddig was known to be "an associate of Mohammad Salameh and Nidal Ayyad" who would soon take part in the bombing of the World Trade Center.[46]

Final approval for the operation was received from Tehran via Khartoum only a few days before the actual operation. In Khartoum on February 19, Iranian terrorist experts who had just arrived from Tehran and members of AIM's Higher Liaison Committee met to closely and thoroughly study the posture of the New York networks. Satisfied with the preparations, they ordered the operation carried out.[47]

The background of the Khartoum meeting, under cover of which the final approval for the World Trade Center bombing was given, testifies to the extent of the Iranian control and advanced preparations:

More than three months earlier — in late November 1992 — Tehran and Khartoum decided to conduct a major and thorough re-examination of the current situation and future plans in February 1993. These consultations would take place in the context of a conference of nineteen Islamist movements "linked with the Islamic Revolution in Iran" that Turabi would convene in Khartoum.[48] In early December it was learned by informed sources that the Khartoum conference was supposed to address, among other subjects, the long-planned revival of Islamist international terrorism in Western Europe and the United States.[49]

The timing of the decision to convene the February conference in Khartoum is significant: it was in late November that Tehran, having successfully "solved" the problem of Ian Spiro, authorised the continuation of active preparations for the terrorist strike in New York. Only an intimate knowledge of the details of the actual preparations in New York and the political considerations involved could have permitted such an accurate estimate of the time needed to complete the preparations for the strike.

Therefore, the ability of Tehran and Khartoum to so accurately time and prepare the cover conference in February implies an intimate knowledge of events in New York and, thus, direct involvement and sponsorship.

COUNTDOWN

The final preparations began almost immediately after the go-ahead was given in Khartoum on February 19. On February 22, the Iranian and Sudanese intelligence operatives in Toronto purchased airline tickets for Abouhalima and other terrorists expected to flee New York in the wake of the operation.[50]

As the spiritual leader, Sheikh Abdel-Rahman must have given his blessing to the operation, promising eternal afterlife to all involved. Within the organizational framework of the Islamist international, Abdel-Rahman "inspired" the bombing, and may have issued a formal *fatwa* concerning the personal fate of the participants.[51] In an interview in early August 1993, El-Sayyid Nossair stated unequivocally that "without [the Sheik's] blessing there would have been no actions."[52]

However, only Tehran could issue the final operational order.[53]

The professional terrorists began their preparations. Many Arab men visited and stayed in the Youssuf and Salameh's apartment, especially at night; there was a lot of activity at night. Boxes were taken in and out of the apartment. Several young Egyptians who lived in nearby apartments suddenly left for Egypt during the week of the bombing.[54]

The time was ripe to expose the "expendables." Salameh and Ayyad rented the Ryder Company's Ford Econoline van used to plant the bomb.[55] On February 25, the day before the bombing, Salameh reported to the police that the Ryder van he had just rented had been stolen.[56] On February 25, Nidal Ayyad ordered three tanks of compressed hydrogen. They were delivered to Salameh at the storage locker.[57]

The explosives were mixed from the nitric and sulfuric acid and the urea. The 1,000-pound bomb was made on the eve of the operation. The explosive was in the form of a thick paste which was loaded into cardboard boxes. They were piled in the truck. The main explosive charge was to be ignited with several smaller nitroglycerine bombs, which in turn were activated by simple blasting caps. A lot of expertise was needed in rigging the bomb in order to ensure near-simultaneous detonation. Bottles of compressed hydrogen gas were placed on top of the explosives to create a destructive fireball when detonated. In order to ensure enhanced blast, the half-a-dozen or so cardboard boxes had to be specially organized and the nitro and caps precisely placed.[58]

While Salameh, Ayyad and Abdel-Rahman Yassin might have been capable of mixing the chemicals — and there is evidence they had done so at one time or another — it would take an expert to place the nitro and caps. According to Abouhalima, two Iraqi expert terrorists showed up a few days prior to the bombing to coordinate the operation and ensure the technical details of the bomb. He identified Youssuf, whom he knew only as "Rashid", as one of them.[59] Indeed, Youssuf's fingerprints were found on several key components and tools that could have been used for the construction of the bomb, strongly suggesting that he was involved in making the bomb.[60] Moreover, the combination of explosives and compressed gases is a classic Iranian-style bomb of the kind used from Beirut to Kuwait to Paris.

The terrorist experts — Youssuf, Abouhalima, and the other Iraqi — must have installed the detonators. It is highly likely that it was a combination of a remote control device, most likely the modified Swiss-made telephone pager, and a simple timer made from an alarm clock, as a back-up system.[61]

On February 26, the van-bomb was then driven

to the World Trade Center and placed in the exact location. A second car was used to drive away the van driver and any other terrorists involved.[62] The two expert terrorists, Youssuf and Abouhalima were directly involved in the final preparations as well as the actual placement and activation of the bomb. Abouhalima was seen with Salameh in the New Jersey storage area, driving a van on the night of the 25th, as well as in and around the van at dawn on the 26th. Youssuf was also seen in a van on the 25th.[63]

At 4:00 a.m. on the morning of February 26, Salameh, Abouhalima and Youssuf were seen purchasing gas for the yellow van-bomb while another car, a blue Honda, was seen parked near by. The Honda is believed to have been used as the getaway car.[64] According to Theodore Williams, a cellmate of Abouhalima, Salameh drove the van and planted the bomb while Abouhalima waited for him outside. Youssuf was in the passenger seat next to Salameh, while Abouhalima drove the other car.[65] Salameh is reported to have a fairly strong alibi for the period of time immediately before and during the World Trade Center explosion.[66] According to Williams, after parking the van, Salameh and Abouhalima went to a record store in nearby Park Row and waited for the explosion.[67]

If correct, this information strongly suggests that indeed expert terrorists — primarily Youssuf — placed the bomb-van in the right spot, then inspected and armed the bomb. With Salameh and Abouhalima in the record store, the whereabouts of Youssuf, who had arrived with them, are unknown. One might surmise that, having ensured that the bomb was readied, Youssuf walked to a nearby phone, perhaps a pay phone overlooking the World Trade Center, and calmly dialed the beeper....

THE EXPLOSION AND THE SHOCK

The bomb that exploded on Friday, February 26, 1993, at 12:18 pm, on the B-2 level of the underground parking garage of the World Trade Center did not just happen to be in that location. The explosion paralyzed the emergency systems of the buildings. The blast ripped a 180-by-12-foot hole in a wall above the underground train station, creating a 200-by-100-foot crater in the garage below the Center's Vista Hotel. The hotel's first floor was gutted and the building suffered severe structural damage. Smoke reached up as high as the 96th floor in the 110-story twin towers. Six people were killed and over 1,000 injured, mostly from smoke inhalation.[68] The bomb was well placed, for it knocked out the entire communications and fire control systems for the buildings, broke five of the eight electrical feeder cables and caused a flood that drowned the backup generators meant to handle any emergency.[69]

Notwithstanding press reports to the effect that the bomb was amateurish, in reality only an expert would know where to place such a bomb, how much explosives to use, and how to direct the blast-and-heat wave to cause maximum damage. Indeed, the logic behind the explosion — that of using the structure of the building to echo and reinforce the blast-and-heat wave — is characteristic of the bomb-making techniques taught in Iran. The same approach to designing and placing bombs has been used repeatedly in HizbAllah-affiliated operations in Beirut and Buenos Aires.

Meanwhile, Tehran demonstrated for the entire Muslim world that it was actually responsible for the New York bombing. This was done in a unique, indirect manner that speaks volumes in the conspiratorial environment of the Middle East:

On February 26, the main Friday sermon in Tehran was delivered by Iran's spiritual leader, Ayatoallah Khamene'i. A major portion, which was repeated around 8:30 a.m. (EST) by Iran's international media for the benefit of the entire Muslim world, was devoted to the plight of the Muslims of Bosnia and Iran's position on the issue.

Khamene'i started by acknowledging the inability of Iran and other Muslim communities to send enough volunteers and military assistance to Bosnia. "We regret that we cannot defend that nation. We regret the Muslim youth cannot reach there for defense because the roads are blocked," he said. Khamen'i attributed this sorry situation to an intentional anti-Muslim campaign on the part of the West, led by the United States. However, he emphasized, these constraints should not prevent Iran and the Muslim world from actively assisting the Bosnian Muslims. "We must protect them as much as we can," he declared. "And I don't mean financial or material help, though that may also be necessary. We must give them all [types of] political support, we must endeavor [to do it]," Khamene'i exclaimed, adding that this assistance must ensure that the West will stop its assault on the Bosnian Muslims, as well as be punished for causing their current plight.[70]

Immediately after the explosion, there were numerous calls claiming responsibility, many of them in the name of warring factions in the former Yugoslavia. In the first news reports, these claims were given prominence in the American media. A "Serbian Liberation Front" was singled out by the press, even though there was no previous knowledge of this group and its statement differed from all known patterns of Serbian rhetoric.[71] Even the authorities paid special attention to the possibility of a Balkan motive. "That is that the Bosnians, the Serbians, Croatians, the Muslims, all these conflicts in the area might lead you to the conclusion that because they [the parties to that conflict] are meeting in New York there might be some connection with the explosion there," then-FBI director William Sessions said.[72] These reports reverberated throughout the Muslim world immediately.

The significance of the Khamene'i sermon is that it provided a very explicit warning that the Bosnian cause was about to hit world attention about four hours before the explosion in New York, promptly claimed in the name of the Bosnian Muslim plight, went off. In the byzantine conspiratorial atmosphere of the Muslim world, this chain of events constitutes a confirmation of Iran's responsibility for delivering the terrorist strike at the heart of America.

Meanwhile, in New Jersey Salameh continued to follow his instructions. Soon after the explosion, he again reported the van stolen, approached the rental agency and insisted on having his $400 deposit returned. He continued to press for it even as the media hinted that identifiable parts of the van had been recovered. Salameh was arrested as he came to pick up the deposit.[73] Traces of nitrate were found on the rental document.[74]

EXPENDABLES AND RED HERRINGS

Although Salameh's speedy discovery and arrest were widely described as "a case of dumb luck,"[75] his entire behavior in the aftermath of the explosion clearly indicates that it was only a matter of time before he was identified and caught. "He is either dumb or some kind of martyr," remarked one senior law enforcement official.[76]

Quite true. And he is not dumb. Salameh is a martyr.

An illegal alien, he lived for years in complete anonymity, avoiding the routine notice of the law. Had he not reported the van stolen, it would have been written off by Ryder as one of many of their vehicles stolen or lost every day . The overworked police, even if they did pay timely attention to the case of a missing Ryder van, would have run into a dead end. Salameh did not live at the address he had given; in fact, officially he did not even exist in the United States. Moreover, he could even have reported the van stolen to the Ryder Company and still melted away into anonymity if he had foregone getting his deposit back. But he persisted in fighting for his deposit, registering with the police, and attracting unnecessary attention to himself. This is most unbecoming behavior for a veteran of more than four years of living obscurely as an illegal alien.

No, Salameh is not stupid. He was following his instructions to the letter. His assigned role was to be captured so that the Islamists can transform his trial into a politicized show trial demonstrating American conspiracies against Islam.

Things appeared to go badly for the other conspirators. Ayyad's card was found in Salameh's possession. Elgabrowny could have avoided exposure and arrest by simply denying any knowledge of Salameh. However, ostensibly enraged, he swung at the police and was arrested for that. (His direct involvement in the bombing would emerge only subsequently.) Elgabrowny incriminated himself when, after asking to go to the bathroom, he dipped his hands in a toilet bowl filled with his urine, thus making a nitrate trace examination impossible and bringing himself under suspicion. And he did this at a point at which there was no evidence that he had been involved with the bombing.

Why then would he get himself into avoidable trouble? It is probable that, in accordance with the original plan, Elgabrowny had to go to jail to assist in the deliberate sacrifice of Salameh, Ayyad and possibly other pawns. Arrested, Elgabrowny would be the local senior commander who would supervise the other martyrs' "proper behavior" in jail,[77] as well as ensure the proper conduct of a "show trial" when the time arrives.

By the time the expendables were caught, the expert terrorists — the "masterminds" — were long gone. Most likely they safely escaped to the Middle East. One investigator believed that the terrorist masters "left him [Salameh] behind as a signature. Maybe it was their game plan all along to leave him behind." If this was the case, the plan to attract attention to Salameh worked perfectly, for the experts got away.[78] During the days immediately preceding and following the bombing, Ramzi Ahmad Youssef and the young Egyptians who had lived near Salameh vanished. The Egyptians left for Egypt.[79] Youssuf left for Karachi, Pakistan, on the day of the explosion, carrying a passport under the name "Abdul Basit."[80] He was last believed to be in Iraq.[81] Abdul Rahman (or Abboud) Yassin and another follower of Abdel-Rahman who were on the fringes of the network and provided material to the FBI shortly after the bombing have since disappeared and are believed to have fled to Iraq.[82]

Mahmud Abouhalima suddenly left New York on March 6, two days after Salameh's arrest.[83] Fearing that the law enforcement authorities were closing in on him, he chose not to utilise the Toronto-Stockholm escape route even though local operatives in Canada had purchased an airline ticket for him four days before the bombing.[84] Instead, using his German passport, Abouhalima flew to Pakistan, the site of the headquarters of Sheikh Abdel-Rahman's Islamic Group, via South Africa and Germany. One or two accomplices probably also flew out with him, apparently using false passports. The three bought their tickets at the last minute just to get out of North America.

Abouhalima had been the driver of the car that escorted the van and evacuated whoever was with the van. An "Afghan", he was one of the principals, the on-site professional leader activated for the operation, and provided direct support services to the expert terrorists who arrived from overseas. If captured he would be able to identify them; hence the urgent need to get him out and away.[85]

Unluckily for him, Abouhalima arrived in Pakistan on March 8, just as Washington was debating putting Pakistan on the list of states supporting terrorism. With both Abouhalima's identity and the FBI's search for him known all over the world, Islamabad could not afford to shelter him and he was ordered to leave the country. Realizing that capture was ultimately inevitable, Abouhalima travelled to Saudi Arabia in order to make a *hajj*, the pilgrimage to Mecca which all Muslims are required to make at least once in their lifetime. He then continued to Egypt on March 13. There, on a tip from the Pakistani ISI, Egyptian authorities seized his younger brother, Sayed, who in turn divulged his brother's hiding place.

Abouhalima was arrested on March 14 and tortured for some ten days before being extradited to the United States on March 24.[86]

(Pakistan had had no alternative but to surrender Abouhalima, considering that certain other recent arrivals — Mir Amail Kansi, other still-unidentified travellers from the U.S. and the Memon family, responsible for the murderous bombing that had just occurred in Bombay — had all received shelter in Pakistan, making Islamabad's denial of any involvement with terrorism, let alone support for it, questionable at best.)

Meanwhile, it had not taken long for the magnitude of the New York operation to become clear to the investigators. Traces of nitrate were immediately found at the site, concrete evidence of a bomb, and Police Commissioner Raymond Kelly identified it as a bombing on the basis of "the magnitude of the explosion, the fact that a significant amount of heat was generated, and the fact that traces of nitrate were found."[87]

Gilmore Childers, Assistant U.S. Attorney, characterized the bombing as "the single most destructive act of terrorism on American soil."[88]

Within a few days, James Fox of the FBI was telling the press that investigators thought the bombing had been carried out by "a large, well-known terrorist group, a group that knows what it's doing."[89]

By early March, investigators were acknowledging that there was evidence that Salameh had been recruited by a terrorist group, one that was most probably Iranian-sponsored[90], and that he was "part of a conspiracy." [91] Abouhalima would eventually describe the bombing as Iranian-sponsored.[92]

And in late June, the CIA would finally acknowledge that the bombing "was carried out at the behest of a foreign government" — which they would not identify.[93]

Chapter 6

ALMOST A SECOND STRIKE

FIRST REACTION

The Muslim world was stunned but not surprised by the explosion in New York. It was clear that a new era in the relations between the United States and the Muslim world had begun. "Allah knows, but it seems that the American magic is beginning to turn on its master," the Islamists announced. "Regardless of who was behind the recent explosion in New York's World Trade Center, the explosion rang down the curtain on an era of security and stability enjoyed by the United States over the past 50 years."[1]

Mainstream Arabs agreed that "fundamentalism [had]... moved the battle to the very heart of what it calls 'the Great Satan.'" They warned that, as a result of American policy in the Middle East (defined as a "declaration of confrontation" with Islam), "confrontation with the fundamentalist trends will escalate in the Arab world," and may even spread to the rest of the world.[2] Conservative Arabs tried to distance themselves from the Islamist trend, arguing that the New York bombing must have been part of "an organized malicious campaign" against Islam.[3]

Meanwhile, the oblique Iranian claim for responsibility was not lost on the militant Islamists. This was made clear as early as February 28, when Imad al-Alami, one of the ardent Sunni leaders of the HAMAS and its representative in Iran, declared that, in view of "recent developments," the Sunni Islamists now recognized that "there is an identical view in the strategic outlook" between them and Shi'ite Iran. The HAMAS had reached this conclusion because "there were forms of assistance from the Iranian people to help the steadfastness of the Palestinian people in the occupied territories" which went far beyond merely financial and material assistance — which were, instead, in "the Islamic dimension."[4]

Only on March 6, once Salameh was arrested, did Tehran begin a propaganda blitz about the New York bombing. Its overriding theme was that the blaming of Muslims, Islamists and even Iran for the bombing was all a part of a conspiracy aimed at inciting the West to embark on an anti-Islamic Crusade. Tehran warned that the American efforts "to attribute the New York explosions to Muslims have met strong reactions from Islamist groups."[5]

Tehran was becoming increasingly combative and defiant, arguing that "if support for Palestine and the oppressed Palestinians was terrorism, Iran was proud of it."[6] Iran called for a more aggressive policy supporting the export of the revolution in order to further strengthen the commitment to the Islamists and warned that "showing any leniency and flexibility ... would be misinterpreted by the enemy and would further embolden it to pursue its illegitimate objective" and concluded that "this fresh U.S. propaganda aggression should be confronted by further underlining the Islamic-revolutionary stands."[7]

The HAMAS repeated the Iranian line that the accusation of Islamist involvement in the bombing was the beginning of an American-Israeli conspiracy against Islam, and vowed to resist steadfastly.[8]

Starting on March 10, Tehran suddenly shifted its emphasis in dealing with the aftermath of the World Trade Center bombing to a posture of defiance and taking the initiative. In a well-publicized sermon, Ali Akbar Nateq-Nouri, the speaker of the Majlis, called American accusations of Iranian involvement with terrorism "psychological warfare with specific political aims" and called for stern counter-measures. "The resistant nation of Iran does not fear a psychological war and will march toward sacred goals of the Islamic system with greater unity and solidarity," he declared. "Experience has shown that the more pressure exerted by enemies on us, the stronger our people become."

More than two-thirds of the members of the Majlis issued a statement urging an immediate escalation of the struggle against the United States that would climax on *al-Quds* Day (Jerusalem Day, March 19, 1993). "We deeply believe that obliteration of Israel and downfall of the world arrogance headed by the United States are possible. The United States is trying in vain to take advantage of every incident against Islam and Muslims," the statement said.[9]

Defining the United States as "the world's most dangerous state sponsor of terrorism," Tehran outlined its own anti-terrorist policy: Iran did not condemn the New York bombing, though it declared that it was morally and politically wrong to rejoice over killing of innocent people by bombs in Western countries — but in the context of reiterating its enduring support for the export of the Islamic revolution: "Just as we support the liberation struggle of the people around the world, we are not prepared to support terroristic and deviant actions or even express pleasure about them." Then, reaffirming the validity of the *fatwa* urging the killing of Salman Rushdie, Tehran used the occasion to stress that at times violence can be in accordance with the objectives of Islam.[10]

Islamist terrorist leaders echoed the Iranian call for jihad. Most important was a March 11 speech by Sheikh Asa'ad Bayyud al-Tamimi, the leader of the Tehran-sponsored Islamic Jihad — *Bayt al-Maqdis* (also known as HizbAllah-Palestine), who had been intimately involved in preparing for Islamist terrorism in the U.S. during the Gulf crisis. He connected what he described as the Western hate for the Muslims in the wake of the New York bombings and the forthcoming commemoration of *al-Quds* Day through jihad. "There is fury, fury everywhere," he thundered. "I call on the West to understand this — that Islam is escalating and cannot be resisted. An oppressed person will hit his enemy in any place. I pray that Allah may tear apart America just as the Soviet Union was torn apart, because it leads injustice in the world." [11]

The Islamists' expectations that terrorist violence in America would be resumed were not without reason. It would not take long for other cells of the New York Islamist network to begin preparing for their contribution to the jihad.

ENTER THE SECOND CELL

In the fall of 1992, while the planning for the main strike that would become the bombing World Trade Center was advancing on-track, Siddig Ibrahim Siddig Ali was ordered to prepare plans for the bombing of alternate objectives, both as a fallback plan to be used in case of a failure of the main strike and as a series of follow up strikes if the main strike succeeded. The various assassination plans were also revived.[12] The actual preparations for the bombing operations of the second cell began before the bombing of the World Trade Center took place.[13] In early 1993, both before and after the World Trade Center bombing, Siddig Ibrahim Siddig Ali surveyed several military installations, inspecting them as objectives for future bombings.[14]

As mentioned above, some of the professional preparatory work, most notably determining the type of the home-mixed explosives and actually testing them, was done jointly with the other major cell under the supervision of the expert terrorists.[15] Indeed, Mahmud Abouhalima, the leader of the first cell, would also have been involved in the second plot if he had not been arrested. And in fact, he continued to have some role even from jail.[16]

The command structure of the second Islamist terrorist cell committed for the summer spectacular operation in New York continued to evolve between the fall of 1992 and the spring of 1993. This was because the posture of their intended operations was changing: from a fallback operation it was becoming a main event to be made up of a series of spectacular major strikes delivered simultaneously. Although Iran remained responsible for the operation, because of the Sudanese character of the network the commands and instructions were now transmitted primarily via Sheikh Turabi in Sudan and Sheikh Abdel-Rahman.[17] (Some three of the "Sudanese" members of the network may actually have been Egyptian terrorists using Sudanese papers provided by Khartoum.)[18]

However, like all major Iranian-controlled networks, the second New York cell was also made up of four key commanders, each of a different background and distinct responsibility:

1. Muhammad Rezah Shalchian (or Chalagian) Tabrizi was the senior Iranian intelligence commander. Operating under his cover as financial comptroller of Iran's UN mission, he is the senior officer of the IRGC Intelligence responsible for support of, and oversight over, the Islamist terrorist infrastructure in the United States. Another figure,

Sarag (or Siraj) al-Din Hamid Youssuf, Turabi's personal representative and officially the Counselor of the Sudanese mission to the United Nations, gradually assumed prominence, since the planning involved the active cooperation of the UN mission.

2. Initially, Ramzi Ahmad Youssuf was the senior terrorist expert and the professional commander for the second cell as well as for the first one. When Youssuf had to flee the U.S. after the World Trade Center bombing, Fadil Abdelghani (Abd-al-Ghani), a "submarine" expert terrorist already in America, was activated and assumed command over the several expert terrorists who were planning and facilitating the operation. Abdelghani was in charge of the professional aspects of the operations, from building and rigging the bombs so that they would inflict the anticipated damage, to their correct placement and activation, to the timely, safe and secure exfiltration of all the expert terrorists.

3. Siddig (Siddiq) Ibrahim Siddig Ali was the leader of the New York-based network in his capacity as the representative of Sheikh Umar Abdel-Rahman, ensuring that all the religious decrees and professional instructions were carried out and making progress reports to the Sheikh while at the same time creating a hedge of deniability between the spiritual leader and his terrorist disciples. He was one of the on-site professional leaders activated for the operation and provided direct support services to the expert terrorists who arrived from overseas.

4. Ibrahim A. Elgabrowny was to have been in charge of the support team for the second cell as he

had been for the first one, providing logistics for the quality operatives and terrorists while controlling and maintaining discipline among the expendable "martyrs". After his arrest in connection with the World Trade Center bombing, Emad Salem, who would become the FBI's informant, assumed this role.

THE SUDAN FACTOR

The operational planning of the second cell brought to the fore the terrorists' close relations with Sudan, a major terrorist sponsoring state, and the extent of assistance the terrorists were to receive from the Sudanese UN mission. The extent of Sudanese involvement that is currently known strongly suggests that the highest levels in Khartoum were involved in the terrorist network in New York.[19] The pattern of this direct involvement fits closely with Sudan's growing involvement in, and contribution to, the Iran-led international Islamist terrorist system.

Ever since his rise to power in Sudan in a military coup on June 30, 1989, General Umar al-Bashir has been trying to impose an Islamist regime he has defined as "a twin of the Iranian Revolution."[20] He has repeatedly emphasized his support for pan-Arab causes and expressed hope for Arab support for Sudan's designs in Africa and the Red Sea.[21]

The most important factor in Sudan was the rapid emergence of Sheikh Hassan al-Turabi as its spiritual leader. In August 1989, Turabi arranged for Sudan to become an Islamist "springboard to Arab and African countries" in return for substantial financial assistance from Islamists.[22] Eventually Turabi was able to provide a crucial link between the Islamist Sunni militants and the Shi'ite militants of Tehran.[23]

Turabi identifies the essence of Sudanese foreign policy as "a program for the Islamic Call" and the manifestation of "the policy of the Islamic Movement, which is of the [entire] ummah or rather, cosmic and universal."[24] Following the example of Iran, Turabi was able to transform the Sudanese diplomatic service into a terrorist support infrastructure answering to him.[25] Indeed, in the spring of 1993, when Ahmin Suliman, Sudan's ambassador to the United Nations, learned about the support given to the New York network, it was Turabi, not Gen. Bashir, he called to complain. Turabi told him to mind his own business.[26]

Sudan's profound shift toward Iran occurred in the early spring of 1991, in the wake of the Gulf Crisis and, especially, Saddam Hussein's failure to conduct the war as a genuine Islamic jihad. Turabi announced the creation of "a universal framework for the Islamic movement" operating from sanctuary in Sudan. The Islamic Arab Peoples' Conference was established in Khartoum in April 1991 with Turabi as its permanent leader,[27] a congress of a wide variety of terrorist organizations and popular Islamist movements from 55 countries.

This was the first serious attempt to coordinate a Sunni Islamist assault on the Muslim world and against the West.[28] The Conference "stressed the need for unity to solve conflicts in the Arab and Islamic region and [stressed] that a comprehensive solution is the answer to achieving stability."[29]

The Arab Islamic Peoples' Conference resulted in the establishment of the first real Sunni Islamist revolutionary international — The Popular International Organization [PIO]. "This is not a coterie, or an official banquet, which convenes the gentlemen under the aegis of the sultan," Turabi declared in his address to the Conference. "Its objective is to work out a global action plan in order to challenge [and] defy the tyrannical West, because God can no longer remain in our world, in the face of the absolute materialistic power."[30]

The Iranians were duly impressed with the zeal and commitment displayed during the Arab Islamic Peoples' Conference and Tehran Tehran decided to provide Turabi with professional assistance that would enable him to effectively spread the Islamist revolution throughout the world. The most important such step was the establishment of a headquarters for Turabi and the PIO: located in the Hall of Friendship in Khartoum, it is formally known as Bureau No. 7.

In April 1991, immediately after the Conference, Colonel al-Fatih Urwah of Sudanese intelligence went to Tehran to be trained to run it. There he was given several courses on staff management and communications techniques. He brought back a variety of communications equipment (including "electronic jamming equipment") to facilitate safe and secure PIO communications with the many Islamist movements. Clandestine techniques and communication codes were taught in Khartoum by newly-arrived experts from Iran, by the HizbAllah, and by Egyptians who had defected from the *Mukhabarat*. With their help, Turabi was able "to create a code which would allow him to contact fundamentalist organizations in the Arab World and abroad without being decoded by the [Western] security organs."[31]

And indeed, soon a stream of coded instructions began to flow from Khartoum and Tehran to Sheikh Abdel-Rahman in New York, providing the local network with specific instructions for virtually all their activities in the New York area. This stream of instructions, which were reportedly intercepted and deciphered by the Israeli and Egyptian intelligence services and then shared with the United States, continued virtually until the indictment of Sheikh Abdel-Rahman and his followers in late August 1993.[32]

The final consolidation of the strategic alliance that transformed Sudan into an Iranian fiefdom was completed in mid-December 1991 during a visit to Khartoum by a delegation of 157 Iranian senior officials led by President Hashemi-Rafsanjani to "boost relations between the two fraternal countries and widen horizons of cooperation and cohesion."[33] Hashemi-Rafsanjani predicted that "the Islamic revolution in Sudan would undoubtedly seriously affect the entire Arab world, Africa, and the world of Islam."

Hashemi-Rafsanjani stressed that "the two Islamic revolutions of Iran and Sudan, with regards to the strategic importance they enjoy in Asia, Africa, and the Middle East, undoubtedly can be the source of movement and revolution in the Islamic world."[34] Sudanese Foreign Minister Ali Sahlul said that Iran and Sudan "are facing the same threats" from the West and that both countries are working to expand "the reconciliation, cooperation, and solidarity between the states facing the dangers and threats we are facing."[35]

Meanwhile, Turabi was improving the leadership and command and control elements of the Islamist movement. In late 1991, he established a supreme council for the PIO and the International Muslim Brotherhood in Khartoum. Some 350 functionaries and leaders from several countries who were now living in Khartoum were to receive specialized training so that they could carry out their leadership roles. As noted above,* Sheikh Umar Abdel-Rahman, Rachid Ghanouchi of Tunisia, and Abbas Madani of Algeria (despite the fact that he was in jail) and of course Turabi were named as the top leaders of the organization, with Abdel-Rahman in New York and Ghannouchi in London as the senior representatives overseas, authorized to task their cells to commit specific terrorist attacks in accordance with a master plan and agreed-upon priorities and strategy.[36]

Thus a new "Islamist International" emerged in early 1992, unifying and better coordinating the various Sunni militant Islamist movements from West Africa to the Far East, which were now spreading rapidly throughout non-Muslim areas as well

* See Chapter 3

as in the Muslim world. This new "Islamist International" is now the dominant force in, and the spearhead of, a widespread campaign of Islamic proselytizing, a force which is actively involved in numerous armed clashes and subversions all over the world. The new organization is an outgrowth and expansion of the already extensive military-political networks of the Muslim Brotherhood.[37] To lead this Islamist revival, the Sudanese and the Iranians established a Higher Liaison Committee in Khartoum which task is to supervise extremist Islamist groups and organizations, coordinate and support their operations.[38]

In Sudan the Iranians have established an extensive, sophisticated system of terrorist training and support facilities ranging from training camps to international communications centers.[39] Thus, Egyptian sources lament, "the Sudanese regime is indeed the country that sold the Sudanese people's sovereignty by letting the Iranians build terrorist camps on Sudanese territory" in order to further what is essentially an Iranian strategic aspiration.[40]

George Logokwa, the Sudanese Labor Minister who defected in Egypt in August 1992, emphasized the centrality of terrorist infrastructure organized by Turabi's National Islamic Front to the future of Sudan and the region as a whole. "These camps," he said, "are located outside Khartoum. The Islamic Front has spent millions of dollars to establish them with the help of the Iranian Revolutionary Guards, who are in charge of training the terrorist cadres from extremist groups and *al-jihad* organizations in Arab countries, some Iranians, and Afghans.

They receive tough training in all types of combat, violence, and assassinations — to be sent, from time to time, to some neighboring countries to explore the situation, carry out limited and swift operations, and await the major plan devised by the Front to send its members to the countries chosen as targets for intensive activity."[41]

It should be noted that in 1992 a special squad of HizbAllah and Islamist terrorists were trained in Sudan for the construction and placement of extremely powerful booby-trapped bombs, including car-bombs, in urban centers in the United States and Western Europe.

They have already been deployed to their destinations.[42]

The rise of Turabi's Sudan as a central power player in international Islamist terrorism has had a direct impact on the Sudanese Islamist community in America, including their willingness to take part in terrorism. As of 1990, that community was transformed into active supporters of the Turabi regime and close followers of Sheikh Abdel-Rahman. Siddig Ibrahim Siddig Ali is the head of the New Jersey and New York branch of Turabi's National Islamic Front (NIF).[43] Fares Khallafalla and Tarig Elhassan, who would be implicated in the summer 1993 conspiracy, are also active members of NIF.

Siddig traveled frequently to Sudan.[44] He also arranged for several recruits to go to Sudan for advanced terrorist training. Indeed, "several" of those arrested in late June 1993 in connection with the July bomb plot had been trained in the camps in Sudan, including those run by the Iranians.[45]

It is hardly surprising that Siddig Ibrahim Siddig Ali was confident about Khartoum's support for the New York terrorist network. At one point, when Emad Salem asked him, "The brothers who are in the Sudanese embassy — are they going to be with us?" Siddig told him, "God willing, yes. There is someone who is going to help me. High level man." He was referring to Sarag al-Din Hamid Youssuf, a.k.a. Siraj Yousif. Officially the Counselor of the Sudanese Mission to the United Nations, Sarag/Siraj is in fact, as noted above, Turabi's personal representative and as such a senior intelligence officer and the actual head of mission.

Siddig was therefore confident that after the terrorist strikes were carried out, the Sudanese would provide the conspirators with shelter, visas, and assistance to leave the US.[46]

THE WORKING OF THE SECOND CELL

The unfolding of the active preparations for the new cycle of bombings in New York was followed closely by the terrorist masters in Tehran and Khartoum. The senior terrorist commanders repeatedly convened, consulted, and reached decisions before any major development in the active preparations in New York could take place. As in the case of the World Trade Center, Iran was in charge of and responsible for the entire operation. This time, however, specific commands were transmitted primarily via Sheikh Turabi in Sudan to Sheikh Abdel-Rahman in New York.[47]

Despite all these precautions, the first step taken by the cell's leader, Siddig Ibrahim Siddig Ali, was to prove fatal to the cell and the operation. With Elgabrowny in jail, he asked Emad Salem, 43, a retired Egyptian colonel believed to be very close to Sheikh Abdel-Rahman, to take over the support system. Salem, however, would immediately become the FBI's informant, betraying the operation.

The American authorities learned about the conspiracy in early May when Salem suddenly appeared on the scene and offered his services as an informer.[48] It is perhaps ironic that Siddig Ibrahim Siddig Ali was the member of the network most preoccupied with the possibility of a security leak. For example, in one of the discussions about the planned assassination of Egyptian President Husni Mubarak, Siddig argued that the reason Mubarak did not arrive in New York as planned in the spring 1993 was because of a leak in their network. Haggag, then in charge of the assassination project, became convinced that Siddig himself was the informant. He then approached Salem, whom he trusted, and asked for help in dealing with the leak.[49] The issue of mutual suspicion ended up in a shouting match in front of Sheikh Abdel-Rahman, who cleared Siddig Ibrahim Siddig Ali and sternly admonished Haggag.[50]

Meanwhile, Iranian and Sudanese preparations for the conduct of yet another round of terrorist strikes in the United States began in late April 1993. Around April 25, Hussein Sheikh-ol-Islam, a veteran terrorist master who had been involved in such operations as the bombings of the American Embassy and the Marines' barracks in Beirut, chaired a two-day terrorist summit in Tehran aimed at formulating the escalation strategy for the impending jihad against Israel and America at which senior Palestinian and other Arab terrorist leaders met with senior Iranian intelligence, security, and military officials to discuss joint operations and coordination of overseas operations.[51] During the conference a small inner circle met secretly to discuss impending operations and issue activation instructions.[52]

Thus, although the second cell of the New York network of Islamist terrorists began preparations to resume operations soon after the explosion in the World Trade Center and the first round of arrests, it became truly active in late April. It was then that evidence of a "second cell" connected with the World Trade Center bombing network surfaced. Authorities learned at the time that the objective of these terrorists was the assassination of key New York area leaders popularly associated with support for Israel.[53]

The first of these targets was U.S. Senator Alfonse D'Amato, who was warned by the FBI in early May that he had been targeted by Islamist terrorists. The threat was sufficiently serious to warrant the Senator's cancellation of his customary participation in the forthcoming "Solidarity with Israel" parade in Manhattan. About the same time, several other legislators were also warned.[54] When the terrorists realised that Senator D'Amato was being protected, they diverted their attention to an individual who might have less protection. Their new target for assassination was Brooklyn Assemblyman Dov Hikind, who is known for his active participation in pro-Israel and Jewish affairs. Nossair insisted that Hikind be killed as a follow-up to his own assassination of Kahane. On May 17, Hikind was also assigned around-the-clock police protection.[55]

As attention was being focused on the assassination plots, the leaders of the second cell were gearing up for a series of spectacular explosions all over New York planned for the Fourth of July. In order to enhance the shock of the spectacular follow-up to the World Trade Center bombing, the July bombings were to take place in quick succession all over New York City, causing tremendous numbers of civilian casualties.[56] On May 18, Siddig declared at a meeting of the terrorists in New Jersey that the World Trade Center bombing was merely a message that "we can get you any time," and that the next cycle of bombing would demonstrate the wrath of Islam.[57]

Nevertheless, the cell continued to study additional options. Siddig Ibrahim Siddig Ali again brought up with Emad Salem the possibility of assassinating FBI agents and taking hostages in the U.S. in order to bring about the release of the World Trade Center prisoners.[58] "Should our brothers be condemned to life in prison or to any other foolhardy sentence, they [the Americans] shall receive a blow of the kind they've never experienced in their life. It will be a blow whereby we'll hit them with missiles and take hostages," Siddig declared.[59] On

May 23, the conspirators briefly considered the possibility of targeting Henry Kissinger and former President Richard Nixon as potential hostages. The proposed taking of hostages was to be a part of a conspiracy broader than the series of bombing in Manhattan.[60]

While the Siddig cell was increasingly preoccupied with preparing for a series of spectacular bombings, preparing the assassination of Mubarak remained entrusted to the hands of Abdel-Rahman Haggag (Abdo Mohammed Haggag).[61] In the spring and summer of 1993, Haggag, Siddig, Hampton-El and possibly ten others were planning a "suicide mission" to kill Mubarak during his next visit to the United States, then scheduled for September 1993. The new assassination plan was a refinement of the previous plan. Like the previous plan it called for an attack on Mubarak by assassins dressed in hotel uniforms. Siddig Ibrahim Siddig Ali and Hampton-El met with Haggag several times in 1992 and 1993 to discuss the plot. Most important were several consultations that took place between Haggag, Siddig, Hampton-El, and Salem between April and June 1993, in the course of which Siddig acknowledged that he, Haggag, and other members of the network had received special training for a secret mission — the Mubarak assassination. Hampton-El agreed to provide the weapons and ammunition for the conspirators.

Throughout the entire process, it was clear to the participants that the assassination would have to be a suicide mission.[62]

Meanwhile, the preparations for a series of spectacular explosions were accelerating. On May 7, Siddig and Salem first discussed possible terrorist operations in the New York area. Among the options they examined was driving a car bomb into the United Nations Secretariat building. Siddig was to be responsible for the professional aspects of the operation — planning the strike, "building bombs, getting timing devices," recruiting the bombers, and other aspects of the operation.[63] The terrorist leaders also prepared false passports and escape routes for the principals.[64] Over the next few days, Siddig and Salem discussed various options for the UN building operation, including the acquisition of high explosives and gun powder and testing a timer. On May 18, they discussed the possibility of blowing up the Federal building where several law enforcement agencies have offices.[65] The next day, Siddig instructed Salem to rent a safehouse in Queens to be used as their bomb factory.[66]

What the network seemed to lack at this point in mid-May was focus and professional guidance. It is still unclear how many of the expert terrorists who had been infiltrated into the United States during the autumn of 1992 remained in the New York area after Youssuf and many others fled the country in March 1993. The New York conspirators were enthusiastic and dedicated — but not practical. They could not limit themselves to a few specific plans and concentrate on carrying them out. Harnessing and disciplining the cell would require a terrorist authority whom, at that point, they were definitely lacking. The terrorist masters, with whom the principals of the second cell had contacts, could not have missed the problem. A "submarine", an on-site long-term plant, was therefore activated to assume command as the expert terrorist.

Enter Fadil Abdelghani (Abd-al-Ghani), a 31-year-old Sudanese. Although he came from an affluent family of Khartoum's elite and was a qualified medical laboratory technician, he chose to work as a cab driver until his license expired in April 1992.[67] Since then, he had stayed on the fringes, reportedly involved in organizing the Islamist underground network for AIM.[68] He continued to worship at the al-Salam Mosque in Jersey City.[69]

Although without any visible means of income, Fadil Abdelghani was able to go to Sudan every year for "technical training," i.e., terrorist training updates. He also travelled frequently to Egypt, South America and the Netherlands.[70] A true professional, he stayed out of sight, and out of the reach of the FBI's microphone, until the last phases of the operation, at which point he surfaced anew. In the last days prior to the FBI break-up of the cell, Fadil Abdelghani emerged as a dominant figure, discussing specific bombing plans and other technical matters in the Queens safe house full of explosives.[71]

Fadil's cousin, Amir Abdelghani (Abd-al-Ghani), a.k.a. Abdou Zaid, 33, a Sudanese cab driver who had been in the U.S. since 1985, seems to also be a trained terrorist. He too traveled to Sudan once a year, ostensibly to visit his wife and child.[72] Eventually, developments in the planning for the series of bombing operations would give Amir Abdelghani an important position.

The bombing of the UN building was to be the

first attack in the chain of bombings planned for the Fourth of July. Reconstruction of the terrorists' plans suggests that they intended to count on various reactions to an explosion at the UN building in order to maximize the damage and casualties in the other bombings.[73] Siddig wanted to make the destruction of the UN building the priority objective because it is "the world's government" which he sees as anti-Islamic.[74] "All UN resolutions are oppressive," he said. "It is against Islam and Muslims." [75] Sheikh Umar Abdel-Rahman considered the UN to be "the Americans' UN" and therefore a hostile organization[76]; he was quite explicit in his endorsement of the planned attack on it.[77]

Siddig's plan called for a large car bomb to be placed against a major structural element of the building[78] and he had an ingenious plan for getting the car bomb into the UN building's underground garage.[79] An Egyptian limousine driver in his 40s (who is still missing) would provide the car[80], a limousine with diplomatic license plates that would facilitate its entry into the UN compound "without inspections."

The diplomatic plates would be provided by two senior members of Sudan's UN delegation who are in fact intelligence officers responsible for supporting terrorist operations.[81] Ahmad Youssuf Othman, a.k.a. Ahmed Mohammed, officially the Third Secretary responsible for consular affairs, is the Sudanese intelligence officer who served as Siddig's point of contact. Othman serves directly under Sarag al-Din Hamid Youssuf, who is, as indicated above, Turabi's representative and the senior intelligence officer.[82] These two, along with a Libyan officer also serving as a member of his country's UN delegation, were also expected to help get the car bomb admitted to the UN compound in case of any problems at the gate.[83]

Since the bomb in the limousine would have to be very powerful but small enough to be concealed from possible inspection at the gateway to the UN grounds, the terrorists initially decided to make it from plastique high explosives. In mid-May, Hampton-El was assigned to find "powerful explosives," preferably C-4 plastique, through his Fuqra connections. As a result Siddig went to Philadelphia to meet with a 27-year-old Fuqra member called Earl Gant (a.k.a. Abd Rashid and Abd Jalil) who was supposed to provide the high explosives; but Siddig returned to New York empty handed. Hampton-El then tried, without success, to obtain high explosives plus two grenades from another source.[84]

On May 30, Siddig, Hampton-El and Salem met in Brooklyn to discuss obtaining high explosives for the UN operation. Hampton-El, still responsible for the explosives acquisition, reminded Siddig that home-mixed explosives work very well, as they both had seen in the test explosion prior to the World Trade Center bombing.[85] In order to better understand the home-mixed explosives, Hampton-El took home manuals for making bombs identical to those of Ajaj and Youssuf recovered by authorities.[86] Because they might have to use a larger volume of home-mixed explosives, the terrorists decided to use the larger van of the Sudanese embassy instead of the limousine as their car bomb.[87]

Because of the overriding importance of the timing of the UN explosion, the terrorists debated the detonator question. Salem suggested a single action key fuse in which the timer begins to count at the push of a button.[88] The question of a remote control was studied but (as in the case of the World Trade Center) the terrorists must have known by now that most radio remote controls were ineffective inside buildings. Indeed, the issue of using beepers came up repeatedly in early May in various contexts.

Ultimately, because of the crucial importance of the explosion under the UN building, the possibility of a suicide operation was raised. Siddig acknowledged that "this [will] blow while they [the perpetrators] are inside." He had no problem with such an operation. "We say that we are ready [to] sacrifice anything. We enter and we don't get out."[89]

Sheikh Umar Abdel-Rahman has the authority to approve and bless suicide operations in the United States.[90]

As the terrorists settled on the use of proven home-mixed explosives, their operational plans became more focused and their bombing plans more specific and detailed. In order to overwhelm the authorities, at least three bombs would be blown up on the same day at different places and in a specific sequence. The primary objectives would be the UN building, the Federal building, and either the Holland or the Lincoln Tunnel (or preferably both).

Siddig expected that the only way to get the car bomb into the Federal Building would be by shooting the guards and driving straight into the ground floor. That assault on the Federal Building would require three cars. The conspirators discussed ways to get these cars, ranging from the possibility of renting cars under false names to acquiring stolen cars. They settled on buying stolen cars.[91]

The time arrived to activate the local expendables. Since all of them worshipped at the al-Salam Mosque in Jersey City,[92] they must already have been identified, vetted, and even recruited by 1992. The terrorist leaders considered a diverse group of individuals — Palestinians, Egyptians, Iraqis and Sudanese — from among whom to make their selection. Siddig explained that for security reasons, the expendables would be ordered to come for "regular training" and would not be told that they were actually "implementing the plan... till the last moment."[93]

The expendables included: Fares Khallafalla, 31, a Sudanese who worked as a driver for a medical delivery company; Victor Alvarez, a.k.a. Mohammad, 32, a Puerto Rican convert who had become a devout Muslim; and Mohammad Saleh, a.k.a. Mohammad Ali, 40, a Palestinian from Jordan who owns a gas station.[94]

One of the key expendable cell members were Tarig Elhassan (Tariq al-Hassan), 38, a Sudanese cab driver who had been in America since 1986 and had become a devout Muslim in recent years. Elhassan was living in a safe house, suggesting that he may have been involved in providing some support functions for some time.[95]

Another member, Matharawy Muhammad Said

Saleh, 44, is an Egyptian welder who was convicted as a heroin dealer in Detroit in 1988. Saleh, who arrived in the U.S. legally in early 1980s, had military experience in Egypt and may be an explosives expert. He was to get the cars for the bombings without being detected.[96] Saleh also uses the name "Wahid Ahmad"[97], and as "Wahid" he met twice with the conspirators in the Queens safe house and was among those indicted in connection with the plan to blow up the UN building.[98]

Also involved, apparently marginally, was Abu-Ubaydah Yahyah, 39, an American black Muslim and a martial arts specialist. An activist and an acquaintance of most of the conspirators, he had even volunteered for service in Bosnia. On the day the network was captured, he left a warning note for Hampton-El on his car window, indicating his advance knowledge of the terrorists' plans.[99] Also arrested was Ashraf Mohammad, who planned to assist in Matharwy Saleh's escape to Florida.[100]

The terrorist plan went into its final implementation phase in late May. Siddig, Salem, Khalafalla and Amir Abdelghani met in the Queens safe house to test the timing devices they would use in the operation. On May 29, Siddig and Emad Salem drove Amir Abdelghani around to visit the possible targets in Manhattan. During the ride, Siddig identified the Holland and Lincoln Tunnels as additional targets for the same day, immediately after the bombing of the UN and Federal buildings.

The men discussed possible locations for the placement of bombs as well as the possibility of starting fires as diversions. One of the conspirators suggested setting off a bomb at 47th Street and Fifth Avenue, in the heart of the jewelry district, because so many Jews work there. Siddig called it "the heart of Israel here in Manhattan," and added, "Boom — broken windows, Jews in the streets."[101] On June 4, Mohammad Saleh, the gas station owner, told Siddig and Salem, who were visiting him in Yonkers, that he would participate in the operation, providing the required fuel.[102]

By early June, the plans and preparations had reached an advanced stage and were on the verge of implementation. Determined to be capable of striking by the end of June, the conspirators believed that they were on the threshhold of the operation, just before the point of going into action with the final preparations. It was time for the terrorist experts in Tehran to carefully check the situation in the U.S. The pressure of time and the realization that, in the wake of the World Trade Center attack, American law enforcement authorities were investigating the Islamist community of the New York area thoroughly, made it imprudent to send intelligence operatives in a concealed and clandestine manner. Tehran therefore decided to send its experts under the cover of a diplomatic delegation.

Thus, although in early June Tehran was in the midst of a campaign urging an activist anti-American policy,[103] (see below), Hashemi-Rafsanjani dispatched a diplomatic delegation to the United States, ostensibly to initiate an "unofficial dialogue" with the Clinton administration. The delegation was headed by Muhammad Javad Larijani, Hashemi-Rafsanjani's adviser, and included Abdolkarim

Surash, Mohammad Bahrololum, and other senior
officials affiliated with the ideological struggle and
intelligence operations. The delegation arrived in
New York on June 9.[104] Intelligence officers in the
ranks of the delegation were in position to personally assess the terrorists' plans and capabilities.[105]

The experts' findings and conclusions were discussed and approved in clandestine meetings conducted in Khartoum on June 12 and 13.[106] These
consultations were conducted under the cover of a
special session of the People's Arab and Islamic
Congress chaired by Turabi and dedicated to con-
demning "U.S. genocide" against Muslims as
demonstrated in Somalia and Palestine.[107] By mid-
June, the network in New York had been given the
green light to proceed to implement their plans.

The pace of preparations in New York picked
up soon afterwards. In the next few days, Siddig,
Amir Abdelghani, Khalfalla, Alvarez and Elhassan
began mixing the explosives at the safe house in
Queens. The explosives were made of acids and fer-
tilizer with fuel added to enhance heat, essentially
identical to the mixture used for the World Trade
Center. On June 20, Siddig and Salem went to the
woods near Naugatuck, Connecticut, to explode a
test sample of the mixture. Satisfied, they ordered
the mixing of larger quantities. On June 23, two
men transported fuel from Mohammad Saleh's gas
station in Yonkers to Queens to complete the mixing and preparation of the bombs.[108]

Meanwhile, Amir Abdelghani had been given
$200 to buy stolen cars for the operation.[109] He and
Khalafalla also gave Alvarez another $300 for other

stolen cars. On June 22, Salem and Alvarez went to New Jersey to obtain the firearms needed for the operation.[110]

The terrorists were mixing the explosives in 55-gallon drums. The chemicals used were worth some $900. They had acquired some 2,000 lbs. of bomb ingredients, enough to make some 500 lbs. of explosives. Such a quantity is sufficient to heavily damage a building or bring down a section of a bridge or a tunnel.[111]

On the night of June 23-24 the active preparation of the bombs in the safe house in Queens was interrupted by an FBI raid. Eight drums containing 180 gallons of explosives were seized. [112] The terrorists were arrested in the early hours of the morning of June 24 as they were mixing the explosives.[113]

Chapter 7

ONLY THE BEGINNING

The bombing of the World Trade Center was a milestone of historic significance in global terms. It pushed the Islamist community, not only in the U.S. but around the world, across a crucial line. The terrorist bomb in New York demonstrated that it was now both permissible and possible to strike at the heart of America.

The primary legacy of the bombing is its invitation and encouragement for the like-minded to follow suit. Indeed, French experts view the New York bombing as "the beginning of a 'war' between radical Islamism and the United States."[1] The activities of the Islamist terrorist networks in New York must therefore be considered a strategic operation; they ought to be examined in the context of the ongoing development of the entire Islamist movement, its internal dynamics and its policy, both as a whole and within each of its constituent parts, vis-á-vis the United States.

Led by the terrorist-controlling states, the Islamists have been preparing for this step for a long time.* From their point of view, the strike in New York is but one milestone— and an early one — in a long-term historical process that will not be decided by any single event, no matter how cataclysmic it might be. Abd al-Muhsin Fadlallah, a cousin of the HizbAllah's spiritual leader, Ayatollah Muhammad Hussein Fadlallah, defined the Islamist approach to the struggle against the United States: "People who believe in God and see things in the long term, they will win. People who think only of the next hour, of their immediate surroundings, they will not win."[2]

Fully aware of the magnitude and complexity of the tasks ahead, the Islamists have embarked on a prudent and protracted process of preparing for, and waging, their kind of war against the West and especially the United States. International terrorism is the Islamists' most effective weapon. To employ it, highly professional and proficient terrorist cells and networks are already in place in the United States, Canada, Western Europe and elsewhere in the world, ready for such an escalation. Instruments of state policy, these Islamist terrorist networks await orders from Tehran, Damascus, and Khartoum before launching their operations.

* *Target America* details the relationships among the several governments sponsoring and directing terrorism, their respective roles and authority within the system, the major terrorist organizations, and the creation of the international network of trained agents now in place and operating worldwide.

The most important question emerging from the New York case is: Will they strike again? The answer involves a combination of several factors affecting the functioning of all Islamist terrorist networks operating in the West — the decisions of the sponsoring states, the availability of spiritual leadership and guidance, and the availability of dedicated and capable terrorists. Thus, in order to better understand the importance and the legacy of the New York Islamist terrorist network, the following key factors should be examined in a larger context:

o The role of the spiritual leader, especially Sheikh Abdel-Rahman;

o The potential for Islamist terrorism in America in the wake of the arrests and indictments;

o The policy of the controlling states and their interest in escalation.

THE ROLE OF SHEIKH UMAR ABDEL-RAHMAN

One of the lingering questions concerning the operations of the New York Islamist terrorist network is, how much did Sheikh Umar Abdel-Rahman know, and when? He himself repeatedly denied any connection with the terrorists. Following the World Trade Center bombing, he told an interviewer flatly, "I had no knowledge of this explosion, and I'm not responsible for it."[3]

However, less than a year earlier, in the summer

of 1992, as part of the further consolidation of the PIO and AIM, Sheikh Umar Abdel-Rahman was named a senior member of the supreme leadership and authorized to act as the Islamists' senior representative in North America. As previously noted, in this capacity he is authorized to assign the local cells to commit specific terrorist attacks in accordance with a master plan and agreed-upon priorities and strategy that are determined in Khartoum and Tehran.[4]

At the same time Sheikh Abdel-Rahman, and only he, was authorized to issue *fatwas* permitting suicide operations in North America, thus significantly simplifying the Islamists' ability to conduct spectacular terrorism there. Indeed, in late 1992, Sheikh Abdel-Rahman was recognized along with Sheikh al-Turabi as "the most prominent" leaders of the Islamist international. In the case of Abdel-Rahman, this was because of his control of terrorist operations in America.[5]

Sheikh Abdel-Rahman's unique authority to bless suicide operations in North America is of crucial importance in assessing his involvement with the terrorist plans. Since both the bombing of the United Nations building and the assassination of President Mubarak were to be suicide operations,[6] the conspirators must have been certain at that point of their ability to get the necessary blessing and authorization from Sheikh Abdel-Rahman.

Indeed, a close examination of the relationship between the New York Islamist terrorists and their spiritual leader during the active preparations for the operations of the summer of 1993 clearly indicates that Sheikh Abdel-Rahman knew at least some details of the planning for bombings in New York — at least the preparations exposed in late June 1993.[7] His voice is on the tapes recorded during the investigation,[8] and what he is heard saying may amount to a discussion of possible bombing plans.[9]

Sheikh Abdel-Rahman also clearly and explicitly expressed his opinion about terrorism in the United States in principle. For example, he told Siddig that "American blood should be spilled on its own soil."[10]

The followers of Sheikh Umar Abdel-Rahman unquestionably paid very close attention to the positions he took and sought his approval for all their activites. As mentioned above, in August 1993 El-Sayyid Nossair told an interviewer emphatically that without Abdel-Rahman's blessing "there would have been no actions. The Sheikh inspires people to fight," Nossair explained. "He is a brilliant scholar and a brilliant speaker, but he always is talking of fighting. The Sheikh believes in fighting more than anyone else." Nossair was adamant in his insistence that the perpetrators of any terrorist operation from the New York area network would have gone to the Sheikh to "request his blessing."[11] Similarly, Abouhalima stated that "[Abdel-]Rahman was told of the [WTC] bombing plans and approved them."[12]

It is hardly surprising, therefore, that Siddig Ibrahim Siddig Ali and Emad Salem had several discussions about the role of Sheikh Umar Abdel-Rahman, with Salem trying to learn the extent of the Sheikh's knowledge of the conspiracies and the extent of his support. Most revealing is their discussion on May 18, 1993:

Siddig: "Sheikh doesn't know anything about you or about this subject at all. We intend to make the Sheikh as a headline only."

Salem: "He doesn't interfere."

Siddig: "No, no, he doesn't interfere and he has no relation with it. You don't put him in the middle, you simply ask him a general question. That's all."

Salem: "What does he think of the Big House?" [the UN Building]

Siddig: "Of course he approves, of course. Don't be so doubtful. Believe me, your brother is very smart, thank God. I don't make a step unless I check with the law of our religion from Sheikh Umar. He was asked if the [inaudible] was an Islamic move. He said of course it is."[13]

(The subsequent course of the discussion strongly suggests that Siddig was referring to the World Trade Center.)

Indeed, in a subsequent meeting that Salem attended, Sheikh Umar Abdel-Rahman demonstrated a knowledge of the intention to blow up the UN building, suggesting that it be carried out later in order to bomb military installations first.

In the same meeting, he also told Salem to proceed cautiously with the plot to blow up the Federal building (which houses FBI offices in New York).[14] In discussions with Salem, Abdel-Rahman referred specifically to the planned bombing of the United Nations building, saying, "It is not forbidden, but it will put the Muslims in bad light." In a May 23 meeting, Sheikh Abdel-Rahman urged prudence and caution on the part of his followers, but he did not discourage them from carrying out their plans. "Go slow," he said. "The person who killed Kennedy was in training [? because inaudible] for three years. We don't want to do anything in haste."[15]

The key to a full understanding of the role of Sheikh Umar Abdel-Rahman lies in his relations with the Egyptian Islamist terrorists. There is a track record of recent operations in which the Sheikh's exact role and responsibility can be ascertained.

In the summer of 1992, Sheikh Umar Abdel-Rahman was living and preaching in New York; he announced that he would return only 2to an Islamist Egypt ruled by "Islamic Government based on the *Shari'ah* [Islamic law]. The primary principle of the *Shari'ah* is that 'only Allah rules.'"[16] He urged his followers to expedite the creation of such conditions and issued a general *fatwa* calling for the assassination of pillars of Egyptian society.[17]

Egyptian security authorities uncovered five hit lists of individuals drawn up by Islamist organizations, mainly those affiliated with Islamic Jihad. On one of these lists "journalists and thinkers" were defined as priority targets.[18]

On June 12, 1992, the assassination of Dr. Faraj Fudah, a writer and intellectual, in Cairo confirmed the reality of the threat. The Islamists consider it a prelude to an Islamist coup conceived by the Islamic Jihad.[19] And indeed, the Islamists in Upper Egypt were planning to conduct a wave of terrorism and assassinations following the death of Fudah.[20]

However, the most important aspect of Dr. Fudah's murder is its clarification of the role of the spiritual leader and the military commander.

From his exile in New York, Sheikh Umar Abdel-Rahman issued the *fatwa* sanctioning/ordering the assassination. The actual assassin was one Abdel-Shafi Ahmad Ramadan of the Al-Jihad Organization. The operational plans were made by the jailed leader of Islamic Jihad Sawfat Abdel-Ghani. His lawyer, Mansur Ahmad Mansur, used their meetings in jail to inform Abdel-Ghani about developments and to carry Abdel-Ghani's plans out to the actual killers. Upon receiving a message from Abdel-Rahman, Abdel-Ghani gave the "go" order for the specific operation — the implementation of the *fatwa*.

The Islamic Jihad's adherence to leaders so far apart "means [that] the organization maintains a strong, accurate, and well-organized communications network at home [in Egypt] and abroad." Fudah's assassination also demonstrated the strength and importance of Sheikh Umar Abdel-Rahman's leadership of and for the Islamist terrorists.[21]

Thus, Sheikh Umar Abdel-Rahman's continued relations with Islamist terrorism in Egypt are indicative of his real position of leadership in the global terrorist establishment. Although he is thousands of miles away in the United States, Abdel-Rahman is considered by all the Egyptian Islamist factions to be their supreme spiritual leader. This further confirms that their seemingly spontaneous actions are actually parts of a master plan;[22] and in fact captured Egyptian terrorists have admitted that "Iran backed them financially to commit terrorist actions inside Egypt." They identified Umar Abdel-Rahman as their supreme leader, who is responsible for their operations.[23]

From his base in New York, Abdel-Rahman also endorsed Islamist terrorism in general. He specifically decreed that in attacking tourists, the Islamic Jihad "was merely doing its duty of forbidding what is sinful."[24] He denied involvement in any organized conspiracy, arguing that his was "not an organization of jihad or repudiation. We are Islamic Groups."[25] At the same time, however, Abdel-Rahman was sending cassettes of sermons calling for Islamic Revolution in Egypt from New Jersey to his followers in Egypt and he had signed the *fatwa* permitting the recent attacks on tourists in Egypt.[26]

One of his "close disciples" operating underground in Egypt acknowledged the Islamic Group's participation in, and responsibility for, the attacks on tourists. He clarified the authoritative role of Sheikh Abdel-Rahman and reaffirmed that there is a constant contact with New York in which specific subjects are decided. "Telephone contact between us and Sheikh Abdel-Rahman takes place daily and lasts for hours. The Islamic Group does not formulate any opinion on any matter without going back to him."[27] Egypt's former Minister of Interior, Maj. Gen. Muhammad Abdel-Halim Mussa, has warned that "Umar Abdel-Rahman ... is residing in the United States as a Khomeyni awaiting return to take power in Egypt."[28]

Cairo determined that the fall 1992 escalation

in terrorist operations, at least in Egypt, was the work of "an international front [that] has been formed to spread terrorism ... which is financed by Iran" and had major facilities in Sudan. Under the leadership of Hasan al-Turabi, "the front is holding regular meetings in Sudan and is being financed, guided and armed by Iran."[29] In that front, Abdel-Rahman was identified as the one who "planned terrorist operations worldwide."[30] This definition fits his role in the United States.

In 1993 the position and power of Sheikh Umar Abdel-Rahman continued to increase. Jamil Husseini Mutawalli, a former local leader of *al-Jama'ah al-Islamiyah* stressed the growing importance of the Sheikh in the rapidly escalating Islamist terrorism in Egypt. "Dr. Umar Abdel-Rahman is the actual and spiritual *amir* [supreme leader] of all the extremist organizations in Egypt. Telephone contacts have taken place between him and the [organizations'] officials, and they exchange audio cassettes by various means."[31]

Abdel-Rahman also provides instructions and actual assistance to the Egyptian terrorists through messengers. In June 1993, Egyptian authorities seized one of his followers, Zakariya Muhammad al-Tuni, an Egyptian with a U.S. passport, trying to smuggle fifteen pistols destined for the local Islamist terrorists in Fayyum, the center of Abdel-Rahman's supporters.[32]

Cairo recognises the crucial importance of the guidance arriving from Abdel-Rahman. In the summer of 1993, Egypt's Interior Minister, Hassan al-Alfi, was convinced that the disruption of the communications between the Islamist terrorists and their leaders abroad is crucial to the possible containment of Islamist terrorism.[33]

The separation between spiritual guidance and specific military operational command also exists with the Egyptian Islamist terrorists. Mutawalli stressed that while the *amir*, Sheikh Umar Abdel-Rahman, is the undisputed leader, a "senior offical in Cairo" runs the actual armed (i.e., terrorist) operations on the Sheikh's behalf and in accordance with his guidance. This "senior offical in Cairo" also personally recruits the terrorists for the spectacular operations. "After being recruited, he [the future terrorist] is subjected to brainwashing, and as soon as he receives the necessary dose, he becomes obedient and ready to carry out orders and implement assassination or sabotage missions."[34]

It is should be noted that the same kind of separation of functions was practiced by the followers of Sheikh Umar Abdel-Rahman in New York. Mahmud Abouhalima and Siddig Ibrahim Siddig Ali both acted as the military commanders while providing their *amir* with a shield of deniability. Still, terrorists recently captured in Egypt identified Abdel-Rahman as their commander and leader. "We carry [out the] order from the Mufti of Al-Jihad, Sheikh Umar Abdel-Rahman, and we will continue to do so," they declared.[35] Their American counterparts would feel the same, whether or not they would say it.

The arrest of Sheikh Umar Abdel-Rahman in New York on July 2, 1993 could not stop the escalation of the terrorist campaign waged by his followers. The Egyptian Islamists are now "engaging in terrorist activity in a violent and threatening way. Umar Abdel-Rahman's group uses the missionary method in its own way. It has also aimed violent acts against the government, security agencies, and against society itself, to forcefully change some social behaviors in communities and neighborhoods."[36]

The professional skills of these terrorists continue to markedly improve. The widespread introduction of highly lethal "booby trapped suitcases" is but one element of "a huge development that has taken place in manufacturing bombs and explosives by the extremist groups."[37] The same trend should be expected in the United States.

WHAT'S NEXT?

It is now quite obvious that the arrests of its first and second network cells are not the end of the terrorist threat from this New York area Islamist network. The conspiracy began before the World Trade Center bombing as a comprehensive long-term undertaking, and only certain components have so far been neutralized.[38] In addition to those arrested, several men still at large were part of the conspiracy. Some are known to authorities who lack the legal evidence needed to make arrests. Others are still unknown.[39] The second cell had at least fifteen members,[40] and five more suspects connected with Sheikh Umar Abdel-Rahman as well as with both the World Trade Center and the planned mid-summer bombings are being sought.[41]

It should be remembered that Abouhalima said that his own cell was "part of a nationwide organization" made up of "300 men across the country who would do anything to hurt the U.S. Government."[42] Siddig Ibrahim Siddig Ali planned to buy in Sudan "RPG's, howitzers" that are "light, but ... heavier than the machine gun, anti-tanks." Some of these weapons would have been diverted to Jordan for operations against Israel — but the rest were to have been smuggled into the United States for the use of the local Islamist terrorist networks here.[43]

Law enforcement authorities believe that they have identified additional terrorist groups in the New York area, all made up of followers of Sheikh Abdel-Rahman who have gravitated around his mosque, but believe that they did not constitute an immediate threat.[44] Authorities discovered a "third cell" related to the two already captured, whose members are "laying low until the smoke clears," avoiding arrest.[45] There is evidence that there are "dozens and dozens" of similar groups around the country.[46] Indeed, the Iranians stress the centrality of the U.S. to the Islamist terrorists, particularly those from Egypt. "The United States is one of the main bases for the activities of the Egyptian combatants" whose leader is Sheikh Umar Abdel-Rahman.[47]

However, what is truly worrisome to the law enforcement authorities is that additional members of the same general population group who are either only loosely connected with any of the known cells — or even not connected with them at all — may still be activated, regroup, and strike soon, primarily in connection with the trials of Abdel-Rahman and his followers, if only in order to prove the viability of Islamist terrorism.[48]

The Iranians control a multitude of Islamist terrorist networks in the U.S., many of them concealed in organizations and groups considered friendly to America.[49] These networks are known to have in the United States large numbers of highly-trained terrorists and a "considerable quantity" of explosives earmarked for use in "a wide range of terrorist attacks" once the order is given.[50] This possibility became very real following the detention of Sheikh Umar Abdel-Rahman on July 2, which resulted in threats of revenge from Islamist circles around the world.[51]

A warning note delivered in New York by the *al-Jama'ah al-Islamiyah* in Egypt parroted the Iranian line, attributing the Sheikh's arrest to the worldwide campaign against Islam:

"As it watched the sensational Rambo-style arrest of Dr. Umar Abdel-Rahman Friday, 2 July 1993, the world did not need more such scenes to clearly see that flagrant exposed American face without its deceptive gloss and without the false masks that Uncle Sam and his feeble slaves have used as pretexts for their new world order... Having seen the actions in the Gulf, Somalia, and Bosnia, and, finally, the actions against Umar Abdel-Rahman, people realized that these slogans were nothing but empty words used to mislead and deceive or used for certain nations but not others." The note then stressed the inherent strength of Sheikh Abdel-Rahman and urged all Muslims to recognise the plight of their situation and the leadership of the Sheikh.[52]

Throughout the Middle East, and especially in Egypt, several Islamist terrorist groups threatened a series of strikes in Egypt and worldwide if anything happened to the Sheikh.[53] In Gaza, where the local Islamic Jihad has close relations with their Egyptian counterparts, slogans painted on walls warned, "We will kidnap Americans if Sheikh Abdel-Rahman is punished or handed over to the Egyptian authorities."[54] In Egypt, *al-Jama'ah al-Islamiyah* claimed that Mubarak was "digging his own grave" because of Cairo's suppression of Islamists and its desire to extradite Abdel-Rahman. The Islamic Group promised to "annihilate the regime of collaborators and apostates" and replace it with an Islamic government.[55]

The warnings increased and became even more credible after Sheikh Abdel-Rahman and his followers were indicted. Abdel-Rahman's Egyptian attorney, Montasser al-Zayyat, warned of dire ramifications the indictment would have. "Humiliating, harming and subjecting the life of Sheikh Umar to danger in this way is a strong provocation to his followers and sympathisers inside and outside Egypt," Zayyat said. "It is very probable they will carry out violent attacks against American interests."

Abdel-Halim Mandour, another of the Sheikh's lawyers, also warned of a violent reaction. "No one can predict what can happen but the followers, friends and students of Sheikh Umar are very angry. They will definitely not have friendly reactions towards the United States."[56]

On August 26, several Islamist groups all over the Middle East issued communiques threatening to hit American citizens and targets all over the world, and especially in America itself, if Sheikh Umar Abdel-Rahman is hurt. Egyptian Islamists rallied to the cause, displaying unity and coordination. In Assyut, a warning statement was issued jointly by the Islamic Group, the Vanguards of Conquest and the Islamic Jihad Organization: "We will take revenge on all U.S. interests and citizens in Egypt or outside if any harm occurs to Sheik Umar ... We will carry out more acts of holy struggle if the [American] regime does not back away from its position on Sheik Umar Abdel-Rahman."[57] The three groups repeated: "We threaten to take revenge against American interests in Egypt or abroad if the U.S. Administration goes ahead with proceedings against our spiritual leader."[58]

Abdel-Rahman's *al-Jama'a al-Islamiya* repeats its threats on a daily basis. "We will take revenge violently, maybe more violently than they can bear. They will regret what they are doing if there is any harm to Doctor Umar Abdel-Rahman."[59]

The most significant of these threats is one put out in Lebanon by a previously unknown organization demanding freedom for the Sheikh and ordering terrorist acts in the United States if their demand is not met. "We warn America against extraditing Sheikh Abdel-Rahman to Egypt and demand that he be freed at once... Otherwise, every American citizen and all U.S. interests around the world will be in danger." The group calls itself "The Partisans of Khalid al-Istambuli" (the assassin of Egyptian President Anwar Sadat). Their communique was issued in Sidon through the channels usually used by the HizbAllah, Islamic Jihad, and other Iranian-controlled organizations, but the office that delivered the message belongs to a local Sunni Islamist organization.[60]

The special importance of this communique lies in the fact that "The Partisans of Khalid al-Istambuli" is the name chosen by the elite of the Egyptian Islamists affiliated with Abdel-Rahman's Jama'at Islami, which is run by Muhammad Shawqi al-Istambuli, Khalid's brother. It is the Lebanon-based detachment of the Egyptian Islamic Jihad that now issues the threats as "Partisans of Khalid al-Istambuli." Operationally, they are part of the elite task force run by the shadowy Abu-Imamah from Qum on behalf of Iran's VEVAK. * Thus, although Sunni, they are fully integrated into the world-wide Iranian-controlled HizbAllah networks. Moreover, as already demonstrated in New York, the Egyptian Islamists are fully integrated into the HizbAllah networks and have agentss in the United States ready and willing to conduct terrorist strikes.

During August, there were a few sporadic and rather amateurish acts of terrorist revenge against the plight of the Sheikh. On August 15, an Arabic-speaking hijacker claiming to have a bomb diverted a KLM Boeing 737-400 on a flight from Tunis to

* See Chapter 3 above.

Düsseldorf, Germany, where he freed first most, and then all, of the passengers and crew. He wanted to fly to New York to demand that Washington free Abdel-Rahman and enforce UN sanctions against Serbia. The hijacker was first described as 55 years old and believed to be an Egyptian who, according to the crew, identified himself as a follower of Abdel-Rahman. "He threatens more attacks if the demand is not met," a spokesman said at Düsseldorf airport. In the predawn hours, officers of the German GSG-9 seized him without any opposition[61] and in a subsequent inspection, no explosives were found on the plane.[62]

The hijacker was identified as one Khalid Abdel-Mun'im Gharib, age 40, a building contractor from the al-Jizah district on the outskirts of Cairo who owned a brick factory and enjoyed a good reputation in his village of Badrasheen. He had left Cairo on August 9 for Tunisia, where he spent several days before hijacking KLM Flight 110. Egyptian police reported that, aside from bouncing a few checks, Gharib had no criminal record. He was devoted to Sheikh Abdel-Rahman but there was no evidence that he belonged to any extremist organization, so it was therefore assumed that he had acted alone.[63]

But closer examination of the Gharib case raises some questions. According to Ulf Steinke, the police commander who handled the eleven-hour hijacking at Düsseldorf airport, Gharib was an "atypical hostage-taker," unusually calm and never aggressive. Steinke said the hijacking appeared to have been premeditated "but I don't think it was thought through to its conclusion." In fact, Gharib does have a history of engaging in Islamist activism and even violence. In recent years, he had made frequent business trips to Western Europe, particularly Germany and the Netherlands. According to an uncle, Abdel-Razik Gharib, he had already been arrested in Holland for protesting in front of the International Court of Justice in the Hague against the killing of the Muslims in Bosnia. The demonstration was not entirely peaceful, for Gharib was arrested for attempted arson and deported from Holland.[64]

According to a cousin, Abdel-Wahab Gharib,"he did not have any activity, neither Islamic, political nor social, but I always felt he had something wrong in his mind."

The reaction of Khalid Gharib's family to the news that he was the hijacker also raises questions. His wife insisted that her husband was traveling in Egypt, and that he had lost his passport three months before. She said he had informed the authorities of his loss and filed a complaint, and that they had the documents to prove it.[65]

This raises the possibility that someone else may have carried out the hijacking using Gharib's passport. The hijacker was estimated to be 55 years old and Gharib is known to be 40. Gharib might have agreed to contribute his passport to a noble cause and then reported it stolen. Such a possibility would make the hijacking the result of a pre-planned conspiracy, in which case it becomes far more meaningful as a warning.

Meanwhile, the Islamists continued with their subtle but meaningful reminders of the reality of their threats. Their next action would to be in the

United States. On August 28, a caller warned that a bomb had been placed on an Alitalia Boeing 747, Flight 661 from New York to Rome. The plane turned back over the Atlantic and landed in Boston. No bomb was found and the plane resumed its flight to Rome. But, although Alitalia spokesman Philip Orlandella insisted that "there was no relation to any terrorist group," there is evidence to the contrary.[66]

Thus the Islamist terrorists have already declared their intentions and indicated their commitment. They certainly have the appropriate skills and capabilities to strike repeatedly both in the United States and elsewhere. Their pin-pricks against civil aviation should serve as a subtle warning and a reminder that their expertise and capabilities go far beyond just blowing up buildings.

THE COMMITMENT OF THE CONTROLLING STATES

The terrorist sponsoring states, primarily Iran, exercise their control over, and guidance of, the Islamist international terrorist movement on two levels, which are interconnected:

The first level is the actual professional command, control, and oversight of terrorist activities and operations. These functions are performed in a clandestine manner, either through direct contacts between Iranian intelligence operatives and the terrorist experts and terrorist commanders in place or under the cover of international conferences.

The second level is the public forum — the ongoing discussion, deliberation, analysis, and explanation of policies and positions in articles, speeches, and sermons. These are usually in Arabic, Persian and other local languages, and the Western public and media are almost entirely unaware of them. Although these public pronouncements are general in nature, they are extremely important to the comprehension of the terrorist high command, both the sponsoring states and the organizations.

Since Islamist terrorism is ideologically-religiously driven, it is imperative for the masters to constantly and conclusively demonstrate the justness of their actions. Although Islamist leaders take unilateral and even arbitrary actions, they must legitimatize the overall character of their action on an ideological and theological level, and this is done in public. Since acts of terrorism are instruments of state policy, they do not occur in a vacuum. They serve and reinforce ongoing policies and processes, as well as serving as the catalysts for the development of subsequent situations and policies. For leaders claiming religious authority (as all Islamist leaders do), in order for these terrorist strikes to be of use, even if they are publicly disavowed, they must be put in context and their impact must be legitimatized. The Islamist leaders must therefore explain and justify their positions to the public at large, including the terrorists.

The declared position of Iran and its closest allies is therefore very important to the understanding of the political dynamics in Tehran. The Islamists' reading and interpretation of the terrorist strikes in New York, and the conclusion drawn about the future course of relations with the United States, clearly expresses Iran's overall perception of, and approach to, relations with America. And since Tehran orders terrorist strikes as part of its overall policy and grand strategy, the Iranian perception of future trends accurately reflects their anticipated the need for further terrorist strikes.

By embarking on and leading the direct jihad against America in early 1993, Tehran has established itself as the undisputed supreme leader of the world's Islamists. The examples set by Tehran have already rejuvenated and changed the Muslim world.

On the eve of the bombing of the World Trade Center, Sayyid Sheikh Hassan Nasrallah, the Secretary General of the HizbAllah, stressed the importance of Iranian influence on the rise and militancy of the Islamist movements. "The Islamic Revolution awakened Muslims and endowed them with prestige, which is evident in nations' strong presence on the scene of jihad and struggle against Western-affiliated regimes. By its support of the oppressed nations against tyranny and oppression, Islamic Iran has affirmed its loyalty to the oppressed."[67]

Now these Islamists rally behind Iran, eager and ready to support and implement its call for a fateful jihad against — and in — America.

The explosion in the World Trade Center in New York came immediately after these observations were made, so they should be considered an integral part of the Islamists' formulation of the new phase of their resolute jihad against the United States. Indeed, Tehran now presents the bombing as a strategic strike that challenges the viability of the Clinton administration, its domestic and foreign policies alike.

Immediately after the World Trade Center bombing, Tehran argued that the bombing in New York and the possibility of retaliation against Iran should be examined in the context of the legacy of Iranian-American relations. Alluding to the failure of the Yazdi initiative with the incoming Clinton administration,* Tehran directly linked the bombing with the lessons of the hostage crisis, which helped lead to the defeat of Jimmy Carter in 1980, and warned Washington of comparable disastrous ramifications for the current Democratic administration. Tehran explained that "the Democrats want to take their chances once again against the Islamic Revolution. The Democratic Party got a taste of the power of the Islamic Revolution when the Shah was toppled and again with the fall of the Nest of Spies [the U.S. embassy]. But maybe the inexperienced bosses in Washington think that their luck might change with a new test, producing different results."[68]

The World Trade Center bombing occurred at the very beginning of the Clinton administration, causing a tremendous economic disaster at exactly the time when the administration was trying to revitalize the American economy. Moreover, they believed, American society and its economy were al-

* See Chapter 5 above

ready in a major crisis, as demonstrated in the 1992 Los Angeles riots — which Iran viewed as a popular uprising. "In such difficult circumstances, the explosion has intensified insecurity and has made it obvious that the economy is exceptionally vulnerable. The explosion in the World Trade Center will have an adverse effect on Clinton's plans to rein in the economy." Tehran emphasized that the New York explosion, just like the Los Angeles riots, should be considered as expressions of despair in, and the deterioration of, the entire United States.[69]

Tehran further argued that the mere association of Iran with the New York bombing in the West was part of an American conspiracy to shift attention away from the collapse of their own position in the Middle East, and to find an excuse to strike at Iran — all in order to prevent the rise of Islam as a dominant force in the world. Tehran remained resolved never to be reconciled with American policy: "Iran does not have to conform to the demands of the new world order. It does not desire liberal Western democracy." In view of this steadfast position, Tehran said, it was only to be expected that Washington would try to blame Iran for its failures in the Middle East and use events in New York as an excuse to strike. "The explosion at New York's World Trade Center can provide the cure for all the woes mentioned above." [70]

Therefore, the Iranians concluded, the bombing in New York was merely the beginning of a violent eruption in the United States. "It is quite likely that any unrest in the future will stem from the erroneous and arrogant policies of the United States at home and abroad. The United States should refrain from their domineering tyrannization of nations and their belligerent interference in the various parts of the world."

The introduction of the international element was significant, for it led Tehran to a discussion of who has the right to take revenge and is likely to do so. Tehran had no doubt that the Islamists were the chosen instrument. "According to the divine traditions, tyranny never goes unpunished in the world. The arrogant U.S. policies are entirely comprised of tyranny and aggression. Even though initially tyranny inflicts anguish on the oppressed, ultimately, divine wrath gives the devout persons the upper hand and they annihilate the tyrant."[71]

Even while denying any involvement in the New York bombing, Tehran left no doubt that it was spearheading the Islamist drive against America. Iran "exposes and impedes U.S. and Western policies in the world. The West and the United States have always felt the need to inflict a decisive and shattering blow to Iran." The recent strike at the very heart of the Great Satan had merely provided an excuse for Washington to go after Tehran. The source of America's enmity, Tehran said, was in objective reasons, namely, Iran's regional and global policies.[72]

But Tehran's overall policy remained consistent, they declared, rooted in uncompromising struggle and defiance. Even with America hardening its position, Iran had no intention whatsoever of abandoning its confrontation with the United States. Tehran warned Washington against taking any initiative against Iran while reaffirming its own commitment to ultimately triumphing over America. "Over the past fourteen years the Islamic Revolution sharpened its claws on both political parties in the U.S., and was victorious in all fields. It defeated all the aggressive American bosses. In this case, if anybody in Washington is still thinking of a new test of strength, they should think hard about this point: Nothing has changed, and America is dealing in this struggle with a nation that knows how to take on its aggressive enemies and bring them to their knees again."[73]

Therefore, since the threat to Iran was increasing, Iran declared that resolute and drastic countermeasures such as strategic terrorist strikes must be implemented. "The threat against the national security of the Islamic Republic of Iran has become more serious. We should not give any pretext to the enemy. Officials are the ones who should speak on the issue and no direct comments should be made." In other words, Tehran should do what is "right" against the United States but keep quiet about it.[74]

Ayatollah Fadlallah, the spiritual leader of the HizbAllah, described the New York bombing as essentially a conspiracy against the Islamists, aimed at arousing and justifying an all-out assault on Islam. The rationale he gave for this assertion is of crucial significance because Fadlallah essentially confirms that the bombing of the World Trade Center was in fact an act of state-controlled terrorism:

Fadlallah ridiculed the accusations leveled against the Islamist defendants in New York on the grounds that Islamists in the United States have no interest in striking out against the government. "Islamists don't benefit anything from it because Islamists living in the United States have freedom of movement. The United States, which fights the freedom of peoples in the Third World through regimes linked to it, grants freedom to these people when they emigrate to the United States." Therefore, it is the oppressed outside the United States who may have had the grievances to deliver such a powerful strike at America.

Fadlallah expects an Islamic revolution at the heart of the Arab world — indeed, he views an Islamist outburst as inevitable. The process only gains strength from American pressure on, and hostility toward, the Arabs, creating favorable circumstances for the Islamist triumph.[75] Therefore, he says, the generation of a cycle of violence between the U.S. and the Arab or Muslim world is bound to expedite the outburst of the triumphant Islamist revolt. The bombing in New York serves as a powerful impetus for such a cycle of violence, which is desired by the Islamists.

On the eve of Al-Quds [Jerusalem] Day, exactly three weeks after the World Trade Center bombing, Iran's spiritual leader, Ayatollah Khamene'i, called on the "dear people and all Muslim nations to hold the international Quds Day ceremonies this year more warmly and enthusiastically than in previous years." In view of the unfolding situation in the Middle East, "the Palestinian strugglers ... need worldwide support," he explained; the events of Al-Quds Day, to be followed by a worldwide Islamist surge, will constitute "a popular manifestation for

resolute rejection of imperialistic and collaboration-
ist plans."[76]

Large numbers of Iranians and foreign volunteers poured into the streets of Tehran on March
19 for Al-Quds Day. The entire Iranian leadership
was present at the ceremonies. A government statement was read, reaffirming the commitment to the
continuation of jihad operations against "Islam's
foremost foes" — the United States, "the occupiers
of Al-Quds," and the "Serb butchers." Tehran urged
Muslim youth around the world to form "resistance
cells," i.e., terrorist networks, against the enemies
of Islam, and promised all possible help.[77]

In Beirut, the HizbAllah conducted a massive
Al-Quds Day rally in which the Iranian strategy was
further elucidated by Sheikh Nasrallah. "The choice
is resistance, the choice is continuing the jihad. We
will continue our resistance until the whole nation
rises and we will present more martyrs from among
our leaders, clerics and warriors," he declared, alluding to the resumption of suicide terrorist operations.[78]

The ultimate objective of demonstrations of defiance like those of the Al-Quds Day ceremonies, as
well as acts of Islamist terrorism in the West (including in the U.S.), is to deliver a message to the audiences throughout the Third World, and the Muslim
world in particular. In the aftermath of the CIA
shooting and the bombing of the World Trade Center, Tehran intensified its propaganda assault on
these primary audiences, both exploiting the lingering impact of the strikes at the heart of the Great
Satan and creating an expectations of further strikes.

In mid-April 1993, as this propaganda struggle was gaining momentum, Tehran provided a succinct analysis of the role of the media in delivering messages to the Near East. Tehran argued that America had unleashed a propaganda war against Iran through the use of mass media in order to persuade world public opinion to side with Washington against Islam. According to Tehran, this offensive was aimed at preventing the consolidation of Iran's hegemony over the Persian Gulf because that would endanger Washington's access to, and control over, the region's oil; and America's main propaganda weapon is the identification of Iran as a supporter of terrorism and subversion in order to frighten the rulers of the Gulf states out of reaching regional arrangements with Tehran.[79]

Iran reiterated its commitment to a defiant confrontation with the United States and its claim to be the only country that is "powerfully defending the rights of Muslims and of oppressed nations" both in word and in action. "This," it declared, "is what constitutes the true threat that Iran poses to the West." For this reason the American propaganda onslaught was only to be expected.

Furthermore, Tehran explained, the building pressure on Iran was being used by President Clinton to divert public attention from the failures of his policies, especially his promised domestic and economic reforms. The Iranians warned Clinton that there were proven ways to overcome the media onslaught and convey the true picture of the situation in America to the American people and the world as a whole.

[257]

(Spectacular terrorist strikes are proven means of getting Tehran's message of a collapsing West and an Iranian reach into the Western media.)

Tehran advised President Clinton to realize that "the uprisings of recent years in various U.S. cities should be a warning to him that, even though he has access to the world's most immense mass media machinery, he cannot overcome his and the U.S. Government's weaknesses, and that the domestic and foreign problem that he is facing and the continuation of this process will have him facing U.S. public rage very soon."[80]

The close interrelationship between policy implementation, including the use of terrorist strikes, and the concentrated preoccupation with certain themes, both in analysis and in propaganda, as well as the use/abuse of Western media through their coverage of terrorism, was made apparent by the timing of the public revival of the Iranian obsession with legitimatizing their hatred of the United States. Tehran's preoccupation with a confrontation and uncompromising struggle with America picked up steam in mid-May 1993, just as the terrorist experts were about to conduct the final check of the preparations of the second terrorist cell in New York for the massive Fourth of July bombings.

In mid-June, with the media battle against the United States expected to intensify in the wake of the planned July attacks, Tehran convened a symposium on psychological warfare under the auspices of the Iranian Voice and Vision Research and Assessment Center led by Muhammad Hashemi, a brother of President Hashemi-Rafsanjani.

Hashemi-Rafsanjani delivered the main address, discussing the growing importance of propaganda and symbolic warfare in which, he said, "Contrary to military warfare, the enemy deploys highly complex and invisible equipment to invade people and society from within and it tries to fulfill its objectives by resorting to such devices as rumors, radios, and false propaganda." He described the most effective theme employed against developing Third World states, especially Muslim countries, as one that destroys their self-confidence in, and commitment to, overcoming their own challenges themselves and solving their own problems in the Islamic way.[81]

Hashemi-Rafsanjani explained that the only way to counter this theme is by demonstrating to the whole world — and through the very same Western media channels — that major problems are not unique to the Third World. (Media reporting on major terrorist strikes at the heart of the West deliver exactly such a message.) In fact, Hashemi-Rafsanjani even alluded to the issue of security in the West. "Developed countries, which exaggerate the problems of the Third World countries out of all proportion, are themselves faced with colossal problems. Some of them are unable to even maintain security in their cities at night."

He promised the Third World Tehran's all-out support and assistance in reversing the impact of U.S. psychological warfare.[82]

By then, Tehran had already defined and outlined its strategy for the anticipated escalation in the struggle with the U.S.

In mid-May, Dr. Muhammad Javad Larijani had described the Iranian reaction to what it calls the escalating Western onslaught on the Islamic world. This "assault" is the aggregate impact of numerous "crimes" like the situations in Bosnia, Israel, and the Arabian peninsula (i.e., securing their regimes against Iran), as well as suppressing Islamist uprisings in Egypt, Algeria, and elsewhere; and of course, it includes the attacks on Iran which are presumably motivated by Iran's tireless support for all the "victims." Larijani stressed that "the answer that the world of Islam should give to the West should go beyond this ... Today, Islam is the target of assault and there is only one answer to this: that the world of Islam should be cleansed of foreign domination!" This objective was so sacred and the struggle so urgent that virtually every means was legitimate: "Defending the revival of Islam and of the movement of Islamism is not an issue we can ignore because we have 'reservations.' In this new field of wheeling and dealing in the world today, we should make defense of this holy wave the biggest weapon and backing of our political activities, but of course in a very calculated and extremely powerful way."[83]

Several Iranian leaders immediately began discussing the most expedient ways and means to implement the new struggle. Ali Akbar Mohtashemi emphasized that Iran must clearly demonstrate its commitment to a confrontation and warned against any appearance of moderation that might create a false impression about Tehran's commitment to the struggle with the United States. "If the Clinton administration harbors false ideas about the Iranian system," he said, "it is playing with fire. The Iranian Government should take no measure that could fan the avarice of the U.S. enemy or cause chagrin to the friends of the Revolution. Even if this is done in a tactical manner, it will be blatant treachery to the strength of the Revolution and of Islam."[84] In view of the fact that Mohtashemi still holds a position of great influence over Iran's terrorist establishment, his warning against any accommodation with the United States is of extreme importance.

Shortly after, Ayatollah Ali Khamene'i again avowed Tehran's total commitment to pursuing Khomeyni's Islamic Revolution.[85] Tehran called immediately for the intensification of Iranian statements of defiance and began alluding to retribution against the U.S. "America intends, through intimidating other states, to keep the so-called leadership of the Western world," but Tehran, by demonstrating the limits to America's power and capacity to intimidate, will not let this happen.[86]

By implication, these pronouncements clarify Tehran's need for a repeat demonstration of Iran's "reach" and its ability to resist the American "onslaught", a demonstration that would be achieved through a spectacular strike in the United States.

On June 2, Tehran again announced — as it had done just before the World Trade Center bombing— that it had given up on reconciliation with the United States. "While Iran on several occasions has shown its good will to Washington ... the American politicians have not only not taken any step to improve ties such as releasing the frozen Iranian assets, but they have even done whatever they could to damage Iran's prestige and credibility, worldwide."

Tehran took special note of Secretary of State Warren Christopher's accusation that Iran supports terrorism and his call for containment. "This new U.S. attempt against Iran will fail. What Mr. Christopher said ... will ultimately become an egg on his face. But should we expect a rational approach toward Iran from a man who the Islamic Revolution put out of a job 14 years ago?"[87]

Tehran declared that Washington has no right to say anything about terrorism because, it claims, the United States has been training *Mujahideen ul-Khalq* terrorists now accused of acts of sabotage in Iran[88] — a recurring theme in Iranian propaganda. Therefore, Tehran argued, "the threats by Warren Christopher and the current U.S. attitude in its approaches to Iran will only culminate in a deterioration of relations and a proliferation of anti-American sentiments in Iran as Iranians have extremely bitter historical memories of U.S. intervention in their country."[89]

Tehran was determined to seize the initiative in this form of confrontational relations with the U.S. and to begin dictating the issues that would be dealt with in the propaganda and media war. Tehran anticipated growing crises "because anti-American feeling and sentiments will continue not only in Iran, but in all the Islamic countries." Drastic measures such as terrorism had to be adopted, if only because "attaching hope to a change in American policy on Iran by resorting to diplomatic levers is extremely naive."[90]

Also on June 2, in a gathering of some 200 high-level visitors from Muslim countries and 4,000 other overseas pilgrims at Khomeyni's tomb on the anniversary of his death, Ahmad Khomeyni proclaimed that "defending the rights of the oppressed Muslims throughout the world is one of the inalterable principles of Iran's foreign policy."[91]

The next day, June 3, Hashemi-Rafsanjani threatened the West with reprisals for "suppressing" Muslims and ignoring the legitimate rights of Islamist movements throughout the world. Iran, he said, has a direct and legitimate reason for that because America and the West were "taking revenge on Bosnian and Palestinian Muslims because of their inability to confront Iran" — but, he went on, Tehran has the means to strike back. "Those who are suppressing Muslim nations under the pretext of fundamentalism, massacring their peoples because of upholding the the banner of Islam, and accusing Muslims of having links with Iran, are mistaken," Hashemi-Rafsanjani warned. "They are repeating the Shah's experience."[92]

The following day, June 4, Ayatollah Khamene'i intensified further Iran's message of defiance, resolve, and combativeness. "Iran will stand steadfast against all plots. Of course in a combat, both sides receive some blows and losses. But the question is that the side which surrenders and accepts defeat will be exposed to the hostilities of the opposite side. ... I say that the people of Iran will stand steadfast with all their strength in the face of this abject plot. We will not allow the principles that are the pillars of the Islamic Revolution and are the cause of the hostility of the enemies to be placed in jeopardy."[93]

Following the aborting of the terrorist strikes planned for New York on the Fourth of July and the arrests of the conspirators, Iran continues to agitate in the Muslim world. Tehran's defiance and warnings increased markedly after the arrest of Sheikh Umar Abdel-Rahman on July 2.[94] Tehran's main theme is that his arrest and "persecution" is an integral part of the confrontation between Islam and America:

"It was quite obvious that Sheikh Umar's arrest was in fact related to the American foreign policy and not really a local or legal issue." Having failed to stop the march of Islam throughout the Middle East, let alone curb Iran's growing influence, "the U.S. Government has stepped in with dubious legal tactics in the hope of creating obstacles for the onward march of the Islamic movements." [95]

Tehran declared these developments to be of an ominous nature. The arrest of Sheikh Umar Abdel-Rahman "marks a new phase in the coordinated and calculated pressure by the U.S. against Muslim combatants in Egypt and elsewhere. The Clinton administration seeks to create the conditions for greater control over the massive public protests in Egypt about the increasing pressure and tyranny." Iran repeats the warnings and the ultimatum issued by the Sheikh's Islamist followers, endorsing their message. "The Islamic Group of Egypt has denounced the U.S. Administration for arresting Sheikh Umar Abdel-Rahman and has announced that if it wants to torture or harass the cleric or to extradite him to Egypt, U.S. interests worldwide will be attacked."[96]

Tehran stresses that the threats of the Egyptian Islamists constitute merely one component of a wider global struggle instigated by what it describes as the "direct U.S. confrontation of Muslim combatants internationally" designed to suppress Islamic revival, and warns that ultimately such a confrontation "creates many problems for the United States, on which the effects will be harmful." But (according to Tehran) Washington will nevertheless continue to pursue such a confrontational policy because it is motivated by domestic crises. "The Clinton administration has lost much of its popularity quickly because of the chaotic domestic situation. By carrying out political international moves, it seeks to shrug off some of the internal pressure and strives to create the conditions to extricate itself on the pretext of foreign political crises. But experience has shown that the Democrats' international actions don't solve their problems; they add to the scale of their political and domestic disarray."[97]

In contrast to what it calls opportunistic American schemes, Tehran insistently portrays Iran's interests in the Muslim world as vital and the advance along the path of Islam (as Iran defines it) as irreversible, explaining that this is why clashes between Iran and the U.S. are quite inevitable. Iran proudly declares its leadership role in the struggle against America, boasting that "in every part of the Third World where there is a fight against the United States and its hegemony, the name of Islam and of

Islamists who are influenced by the slogans of the Islamic Revolution is heard."

Little wonder, then, says Tehran, that the U.S. is determined to silence Iran and the voice of Islamism.[98] But these efforts to suppress Iran and its Islamist followers are doomed to failure because of the inherent nature of the Islamic revival. "Islamism is a 'unique phenomenon' and Iran's powerful leadership has enraged every power center. ... Islamism is the most powerful political-ideological power of the age and is pushing the entire international atmosphere toward great political upheaval." Its confrontation with America and the West is already taking place all over the world. "The United States plays the major role in all the current suppression and hostile stances against Islamism. Soon Washington will witness strong defeats for itself and its world interests."[99]

Tehran leaves no doubt about its determined intention to take part in this struggle, waged by the various Islamist movements all over the world, including America. Indeed, Iran declares defiantly that it will only escalate its universal struggle against Western influence — "The Iranian nation and government will not help the establishment of the U.S.-style peace, rather consider it a duty to caution the world people against the U.S. conspiracies"[100] — and clearly means it to be more than a war of words, for, Tehran stresses, "the enemies of Islam are not safe from Muslims' anger in any part of the world."[101]

On July 13, Hashemi-Rafsanjani visited the headquarters of VEVAK (Iran's Ministry of Intelligence) to inspect "latest achievements of the country's intelligence system" and gave a major speech thanking the senior officers and the service as a whole for their vital contribution to the security of Iran. Although he concentrated on the challenges to Iran's internal security, Hashemi-Rafsanjani also hailed VEVAK's contribution to fighting Iran's enemies overseas, a war usually waged through assassinations and terrorism. He then praised VEVAK's plans for future expansion and promised the senior officers that they would have everything they need for their struggle against Iran's enemies.[102]

The next day, Iran's spiritual leader Khamene'i delivered a speech in front of select members of the *Hizbollahi Ummah*, the Nation of the HizbAllah, which is an international group. His main theme was the inseparability of the worldwide threats to and transgressions against Islam and the national strategy of Tehran. Referring to Bosnia, Khamene'i identified the spread of Western values as "the main factor responsible for the massacre of a Muslim nation in the heart of Europe," but it was above all the United States at the head of "satanic powers" that constituted the greatest challenge to Tehran and Islam as a whole.

Khamene'i attributed the current threats to the entire Muslim world — the ummah — to the "ominous designs" plotted by Washington, and vowed that Iran will take resolute steps to counter and avenge that threat. "The gullibility and naivity of America's present authorities are exposed by the point that they have failed to understand that satanic deeds against our great, courageous and devoted ummah and against the state of Iran with its spiritual power will have no effect other than further disgracing the perpetrators and they will be defeated in confrontation. We will continue the path of Islam with strength and might, as the Revolution and the Imam have taught us."[103]

Expanding on this theme, Ahmad Khomeyni explained that "the growth of Islamic movements in the world is the result of the Iranian people's steadfastness and strength ... America and world arrogance cannot hinder the expansion of the Islamic struggle of the freedom-seeking Muslims. America says it has entered an open fight against Islamic Iran, but our people have repeatedly shown that their determined will to move toward Islamic ideals cannot be altered.[104]

Tehran explained that, despite its efforts, the American-led West remains preoccupied with promoting aggression against Muslims wherever they may be. "This means suffering and continuing to fight enemies armed to the teeth and supported by the arrogant powers. Promoting aggression against the Muslim people has become part of the so-called 'new world order' scenario." For that reason there is no escape from the escalation of the Islamist struggle.[105]

That struggle is currently being waged in the United States in the form of Islamist terrorism. Since the indictment of Sheikh Abdel-Rahman and his Islamist followers, Tehran has continued to raise the ante in its confrontation with America. On August 26, Ayatollah Khamene'i told a gathering of Iran's senior diplomats, "America is the most hated country before the Iranian nation and the conscious people of the world. Therefore the definite policy of the Islamic Republic of Iran is not to have relations or hold negotiations with America."

Khamene'i advised them to expect further crises with the United States because of the mounting points of friction, not only over Tehran's policies but also over the general situation in the Muslim world; and he told them that Tehran would neither budge nor compromise. "We refuse to accept any compromise on the interests of Muslims anywhere in the world," he said.[106]

Conclusions

At present, the Tehran-led Islamists are convinced that they are on the verge of a historic transformation of their fateful jihad against the United States and the West. As symbols of Islam's — and especially Iran's — ability to reach and strike at the very heart of the Great Satan, the terrorists will constitute the Islamists' main weapons. They will be not only symbols but the frontline troops. The growing wrath and might of radical Islam will be expressed through not one or two but many spectacular acts of terrorism.

The bombing of the World Trade Center and the attacks planned for the Fourth of July 1993 were but the first such strategic strikes, intended to demonstrate the Islamists' reach and announce the opening of a new and more violent phase of the Islamist war against America. The bombs in New York were but the prelude to a new terror campaign in which America is the chief target.

During the summer of 1993, Tehran realized that several Islamist causes around the world were suffering setbacks in their confrontations with local authorities. The Iranians pointed to the failures to derail the Arab-Israeli peace process in the Middle

East, to incite a popular uprising in Kashmir, to overthrow the the Egyptian government and to establish an Islamic state in Bosnia-Herzogovina as proof that direct confrontation with the specific enemies in each could not deliver results against resolute and well-armed government forces. Iranian officials conducted several rounds of high-level consultations with key leaders of Islamist terrorist organizations in order to formulate new and innovative solutions to the challenges they see.

Together, they concluded that the only effective way to change the present direction of events would be a massive escalation of international terrorism against the governments — and the societies — they hold responsible for blocking Islamic causes.

That means, primarily, the United States of America.

In early August of this year, Ali Akbar Mohtashemi, one of the founding fathers of the Iranian terrorist system, argued that "the HizbAllah should extend its defensive and aggressive lines all over the region, into Europe, and even in the United States." In view of the repeated examples of Western vulnerability to audacious acts of terrorism, "it is natural that the enemy should not be permitted to dictate or impose the time and place for its confrontation with the Islamic Resistance." Mohtashemi stressed that "actual blows should be dealt to Israel and its American supporters in places they cannot even imagine. This should be done in such a manner that the enemy's power to think and plan is constantly wrested from him as was done in the past."[1]

Iranian terrorist experts are convinced that democratic Western governments are far more vulnerable to the impact of random massive acts of terrorism against "soft" civilian targets than they are to battlefield challenges.

American society itself, its freedoms and values, are the primary target of the Islamists. Sheikh Umar Abdel-Rahman left no doubt that his struggle is with the entirety of American society as the embodiment of Western civilization. Asked about the fact that he enjoys and benefits from such Western values as tolerance and freedom of expression while exploiting democratic freedoms to propagate his anti-Western message, the Sheikh was dismissive: "As for the benefits that the Western cultures have, the opposite is what's happening. The Western culture is the one which opposes the Muslim one. The Western culture is seeking to weaken any Islamic movement."[2] For that reason, confrontation with America, the leader of the West, is an integral and crucial component of the Islamist struggle for the establishment of Muslim states.

While Iran, Syria, Sudan and their allies control the most effective international terrorist networks in the United States (and Europe), the extent of their ability to sustain operations and strike repeatedly depends on the local Islamist communities within which they seek shelter. The record of the terrorists in the New York area to date confirms the existence of a dynamic Islamist conspiratorial structure in the United States, committed to harboring, supporting and recruiting Islamist terrorists, both individuals and networks.

Indeed, Islamist activities continue to expand in the United States. The general trend in the development of the Islamist community in the U.S. is reflected in the evolution of the Islamic Society of North America (ISNA). The Muslim organizations currently most active in the U.S. are those with connections to the International Muslim Brotherhood, and ISNA is the biggest of these organizations.[3] ISNA is an umbrella organization of several more specialized sub-organizations under the central control of the executive council, the Majlis al-Shura, which approves overall policies and future plans, and in effect runs ISNA. Unlike several other Islamic organizations operating in the U.S., "the real difference ISNA has made in the nature of Islamic work is its assumption of a firm ideological structure and Islamic commitment." American Muslim activists point out that "ISNA is considered to be *the* national Muslim organization and generally represents the Islamic mainstream. Though many American-born Muslims have joined its ranks, it continues to be seen by many as an immigrant organization."[4]

Furthermore, Arab sources emphasize, "ISNA is known to be close to the Muslim Brotherhood's current direction and is seeking to be the sole representative of the Muslim association in America." This unique position of ISNA is clearly reflected in the organization's annual conferences attended by thousands of Islamic youth who engage in lively Islamic activities, all perfectly legal and legitimate, as well as conspiratorial activities of a few Islamists under the cover of the conference. The latest

ISNA conference, held in Kansas City, Missouri in early September 1993 and attended by some 5,000 Muslim youth, was not different. In addition to diverse legitimate activities, the conference site was again used as a cover for the Islamist militants.[5]

Meanwhile, the arrests of Sheikh Abdel-Rahman and part of his terrorist network in New York only galvanized the Islamist community throughout the world into undertaking further action against America and Americans. His followers declare that "the arrest of the Sheikh in this manner and with such public fanfare betrays American weakness in the face of the uprising of the Islamic giant of whom Umar Abdel-Rahman is just a symbol."[6]

Law enforcement authorities are now convinced that the New York network is only a fraction of the Islamist threat in the United States. Matthew Fishbein, Chief Assistant United States Attorney, acknowledged, "Whether or not we've identified the major players, obviously there may be others out there that we don't know about."[7]

Now that the masters of Islamist international terrorism have given the order to strike, there should be no doubt that the bombing of the World Trade Center was indeed only the beginning.

Tehran believes that the shock of the Arab-Israeli peace process in the Middle East will galvanize the Islamists everywhere in the world and make the struggle against the United States and Israel more serious by "purifying the front of struggle,"[8] i.e., separating the "true" Muslims from the "hypocrites." Tehran expects Palestinian as well as Islamist terrorist operations to escalate. "The enemies of Islam think they have taken a step forward, but the Islamic world should launch a counter-attack and push them back," Ayatollah Ali Khamene'i told a conference of IRGC commanders. "American and Zionist leaders and the elements who signed the capitulation agreement* should know that Palestinian fists will keep hitting on the heads of the usurpers."[9]

Tehran moved quickly to launch the "counter-attack" Khamene'i had called for. Deputy Foreign Minister Hussein Sheikh-ol-Islam, a veteran of terrorist operations who returned to an active role in the terrorist high command in April 1993, arrived in Damascus on September 18 for a summit with Syrian leaders, including President Assad. He met with numerous terrorist commanders to discuss ways to escalate their common struggle, assuring them of Tehran's unwavering support and the continued cooperation of Damascus. Indeed, when Sheikh Nasrallah of the HizbAllah returned to Beirut from these meetings, he hailed the Syrians as "friends, brothers and allies" in a speech in which he vowed that the HizbAllah would escalate its struggle against America and Israel.[10]

Tehran is adamant about reacting to the latest developments with a wave of terrorism. Muhsin Reza'i declared that the struggle against the United States in connection with the "peace process" was one of Iran's vital interests because "if America

* The agreement between the PLO and Israel

succeeds in this conspiracy it will come to deal with us next."[11] In other words, the attack on America is necessary for the defense of Iran.

All of this adds up to strong indications that Islamist international terrorism — Iran-sponsored, Syrian-supported, and Sudanese-assisted — is about to erupt in a series of spectacular strikes at the heart of its enemies. The United States and Europe—however prepared they become to meet this threat—cannot hope to defend against all attempts to strike terror into the hearts of their citizens. In light of the terrorists' deadly commitment, even with law-enforcement authorities' best efforts, some few attempts will succeed. But however vulnerable the heart of western democracy, it is a tough and tolerable muscle, and its citizens can learn to live with the terrorist threat until peace and the West prevail over radical Islam and its state sponsors.

SOURCE NOTES

INTRODUCTION

1. Blumenthal R., *New York Times*, 27 August 1993; Hetter R., *Wall Street Journal*, 26 August 1993; Getz B., *Washington Times*, 26 August 1993; Michelini A. & Sennott C.M., *Daily News*, 26 August 1993; Smilon M. & Miner C., *New York Post*, 26 August 1993; *Daily News*, 26 August 1993; Tabor M.B.W., *New York Times*, 26 August 1993

2. Miner C. & Smilon M., *New York Post*, 16 July 1993

3. Sachs S., *New York Newsday*, 16 July 1993

4. Melman Y., *Ha'aretz*, 29 August 1993

Chapter 1
COMING TO AMERICA

1. IRNA, 20 July 1988

2. Reinhold R., *New York Times*, 11 March 1989

3. Perry A., *Los Angeles Times*, 11 March 1989; Reinhold R., *New York Times*, 12 March 1989; Engelberg S., *New York Times*, 13 March 1989

4. Wright R., *Los Angeles Times*, 11 March 1989; Perry A., *Los Angeles Times*, 11 March 1989

5. Ben-Yishai R., *Yediot Aharonot*, 10 April 1992

6. Radio Tehran, 5 May 1989; IRNA, 5 May 1989

7. Voice of the Oppressed, 6 June 1989

8. IRNA, 13 June 1989; *Ha'aretz*, 14 June 1989

9. *Tehran Times*, 27 July 1989; *Al-Sharq al-Awsat*, 21 July 1989; *Al-Jumhuriyah*, 22 July 1989; *Tehran Times*, 10 July 1989; NuriZadeh Dr. Ali, *Al-Dustur*, 16 October 1989; Voice of the National Resistance, 26 July 1989; Voice of the Oppressed, 25 July 1989; Tehran Domestic Service, 24 July 1989; IRNA, 24 July 1989; Tehran Domestic Service, 23 July 1989; Voice of Lebanon, 22July 1989; Voice of the National Resistance, 22 July 1989; Tehran Domestic Service, 2 October 1989; Tehran Domestic Service, 3October 1989; IRNA, 3 October 1989; Tehran Television Service, 4 October 1989; IRNA, 4 October 1989; IRNA, 5 October 1989; Tehran Television Service, 7 October 1989; Anderson J. & Van Atta D.,*Washington Post*, 10 October 1989

10. *Jomhuri-ye Eslami*, 10 July 1989

11. Adams N.M., *Reader's Digest*, September 1990

12. Radio Tehran, 7 August 1989; *Yediot Aharonot*, 8 August 1989

13. Tehran Domestic Service, 12 August 1989

14. *Al-'Ahd*, 27 October 1989

15. *Jomhuri-ye Eslami*, 4 November 1989

16. Tehran International Service, 16 December 1989

17. Conference Papers of the Islamic Committee for Palestine

18. Conference Papers of the Islamic Committee for Palestine

19. *Response*, January 1990; Conference Papers of the Islamic Committee for Palestine

20. *Al-Fajr*, 23 August 1987; *Al-Fajr*, 28 August 1987; Kohen O., *Hadashot*, 13 October 1987; *Globe and Mail*, 26 October 1987

21. *Response*, January 1990; Conference Papers of the Islamic Committee for Palestine

22. *Al-Fajr*, 28 August 1987

23. Kohen O., *Hadashot*, 13 October 1987

24. *Al-Fajr*, 23 August 1987

25. *Globe and Mail*, 26 October 1987

26. Iran's Flag of Freedom Radio, 1 June 1990; Radio Tehran, 1 June 1990; Radio Tehran, 3 June 1990; Radio Tehran, 10 June 1990; Tehran International Service, 11 June 1990; Radio Tehran, 11 June 1990; Al-Quds Palestinian Arab Radio, 12 June 1990

27. Iran's Flag of Freedom Radio, 1 June 1990; Radio Tehran, 11 June 1990

28. Radio Tehran, 9 June 1990; Radio Tehran, 10 June 1990; Tehran International Service, 11 June 1990; Radio Tehran, 11 June 1990

29. Radio Tehran, 11 June 1990; Al-Quds Palestinian Arab Radio, 12 June 1990

30. Radio Tehran, 5 December 1990

31. *Kayhan al-Arabi*, 29 August 1991; *Ha'aretz*, 30 August 1991

32. *Al-Sharq al-Awsat*, 11 September 1991

33. *Sawt al-Kuwayt al-Duwali*, 8 August 1991

34. Blumenthal R., *New York Times*, 27 August 1993

35. Ben-Yishai R., *Yediot Aharonot*, 10 April 1992

36. McCoy K., *New York Newsday*, 28 May 1993; Miner C., *New York Post*, 1 July 1993

37. AP, 30 June 1993; *Los Angeles Times*, 30 June 1993; Miner C., *New York Post*, 30 June 1993

38. Duffy B. et.al., *US News & World Report*, 6 March 1989

39. Gertz B., *Washington Times*, 9 March 1989

40. NuriZadeh Dr. Ali, *Al-Dustur*, 12 February 1990

41. *Al-Watan al-Arabi*, 27 November 1992

42. *Al-Sharq al-Awsat*, 10 April 1993; Material provided by Iranian sources

43. *Al-Watan al-Arabi*, 16 October 1992; *Al-Sharq al-Awsat*, 7 November 1991; *Al-Sharq al-Awsat*, 2 November 1991

44. ABC, 16 August 1993; Material provided by Sudanese sources

45. IRNA, 19 March 1990

46. *Keyhan*, 3 May 1990

47. IRNA, 31 May 1990; Radio Tehran, 4 June 1990

48. AFP, 3 June 1990

49. IRNA, 3 June 1990

50. Bkhor G., *Ha'aretz*, 27 June 1993; *Al-Wasat*, 12 July 1993

51. Kepel G., *Muslim Extremism in Egypt*, Berkley CA, University of California Press, 1985, pp. 207-208; *Al-Wasat*, 15 March 1993

52. Peroncel-Hugoz J.-P., *The Raft of Mohammed*, New York NY, Paragon House, 1988, p. 16

53. Heikal Mohamed, *Autumn of Fury*, New York, NY, Random House, 1983, p. 243

54. Sablier E., *Valeurs Actuelles*, 6 April 1987

55. Laroche J.A., *National Hebdo*, 27 February - 5 March 1986

56. Zarai O., *Ha'Aretz*, 24 June 1986; Zarai O., *Ha'Aretz*,23 September 1986

57. Zarai O., *Ha'Aretz*, 23 September 1986; Zarai O., *Ha'Aretz*, 24 June 1986; Material provided by Israeli sources and sources in Europe

58. Khashoqgi Jamal, *Al-Wasat*, 6 September 1993

59. *Rose al-Yussuf*, 24 April 1989; Shaykh Dr. Umar Abd-al-Rahman interviewed by Adil al-Sanhuri, *Al-Anba'*, 13 April 1989; al-Jubayli Ahmad, *Al-Wafd*, 8 April 1989; AFP, 8 April 1989; MENA, 9 April 1989; Voice of the Oppressed, 14 April 1989, AFP, 14 April 1989; al-Jubayli Ahmad, *Al-Wafd*, 15 April 1989; Abd al-Qadir Abd al-Wahid, *Al-Ahram*, 15 April 1989; AFP, 17 April 1989; Ahmad Fikriyah and al-Jubayli Ahmad, *Al-Wafd*,17 April 1989; AFP, 18 April 1989; al-Tarabishi Mustafa, *Al-Ahram*, 5 June 1989; Abdallah Ahmad, *Al-Sha'b*, 5 September 1989; *Al-Wast*, 15 March 1993

60. Hilmi Majdi, *Al-Wafd*, 26 April 1989; Hilmi Majdi,*Al-Wafd*, 27 April 1989; MENA, 30 April 1989

61. Radio Free Lebanon, 14 July 1989; Radio Beirut, 15 July 1989; AFP, 11 July 1989

62. Voice of the Oppressed, 8 August 1989

63. *Al-Sha'b*, 8 August 1989; al-Qammash Ali, *Al-Sha'b*, 25 July 1989

64. Hilmi Majdi, *Al-Wafd*, 12 August 1989; Radio Monte Carlo, 12 August 1989

65. *Al-Wafd*, 13 August 1989; Abdallah Ahmad, *Al-Sha'b*, 5 September 1989

66. Tantawi Hisham, *Al-Watan*, 23 February 1989

67. Jabar Karam, *Rose al-Yussuf*, 5 November 1990

68. Tantawi Hisham, *Al-Watan*, 23 February 1989

69. *New York Times*, 16 December 1990; *Ha'aretz*, 17 December 1990

70. Jabar Karam, *Rose al-Yussuf*, 5 November 1990

71. *US News & World Report*, 12 April 1993; Peterzell J., *Time*, 24 May 1993; *New York Post*, 13 July 1993; Jehl D., *New York Times*, 22 July 1993

72. MENA, 30 October 1990; Jabar Karam, *Rose al-Yussuf*, 5 November 1990

73. Jabar Karam, *Rose al-Yussuf*, 5 November 1990

Chapter 2

EARLY STEPS

1. Khashoqgi Jamal, *Al-Wasat*, 6 September 1993; *Al-Sharqal-Awsat*, 10 March 1993; Mitchell A., *New York Times*, 11 April 1993; Tabor M.B.W., *New York Times*, 11 April 1993 ;Hedges C., *New York Times*, 13 November 1990; Material provided by Afghan and Arab sources

2. Khashoqgi Jamal, *Al-Wasat*, 6 September 1993

3. Khashoqgi Jamal, *Al-Wasat*, 6 September 1993; *Al-Sharqal-Awsat*, 10 March 1993; Waldman P., *Wall Street Journal*, 6 January 1993; Mitchell A., *New York Times*, 11 April 1993; Tabor M.B.W., *New York Times*, 11 April 1993; Material provided by Afghan and Arab sources

4. Manor H., *Ma'ariv*, 10 April 1992; Kifner J., *New York Times*, 7 November 1990; Frank A., *Newark Star-Ledger*, 19 December 1985

5. Hedges C., *New York Times*, 13 November 1990

6. Kifner J., *New York Times*, 7 November 1990; *New York Post*, 7 November 1990; *New York City Tribune*, 8 November 1990; *New York City Tribune*, 9 November 1990; Hedges C., *New York Times*, 13 November 1990; Shamir S., *Ha'aretz*, 14November 1990

7. Kifner J., *New York Times*, 7 November 1990; *New York Post*, 7 November 1990; *New York City Tribune*, 8 November 1990; *New York City Tribune*, 9 November 1990; Hedges C., *New York Times*, 13 November 1990; Shamir S., *Ha'aretz*, 14 November 1990; Frank A., *Newark Star-Ledger*, 19 December 1985

8. Kifner J., *New York Times*, 7 November 1990; *New York Post*, 7 November 1990; *New York City Tribune*, 8 November 1990; Kifner J., *New York Times*, 9 November 1990; *New York City Tribune*, 9 November 1990; Avni B., *Ha'aretz*, 9 November 1990; Hedges C., *New York Times*, 13 November 1990; *New York Times*, 21 November 1990; McKinley J.C. Jr., *New York Times*, 1 December 1990; Kifner J., *New York Times*, 11 December 1990

9. Mitchell A., *New York Times*, 11 April 1993; Kifner J., *New York Times*, 11 December 1990

10. Miner C. & Standora L., *New York Post*, 3 August 1993

11. *New York Post*, 5 March 1993

12. AP, 5 November 1990

13. *New York Post*, 6 November 1990; *New York City Tribune*, 6 November 1990; *Newsday*, 6 November 1990; *New York Post*, 7 November 1990; *Newsday*, 7 November 1990; Avni B. & Aizenberg Z., *Ha'aretz*, 7 November 1990; Miner C. & Murray A.E., *New York Post*, 19 July 1993

14. Shamir Sh., *Ha'aretz*, 12 November 1990; Chang D., *Daily News*, 5 March 1993

15. Dan U., *New York Post*, 6 May 1993; Blumenthal R., *New York Times*, 7 May 1993; Blumenthal R., *New York Times*, 8 May 1993

16. *Washington Post*, 19 May 1993

17. Miner C., *New York Post*, 1 July 1993; *Los Angeles Times*, 30 June 1993; AP, 30 June 1993

18. Waldman P., *Wall Street Journal*, 6 January 1993; Juffe M., *New York Post*, 5 March 1993; Marzulli J. & Sheridan D., *Daily News*, 5 March 1993; *Al-Sharq al-Awsat*, 10 March 1993; Tabor M.B.W., *New York Times*, 11 April 1993; Khashoqgi Jamal, *Al-Wasat*, 6 September 1993

19. Miner C., *New York Post*, 19 July 1993

20. Pierson R. & Rush G., *New York Post*, 22 March 1993

21. Material provided by Egyptian sources

22. *Newsweek*, 22 March 1993; AP, 15 March 1993; Reuters, 13 March 1993

23. Gruson L., *New York Times*, 14 March 1993

24. Kleinfield N.R., *New York Times*, 6 March 1993

25. Nir O., *Ha'aretz*, 15 January 1991

26. *Keyhan*, 18 December 1990

27. Awdah Awdah, *Al-Ra'y*, 5 October 1990

28. *Islamic Horizons*, August 1990; *Islamic Horizons*, September 1990; *Islamic Horizons*, October 1990; Conference papers of the Islamic Society of North America

29. *New York Times*, 1 December 1990

30. Smilon M. & Miner C., *New York Post*, 26 August 1993

31. Farraj Hamdi, *Al-Quds al-Arabi*, 8 October 1990

32. Imad al-Alami to *Filastin al-Muslimah*, December 1990

33. Ginor B., *Matara*, No. 20, 1991; Israeli TV, 11 April 1991; *Ha'aretz*, 11 April 1991

34. Raufer X., *L'Express*, 22 August 1991; *Ha'aretz*, 9 August 1991; Press Association, 23 July 1991; Press Association, 18 July 1991; AP, 17 July 1991; Reuter 17 July 1991

35. IRIB Television Network, 18 March 1991

36. Fadlallah Ayatollah al-Sayid Muhammad Hussayn, *Middle East Insight*, July/August 1991

37. *Al-Jumhuriyah*, 2 August 1992; Husayn Tariq, *Roseal-Yussuf*, 10 February 1992; *Al-Watan al-Arabi*, 6 November 1992; *Al-Watan al-Arabi*, 4 December 1992; *Al-Wasat*, 14 December 1992

38. *Kayhan International*, 5 October 1991

39. Iranian Television, 17 October 1991; Radio Tehran, 18 October 1991; Sharif Imam-Jomeh, Reuter, 19 October 1991; Radio Tehran,19 October 1991; IRNA, 20 October 1991; Iranian Television, 20 October 1991; Iranian Television, 17 October 1991; Radio Tehran, 18 October 1991; IRNA, 21 October 1991; IRNA, 23 October 1991;Radio Tehran, 25 October 1991; IRNA, 20 October 1991;*Ha'aretz*, 18 October 1991; IRNA, 25 October 1991

40. IRNA, 20 October 1991; Reuter, 20 October 1991

41. *Kayhan*, 21 October 1991

42. Radio Tehran, 22 October 1991

43. IRNA, 22 October 1991

44. IRNA, 20 October 1991

45. *Al-Wafd*, 4 December 1991; Robertson R., *Arizona Republic*, 31 May 1993; *Detroit News*, 1 June 1993

46. Material provided by Iranian sources in Europe

47. *Ma'ariv*, 19 March 1992

48. *Keyhan*, 8 August 1985

49. *Hadashot*, 19 March 1992

50. Strenthal S., *Insight*, 10 June 1991

51. *Clarin*, 15 January 1992; *Clarin*, 7 May 1992

52. *ABC*, 21 November 1990; *Le Point*, 23 November 1987; *Il Tiempo*, 6 June 1987; Adams J., *Trading in Death*, London, Huchinson, 1990, pp. 88-100 & 132-134

53. *al-Wasat*, 16 August 1993

54. *Clarin*, 7 May 1992; Tsdaka Sh., *Ha'aretz*, 1 May 1992; Material provided by Israeli sources

55. Noticias Argentinas, 29 March 1992

56. TELAM, 18 March 1992

57. Sadeh D., *Yediot Aharonot*, 27 March 1992

58. Figueroa J., EFE, 20 March 1992

59. *Buenos Aires Herald*, 29 March 1992

60. *Noticias Argentinas*, 6 May 1992; TELAM, 18 March 1992

61. TELAM, 18 March 1992; *Ha'aretz*, 18 March 1992; *Yediot Aharonot*, 18 March 1992

62. *Ha'aretz*, 20 March 1992

63. *Hadashot*, 19 March 1992; *Ha'aretz*, 19 March 1992

64. *Noticias Argentinas*, 6 May 1992

65. *Noticias Argentinas*, 18 March 1992

66. AFP, 19 March 1992

67. Iranian TV, 20 March 1992

68. Radio Free Lebanon, 30 March 1992

69. Voice of Lebanon, 31 March 1992

70. *New York Times*, 9 May 1992

71. Iranian TV, 9 May 1992

72. Radio Tehran, 14 February 1992

73. *Jomhuri-ye Islami*, 9 February 1992

74. Tsdaka Sh., *Ha'aretz*, 1 May 1992

75. Radio Tehran, 2 March 1992

76. Radio Tehran, 2 March 1992

77. Radio Tehran, 3 March 1992

78. *Al-Watan al-Arabi*, 13 March 1992; Bkhor G., *Ha'aretz*, 20 March 1992

79. Raufer X., *L'Express*, 22 August 1991; *Ha'aretz*, 9 August 1991; Press Association, 23 July 1991; Press Association, 18 July 1991; AP, 17 July 1991; Reuter 17 July 1991

80. Hanley R., *New York Times*, 28 March 1992; Hanley R., *New York Times*, 29 March 1992

81. Radio Tehran, 27 March 1992

82. International Day of *Quds* documents; personal observations

83. Voice of the Oppressed, 26 May 1992

Chapter 3

THE FORMATIVE PHASE

1. *Al-Jumhuriyah*, 2 August 1992; Husayn Tariq, *Roseal-Yussuf*, 10 February 1992; *Al-Watan al-Arabi*, 6 November 1992; *Al-Watan al-Arabi*, 4 December 1992; *Al-Wasat*, 14 December 1992

2. Mitchell A., *New York Times*, 15 July 1993

3. *Daily News*, 26 August 1993; Blumenthal R., *New York Times*, 27 August 1993

4. *Al-Jumhuriyah*, 2 August 1992; Husayn Tariq, *Roseal-Yussuf*, 10 February 1992; *Al-Wast*, 15 March 1993

5. *Al-Wafd*, 3 November 1991; *Akhbar al-Jumhuriyah*, 9 November 1991; MENA, 9 November 1991

6. IDF Radio, 13 October 1987; Material provided by Israeli sources

7. Rohani Sayyid Hamid, *Keyhan*, 30 January 1988

8. Bourget J.-M., *Paris Match*, 10 October 1986; Burdan D., *DST*, Paris, Robert Laffont, 1990, pp. 88-90

9. Fusako Shigenobu, *Ryudo*, October 1982

10. Damascus Television Service, 10 July 1985; *Liberation*, 19 March 1985

11. *New York Times*, 28 January 1988; *Wall Street Journal*,11 February 1988; *New York Times*, 18 May 1988; *Los Angeles Times*, 18 May 1988; Kupperman R. and Kamen J., *Final Warning*, New York NY, Doubleday, 1989, p. 10

12. Material provided by Lebanese sources

13. Ryuichi Hirokawa, *Shukan Yomiuri*, 2 October 1983; Ryuichi Hirokawa, *Shukan Yomiuri*, 9 October 1983

14. *New York Times*, 15 April 1988; *New York Times*, 16 April 1988; *Daily Yomiuri*, 18 April 1988

15. Rudolph R., *Newark Star Ledger*, 5 February 1989; Farrell W.R., *Blood and Rage*, Lexington MA, Lexington MA, 1990, pp.xv-xxi, & 212-213; Kupperman and Kamen, op.cit., pp. 10-12 & 84

16. Kupperman and Kamen, op.cit., p. 11

17. Mitchell A., *New York Times*, 5 August 1993

18. Mitchell A., *New York Times*, 9 March 1993; Shamir S., *Ha'aretz*, 23 March 1993

19. Reuters, 5 March 1993; Blumenthal R., *New York Times*, 7 March 1993; McFadden R.D., *New York Times*, 6 March 1993; *New York Post*, 6 March 1993; *New York Post*, 5 March 1993

20. Michelini A. & Sennott C.M., *Daily News*, 26 August 1993

21. Rizq Hamdi, *Rose al-Yussuf*, 10 August 1992

22. Al-Ahram Press Agency, 12 December 1992

23. *Al-Watan al-Arabi*, 4 December 1992

24. Rizq Hamdi, *Rose al-Yussuf*, 10 August 1992

25. Mirghai Uthman, *Al-Sharq al-Awsat*, 3 July 1993; Material provided by Egyptian and Sudanese sources

26. Material provided by Iranian and Arab sources

27. Dan U. & Rothenberg J., *New York Post*, 7 June 1993; Material provided by Iranian and Arab sources

28. *Al-Wasat*, 16 November 1992; *Al-Watan al-Arabi*, 6 November 1992; *Daily News*, 13 March 1993; Shamir S., *Ha'aretz*, 13 March 1993

29. *Al-Jumhuriyah*, 2 August 1992; Husayn Tariq, *Roseal-Yussuf*, 10 February 1992; *Al-Watan al-Arabi*, 6 November 1992; *Al-Watan al-Arabi*, 4 December 1992; *Al-Wasat*, 14December 1992

30. *Al-Wasat*, 14 December 1992

31. Kocieniewski D., *New York Newsday*, 10 June 1993; Blumenthal R., *New York Times*, 8 May 1993; Shamir Sh., *Ha'aretz*, 11 June 1993; Material provided by Iranian and Arab sources

32. Juffe M., *New York Post*, 25 June 1993; Mitchell A., *New York Times*, 25 June 1993

33. Mirghai Uthman, *Al-Sharq al-Awsat*, 3 July 1993; Material provided by Egyptian and Sudanese sources

34. Kocieniewski D., *New York Newsday*, 10 June 1993; ShamirSh., *Ha'aretz*, 11 June 1993; McFadden R.D., *New York Times*, 25 June 1993; Material provided by Iranian and Arab sources

35. AP, 13 March 1993; *New York Newsday*, 13 March 1993; Mitchell A., *New York Times*, 14 March 1993; *New York Newsday*, 14 March 1993; AP, 15 March 1993; Gibson D., *The Record*, 17 March 1993, Carley W.M., *Wall Street Journal*, 17 March 1993; Mitchell A., *New York Times*, 20 March 1993; Lyons R.D., *New York Times*, 24 March 1993; *Al-Ahram*, 25 March 1993; Mitchell A., *New York Times*, 26 March 1993

36. Delattre L., *L'Express*, 6 May 1993

37. Sachs S., *New York Newsday*, 16 July 1993; Hedges C., *New York Times*, 16 July 1993

38. *Al-Ahram*, 25 March 1993; Hubbell S., *Christian Science Monitor*, 26 March 1993; Van Biema D., *Time*, 5 April 1993

39. Kocieniewski D., *New York Newsday*, 10 June 1993

40. Blumenthal R., *New York Times*, 26 March 1993

41. Mitchell A., *New York Times*, 20 March 1993; Lyons R.D., *New York Times*, 24 March 1993; *New York Newsday*, 1 April 1993; Tabor M.B.W., *New York Times*, 11 April 1993; Mitchell A., *New York Times*, 11 April 1993

42. *New York Newsday*, 1 April 1993

43. Khashoqgi Jamal, *Al-Wasat*, 6 September 1993

44. Dan U. & Pierson R., *New York Post*, 25 March 1993 ;Material provided by Arab and Iranian sources

45. Mitchell A., *New York Times*, 25 June 1993; Clines F.X., *New York Times*, 26 June 1993

46. Caspit B., *Ma'ariv*, 2 July 1993

47. *New York Times*, 25 June 1993; Broderick D., *New York Post*, 25 June 1993; *Daily News*, 25 June 1993

48. AP, 25 June 1993

49. Mirghai Uthman, *Al-Sharq al-Awsat*, 3 July 1993

50. Finnegan M., Lambiet J.M. & Sennott C.M., *Daily News*, 25 June 1993

51. Mitchell A., *New York Times*, 25 June 1993; Broderick D., *New York Post*, 25 June 1993; Finnegan M. & McFarland S., *Daily News*, 25 June 1993; Clines F.X., *New York Times*, 26 June 1993

52. Caspit B., *Ma'ariv*, 2 July 1993; Material provided by Sudanese sources

53. *New York Post*, 25 June 1993; *New York Times*, 25 June 1993

54. Kocieniewski D., *New York Newsday*, 10 June 1993

55. Finnegan M., Lambiet J.M. & Sennott C.M., *Daily News*, 25 June 1993

56. Slattery W.T. et.al., *New York Post*, 25 June 1993

57. Miner C., *New York Post*, 17 July 1993; Perl D., *Ha'aretz*, 25 July 1993; Mitchell A., *New York Times*, 1August 1993

58. Dan U. & Miner C., *New York Post*, 22 July 1993

59. Miner C., *New York Post*, 21 September 1993

60. Sachs S., *New York Newsday*, 16 July 1993

61. Hasanyan Abduh, *Al-Wafd*, 2 April 1993

62. Material provided by Iranian sources

63. Tabor M.B.W., *New York Times*, 2 April 1993; *New York Newsday*, 1 April 1993; Smilon M. & Nolan J., *New York Post*, 1 April 1993; Shamir S., *Ha'aretz*, 4 April 1993; *New York Times*, 26 May 1993

64. Blumenthal R., *New York Times*, 8 May 1993; Mitchell A., *New York Times*, 7 May 1993; Tabor M.B.W., *New York Times*, 6 May 1993; *Al-Watan al-Arabi*, 14 May 1993; Neumeister L., AP, 26 May 1993; *New York Times*, 26 May 1993

65. Mitchell A., *New York Times*, 21 May 1993

66. Mitchell A., *New York Times*, 7 May 1993

67. Blumenthal R., *New York Times*, 7 May 1993

68. Material provided by Afghan resistance sources; Van Dyk J., *In Afghanistan*, New York, NY, Coward-McMann, 1983, pp. 98-101

69. Mubarak Hisham, *Rose al-Yusuf*, 24 August 1992; 'Afghans', *Al-Wasat*, 13 July 1992

70. Mubarak Hisham, *Rose al-Yusuf*, 24 August 1992; Yared M., *Jeune Afrique*, 10-16 September 1992; Mubarak Hisham, *Roseal-Yusuf*, 14 September 1992

71. *Al-Watan al-Arabi*, 4 December 1992

72. Shamir S., *Ha'Aretz*, 15 August 1993

73. Gargan E.A., *New York Times*, 11 August 1993

74. Yared M., *Jeune Afrique*, 19-25 March 1992

75. Husayn Tariq, *Rose al-Yusuf*, 10 February 1992

76. Rizq Hamdi, *Rose al-Yussuf*, 23 November 1992; Abu-DahrWalid, *Al-Watan al-Arabi*, 2 April 1993; Egyptian 'Afghans', *Al-Wasat*, 13 July 1992

77. Rizq Hamdi, *Rose al-Yussuf*, 23 November 1992

78. Radio Iran, 24 December 1992

79. Abu Dahr Walid, *Al-Watan al-Arabi*, 2 April 1993

80. Mubarak Hisham, *Rose al-Yusuf*, 24 August 1992

81. Sachs S., *New York Newsday*, 16 July 1993; Nakhoul Samia,Reuter, 15 July 1993

82. Hedges C., *New York Times*, 16 July 1993

83. Tabor M.B.W., *New York Times*, 2 April 1993

84. Blumenthal R., *New York Times*, 11 March 1993; BlumenthalR., *New York Times*, 12 March 1993; Behr P., *WashingtonPost*, 12 March 1993; Reuters, 13 March 1993; Pierson R., & WeissM., *New York Post*, 13 March 1993; AP, 15 March 1993; Blumenthal R., *New York Times*, 25 April 1993

85. Sachs S., *New York Newsday*, 16 July 1993; Hedges C., *New York Times*, 16 July 1993

86. *Al-Sharq al-Awsat*, 10 April 1993; Dan U., *New York Post*, 6 May 1993; Material provided by Iranian sources

87. Shaqed R., *Yediot Aharonot*, 8 March 1993; Hedges C., *New York Times*, 8 March 1993

88. Zarai O., *Ha'aretz*, 31 July 1986; 'Afghans', *Al-Wasat*,13 July 1992

89. Shaqed R., *Yediot Aharonot*, 8 March 1993

90. *New York Times*, 5 March 1993; Kleinfield N.R., *New York Times*, 6 March 1993; McFadden R.D., *New York Times*, 6 March 1993; Hedges C., *New York Times*, 8 March 1993; *New York Post*, 8 March 1993

91. Kleinfield N.R., *New York Times*, 6 March 1993; Broderick D., *New York Post*, 5 March 1993; *New York Times*, 5 March 1993; Shamir S., *Ha'aretz*, 23 March 1993

92. *New York Times*, 26 May 1993

93. Mitchell A., *New York Times*, 11 March 1993; Pierson R., *New York Post*, 12 March 1993; *New York Times*, 14 March 1993; Nazzal Khawlah, *Al-Majallah*, 24 March 1993

94. Blumenthal R., *New York Times*, 12 March 1993; Pierson R., *New York Post*, 12 March 1993; Broderick D., *New York Post*, 12 March 1993

95. Mitchell A., *New York Times*, 5 August 1993; Blumenthal R., *New York Times*, 10 June 1993; Ghazzawi Kamil, *Sawtal-Sha'b*, 26 May 1993

96. Tabor M.B.W., *New York Times*, 2 April 1993; Smilon M. & Nolan J., *New York Post*, 1 April 1993; *New York Newsday*, 1 April 1993

97. Mitchell A., *New York Times*, 26 March 1993; Smilon M. & Pierson R., *New York Post*, 26 March 1993

98. Nir O. & Shamir S., *Ha'aretz*, 26 March 1993

99. Mitchell A., *New York Times*, 20 May 1993

Chapter 4
TRIALS AND ACHIEVEMENTS

1. Hewitt G., *Terry Waite and Ollie North*, Boston, MA, Little Brown and Company, 1991, pp. 32-33, 54, 67, 76, 107, 178, & 200

2. *Los Angeles Times*, 12 November 1992; Feldman P., *Los Angeles Times*, 30 November 1992

3. Granberry M., *Los Angeles Times*, 14 February 1993

4. Feldman P., *Los Angeles Times*, 20 November 1992

5. Feldman P., *Los Angeles Times*, 30 November 1992

6. Coughlin C., *Hostage*, London, Little Brown and Company, 1992, p. 228

7. *Los Angeles Times*, 25 November 1992

8. Reza H.G. & Lowrie K.B., *Los Angeles Times*, 18 November 1992

9. *Los Angeles Times*, 25 November 1992

10. Feldman P., *Los Angeles Times*, 30 November 1992

11. Feldman P., *Los Angeles Times*, 20 November 1992

12. Feldman P., *Los Angeles Times*, 30 November 1992

13. Feldman P., *Los Angeles Times*, 30 November 1992

14. Gaw J., *Los Angeles Times*, 10 November 1992

15. Feldman P., *Los Angeles Times*, 30 November 1992

16. Reza H.G. & Lowrie K.B., *Los Angeles Times*, 18 November 1992; Feldman P., *Los Angeles Times*, 30 November 1992

17. Abrahamson A., *Los Angeles Times*, 15 December 1992

18. Romney L., *Los Angeles Times*, 9 November 1992; *Los Angeles Times*, 12 November 1992; Reza H.G. & Lowrie K.B., *Los Angeles Times*, 18 November 1992; Feldman P., *Los AngelesTimes*, 30 November 1992

19. Feldman P., *Los Angeles Times*, 30 November 1992

20. Romney L., *Los Angeles Times*, 9 November 1992; Gaw J.,*Los Angeles Times*, 10 November 1992

21. *Los Angeles Times*, 12 November 1992; *Los Angeles Times*, 14 November 1992; *New York Newsday*, 15 November 1992

22. Abrahamson A., *Los Angeles Times*, 15 December 1992

23. Reza H.G., *Los Angeles Times*, 13 January 1993; Reza H.G., *Los Angeles Times*, 29 December 1992

24. Reza H.G. & Lowrie K.B., *Los Angeles Times*, 18 November 1992; Feldman P., *Los Angeles Times*, 30 November 1992

25. Granberry M., *Los Angeles Times*, 14 February 1993

26. *Los Angeles Times*, 25 November 1992

27. Lowrie K.B., *Los Angeles Times*, 5 March 1993

28. *Mednews*, 7 December 1992; Doron A., *Ma'ariv*, 25 December 1992

29. Granberry M., *Los Angeles Times*, 14 February 1993

30. Feldman P., *Los Angeles Times*, 30 November 1992

31. Material provided by Lebanese sources

32. Based on material provided by Lebanese, Iranian, and Arab sources

33. Adams N.M., *Reader's Digest*, December 1993

34. Ilm-al-Din Riyad, *Al-Watan al-Arabi*, 19 March 1993

35. AP, 6 November 1992; Radio Tehran, 6 November 1992

36. Mitchell A., *New York Times*, 27 May 1993; Neumeister L., AP, 26 May 1993; *New York Times*, 26 May 1993

37. *New York Newsday*, 3 March 1993

38. Treaster J.B., *New York Times*, 8 March 1993

39. Teller T., *News*, 26 March 1993

40. Teller T., *News*, 26 March 1993

41. Matar Khalil, *Al-Sharq al-Awsat*, 12 March 1993

42. Wendl K., *News*, 1 April 1993; Kamoltz K., *Profil*, 5 April 1993

43. Miner C., *New York Post*, 28 June 1993

44. Stern H., AP, 24 June 1993

45. *Washington Post*, 29 August 1993

46. ABC Nightline, 2 August 1993

47. Tyre P., *New York Newsday*, 16 July 1993

48. *Ha'aretz*, 25 March 1993; Ilm-al-Din Riyad, *Al-Watanal-Arabi*, 19 March 1993

49. *Al-Hayah*, 12 December 1992

50. *Al-Hayah*, 12 December 1992

51. *Al-Ahram Weekly*, 4-10 February 1993

52. Yunus Jamal, *Al-Wafd*, 15 February 1993

53. Haydar Hamid, *Al-Wasat*, 12 July 1993

54. Dan U., *New York Post*, 6 May 1993

55. Tyre P., *New York Newsday*, 16 July 1993

56. Reuters, 24 June 1993; *New York Times*, 25 June 1993; Broderick D., *New York Post*, 25 June 1993; *Daily News*, 25 June 1993

57. Oliver C., *New York Post*, 25 June 1993

58. Clines F.X., *New York Times*, 26 June 1993; Finnegan M., Lambiet J.M. & Sennott C.M., *Daily News*, 25 June 1993; ClinesF.X., *New York Times*, 28 June 1993

59. Wolff C., *New York Times*, 27 June 1993; Blumenthal R., *New York Times*, 27 June 1993; Clines F.X., *New York Times*, 28 June 1993

60. Mitchell A., *New York Times*, 25 June 1993

61. Tabor M.B.W., *New York Times*, 1 July 1993

62. Radio Nejat-i Islam, 23 June 1985

63. Anderson J. & Van Atta D., *Washington Post*, 17 January 1986; Taheri Amir, *Holy Terror*, London, Huchinson, 1987, pp.87-88

64. Kupperman R. and Kamen J., *Final Warning*, New York, NY, Doubleday, 1989, p. 47

65. Robberson T., *Washington Post Magazine*, 16 December 1990 ;Roy O., *The Failure of Political Islam*, Paris, Éditions deSeuil, 1992, pp. 146 & 151; Material provided by Iranian sources in the UK; Pakistani and Afghan resistance sources

66. Clines F.X., *New York Times*, 26 June 1993

67. *Jang*, 14 May 1986; Robberson T., *Washington Post Magazine*, 16 December 1990; Waldman P., *Wall Street Journal*, 6 January 1993; Roy O., op.cit. (Political Islam) pp. 146 & 151; Material provided by Iranian sources in the Europe; Pakistani and Afghan resistance sources

68. Sennott C.M., *Daily News*, 26 June 1993; Finnegan M., Lambiet J.M. & Sennott C.M., *Daily News*, 25 June 1993

69. Finnegan M., Lambiet J.M. & Sennott C.M., *Daily News*, 25 June 1993

70. Finnegan M., Lambiet J.M. & Sennott C.M., *Daily News*, 25 June 1993

71. Material provided by Iranian sources in the Europe; Pakistani and Afghan resistance sources

72. Q. in Van Dyk J., *In Afghanistan*, New York NY, Coward-McCann, 1983, p. 63; In 1986, in a discussion with this author, Rabanni refused to withdraw this decree.

73. Yousaf Brig. Mohammad, *Silent Soldier*, Lahore, Jang, 1991, pp. 76-77

74. Yousaf Brig. Mohammad & Adkin Maj. M., *The Bear Trap*, London, Leo Cooper, 1992, pp. 115-120

75. 'Afghans', *Al-Wasat*, 13 July 1992

76. Raufer X., *L'Express*, 21 August 1992; Yared M., *Jeune Afrique*, 10-16 September 1992; Roy O., *Islam and Resistance in Afghanistan*, 2nd Ed., Cambridge MA, Cambridge University Press, 1990, p. 233; Material provided by Afghan and Pakistani sources

77. Khashoqgi Jamal, *Al-Wasat*, 6 September 1993; Material provided by Afghan and Pakistani sources

78. Radio Islamabad, 24 November 1989

79. Material provided by Iranian sources in the Europe; Pakistani and Afghan resistance sources

80. Ilm-al-Din Riyad, *Al-Watan al-Arabi*, 19 March 1993; Abu-Dahr Walid, *Al-Watan al-Arabi*, 2 April 1993

81. Material provided by Iranian sources in the Europe; Pakistani and Afghan resistance sources

82. *Al-Wafd*, 4 December 1991

83. Yared M., *Jeune Afrique*, 19-25 March 1992

84. Husayn Tariq, *Rose al-Yusuf*, 10 February 1992

85. Kirpekar Subhash, *Times of India*, 28 October 1992; *Indian Express*, 18 January 1993; Material provided by Iranian sources in the UK; Afghan resistance sources; Indian sources

86. Rashid Ahmed, *The Herald*, June 1993; Lodhi Maleeha & Hussain Zahid, *Newsline*, October 1992

87. Finley B., *Denver Post*, 27 December 1992

88. *Denver Post*, 28 September 1993, *Denver Post*, 27 December 1992; *Denver Post*, 1 November 1992; *Washington Times*, 18 October 1992; *Rocky Mountain News*, 16 September 1989

89. Miner C., *New York Post*, 7 July 1993

90. Clines F.X., *New York Times*, 26 June 1993; Wolff C., *New York Times*, 27 June 1993; Tabor M.B.W., *New York Times*, 16 October 1993

91. *New York Post*, 4 August 1993; Treaster J.B., *New York Times*, 4 August 1993

92. Blumenthal R., *New York Times*, 20 July 1993

93. Tabor M.B.W., *New York Times*, 28 July 1993

94. ABC Nightline, 2 August 1993

95. *Yediot Aharonot*, 5 February 1992; NBC Nightly News, 27 February 1992; *U.S. News & World Report*, 30 March 1992; *LeFigaro*, 30-31 May 1992; *Nimrooz*, 12 June 1992; *Kayhan International*, 21 June 1992; ITIM, 2 October 1992; Ilm-al-DinRiyad, *Al-Watan al-Arabi*, 19 March 1993

96. *Yediot Aharonot*, 5 February 1992; *Le Figaro*, 30-31 May 1992; *Nimrooz*, 12 June 1992; *Kayhan International*, 21 June 1992; ITIM, 2 October 1992; Material provided by Iranian and Lebanese sources

Chapter 5

FIRST STRIKE

1. *Al-Wasat*, 5 April 1993; *Ha'aretz*, 11 April 1993; *Kayhan*, 24 December 1992

2. Ilm-al-Din Riyad, *Al-Watan al-Arabi*, 12 February 1993

3. Ilm-al-Din Riyad, *Al-Watan al-Arabi*, 19 March 1993; Material provided by Arab sources in the UK

4. *Washington Post*, 26 January 1993; *Washington Times*, 26 January 1993; *New York Times*, 26 January 1993

5. Lewis N.A., *New York Times*, 10 February 1993; Jehl D., *New York Times*, 11 February 1993

6. Rashid Ahmad & Adams J., *The Sunday Times*, 14 February 1993; Shaka Shakil & Ahbasi Ansar, *The News*, 14 February 1993

7. Ahmad Mushtaq, *Dawn*, 25 May 1988; Navik, *Hurmat*, 16-22 March 1988; Rizvi Dr. Yasin, *Hurmat*, 7-13 April 1988

8. Abbas Samayah, MENA, 13 December 1992

9. Zulfiqar Shahzada, *The Nation*, 12 February 1993

10. *Pakistan Times*, 17 February 1993

11. *Pakistan Observer*, 9 March 1993

12. *The News*, 18 February 1993

13. Shahid Saleem, *Dawn*, 12 February 1993; Zulfiqar Shahzada, *The Nation*, 12 February 1993; Ikbar Anwar, *The News*, 12 February 1993; *Nawa-i Waqt*, 12 February 1993; *The News*, 18 February 1993

14. Material provided by Afghan, Pakistani and Iranian sources

15. Zulfiqar Shahzada, *The Nation*, 12 February 1993; Zulfiqar Shahzada, *The Nation*, 15 February 1993; *The News*, 18 February 1993

16. *The News*, 18 February 1993

17. Material provided by Afghan, Pakistani and Iranian sources

18. Shahid Saleem, *Dawn*, 12 February 1993; Zulfiqar Shahzada, *The Nation*, 12 February 1993; Ikbar Anwar, *The News*, 12 February 1993; *The News*, 18 February 1993

19. *The News*, 18 February 1993

20. Rashid Ahmad & Adams J., *The Sunday Times*, 14 February 1993; Jehl D., *New York Times*, 11 February 1993; *The News*, 18 February 1993

21. Zulfiqar Shahzada, *The Nation*, 12 February 1993; Ikbar Anwar, *The News*, 12 February 1993; AFP, 12 February 1993

22. *Al-Watan al-Arabi*, 27 November 1992

23. *The News*, 16 February 1993; IRNA, 13 February 1993

24. AFP, 25 September 1989

25. Material provided by Pakistani security sources

26. Ilm-al-Din Riyad, *Al-Watan al-Arabi*, 19 March 1993; *Ha'aretz*, 25 March 1993

27. Badamachian Asadollah, *Resalat*, 3 March 1993; *Jomhuri-yeIslami*, 7 March 1993

28. ABC Nightline, 2 August 1993

29. Reza'iyan Majid, *Kayhan*, 17 January 1993

30. Ayatollah Ibrahim Amini-Najafabadi on Iranian TV, 5 February 1993; Shari'atmadari Hussayn, *Kayhan*, 7 March 1993

31. Reza'iyan Majid, *Kayhan*, 24 January 1993

32. Abu-Dhar Walid, *Al-Watan al-Arabi*, 2 April 1993

33. Iranian TV, 26 January 1993

34. Miner C. & Pierson R., *New York Post*, 26 June 1993

35. *Toronto Sun*, 24 June 1993; Reuters, 24 June 1993; *Toronto Sun*, 25 June 1993; *Toronto Star*, 25 June 1993; Material provided by Iranian and Arab sources

36. Material provided by Iranian and Canadian sources

37. Miner C. & Pierson R., *New York Post*, 26 June 1993

38. AP, 3 March 1993; Blumenthal R., *New York Times*, 10 March 1993

39. AFP, 4 March 1993

40. Ilm-al-Din Riyad, *Al-Watan al-Arabi*, 12 February 1993; Rabin E., *Ha'aretz*, 18 February 1993; *Al-Watan al-Arabi*, 19 February 1993; *Evening Standard*, 5 March 1993; *SundayTimes*, 28 March 1993; *Ha'aretz*, 30 March 1993; Blanche E., AP, 7 August 1993; Material provided by Iranian sources

41. Treaster J.B., *New York Times*, 11 March 1993; McFadden R.D., *New York Times*, 6 March 1993; Capeci J. & O'Shaughnessy P., *Daily News*, 7 March 1993; Blumenthal R., *New York Times*, 2 March 1993; McFadden R.D., *New York Times*, 1 March 1993; Blumenthal R., *New York Times*, 6 March 1993; Blumenthal R., *New York Times*, 3 March 1993

42. *New York Times*, 27 June 1993

43. Treaster J.B., *New York Times*, 8 March 1993

44. Reuters, 5 March 1993

45. Mitchell A., *New York Times*, 25 June 1993; Juffe M., *New York Post*, 25 June 1993; *Daily News*, 25 June 1993; *DailyNews*, 28 June 1993; Bell A. & Bell R., *New York Post*, 28 June 1993; Duke L. & Malcolm G., *Washington Post*, 26 August 1993

46. *New York Post*, 25 June 1993

47. Meiri Y., *Hadashot*, 28 June 1993; Material provided by Iranian and Sudanese sources

48. *Al-Sharq al-Awsat*, 30 November 1992; al-Sharif Yussuf, *Rose al-Yussuf*, 14 December 1992

49. Material provided by Iranian and Sudanese sources

50. Miner C. & Pierson R., *New York Post*, 26 June 1993

51. Juffe M., *New York Post*, 5 March 1993

52. Miner C., *New York Post*, 3 August 1993; Shamir S., *Ha'aretz*, 4 August 1993

53. Juffe M., *New York Post*, 5 March 1993

54. Kleinfield N.R., *New York Times*, 6 March 1993; Smilon M. & Nolan J., *New York Post*, 1 April 1993

55. *New York Times*, 5 March 1993

56. Neumeister L., AP, 26 May 1993

57. Mitchell A., *New York Times*, 5 August 1993

58. Treaster J.B., *New York Times*, 11 March 1993; Tabor M.B., *New York Times*, 26 March 1993

59. Mitchell A., *New York Times*, 5 August 1993; ABC Nightline, 16 June 1993; Sachs S., *New York Newsday*, 16 July 1993; Hedges C., *New York Times*, 16 July 1993; Blumenthal R., *New York Times*, 7 May 1993

60. Mitchell A., *New York Times*, 20 May 1993

61. *New York Newsday*, 3 March 1993; Treaster J.B., *New York Times*, 8 March 1993; Teller T., *News*, 26 March 1993

62. AP, 3 March 1993; *New York Newsday*, 3 March 1993

63. Pierson R. & Rush G., *New York Post*, 22 March 1993; Lyons R.D., *New York Times*, 24 March 1993; Smilon M. & Nolan J., *New York Post*, 1 April 1993

64. Tabor M.B.W., *New York Times*, 2 April 1993; *New York Times*, 26 May 1993

65. Tyre P., *New York Newsday*, 16 July 1993

66. Pearl M. & Broderick D., *New York Post*, 9 March 1993

67. Tyre P., *New York Newsday*, 16 July 1993

68. AP, 26 February 1993; Reuters, 26 February 1993; AP, 27 February 1993; Reuters, 27 February 1993

69. Reuters, 27 February 1993; *New York Times*, 27 February 1993; Carley W.M., *Wall Street Journal*, 1 March 1993

70. Radio Tehran, 26 February 1993; IRNA, 26 February 1993; Reuters, 26 February 1993

71. AP, 26 February 1993; Reuters, 26 February 1993

72. AP, 27 February 1993

73. *New York Times*, 5 March 1993; *Daily News*, 5 March 1993; AP, 3 March 1993; *New York Newsday*, 3 March 1993

74. *New York Post*, 5 March 1993

75. *Time*, 15 March 1993

76. McAlary M., *Daily News*, 5 March 1993

77. Tyre P., *New York Newsday*, 16 July 1993

78. *New York Post*, 6 March 1993; Capeci J. & O'Shaughnessy P., *Daily News*, 7 March 1993

79. Kleinfield N.R., *New York Times*, 6 March 1993; Smilon M. & Nolan J., *New York Post*, 1 April 1993

80. Mitchell A., *New York Times*, 5 August 1993

81. Blumenthal R., *New York Times*, 10 June 1993

82. Blumenthal R., *New York Times*, 12 May 1993; *New York Times*, 26 May 1993; Mitchell A., *New York Times*, 5 August 1993

83. Gibson D., *The Record*, 17 March 1993

84. Miner C. & Pierson R., *New York Post*, 26 June 1993

85. Gibson D., *The Record*, 17 March 1993; Carley W.M., *Wall Street Journal*, 17 March 1993; Blumenthal R., *New York Times*, 18 March 1993; *New York Times*, 21 March 1993

86.   Reuters, 24 March 1993; Lyons R.D., *New York Times*, 24 March 1993; Appleson G., Reuters, 25 March 1993; Mitchell A., *New York Times*, 25 March 1993; *Al-Ahram*, 25 March 1993; Blumenthal R., *New York Times*, 26 March 1993; Van Biema D., *Time*, 5 April 1993

87.   AP, 27 February 1993

88.   Reuters, 5 March 1993

89.   Blumenthal R., *New York Times*, 10 March 1993

90.   Dan U., *New York Post*, 8 March 1993; Blumenthal R., *New York Times*, 10 March 1993

91.   Blumenthal R., *New York Times*, 9 March 1993

92.   Dan U., *New York Post*, 6 May 1993

93.   *US News & World Report*, 28 June 1993

Chapter 6

ALMOST SECOND STRIKE

1.   *Al-Quds al-Arabi*, 1 March 1993

2.   Sam'an George, *Al-Hayah*, 6 March 1993

3.   *Al-Sharq al-Awsat*, 6 March 1993; *Al-Fajr*, 8 March 1993

4.   Reuters, 28 February 1993

5.   Radio Tehran, 6 March 1993; IRNA, 6 March 1993; Iranian TV, 6 March 1993; Radio Tehran, 7 March 1993; Iranian TV, 7 March 1993; IRNA, 7 March 1993

6.   *Tehran Times*, 8 March 1993; IRNA, 8 March 1993

7. *Salam*, 8 March 1993; IRNA, 8 March 1993

8. Awdah Awdah, *Al-Ra'y*, 8 March 1993

9. IRNA, 10 March 1993; Radio Tehran, 10 March 1993; Reuters, 10March 1993

10. *Salam*, 10 March 1993

11. Reuters, 11 March 1993

12. Seifman D. & Dicker F., *New York Post*, 25 May 1993

13. McFadden R.D., *New York Times*, 25 June 1993

14. *Daily News*, 26 August 1993; Duke L. & Malcolm G., *Washington Post*, 26 August 1993

15. Mitchell A., *New York Times*, 25 June 1993; Juffe M., *New York Post*, 25 June 1993; *Daily News*, 25 June 1993

16. ABC Nightline, 2 August 1993

17. Dan U., *New York Post*, 26 June 1993

18. *Time*, 5 July 1993

19. ABC, 16 August 1993

20. SUNA, 14 December 1991

21. Hanaqah Ahmad, *Al-Anba'*, 7 April 1990

22. Hasan Tariq, *Rose al-Yusuf*, 22 July 1991

23. Husayn Tariq, *Rose al-Yusuf*, 10 February 1992

24. Madani Nur-al-Din, *Al-Sudan al-Hadith*, 25 November 1991

25. *Al-Watan al-Arabi*, 16 October 1992; *Al-Sharq al-Awsat*,7 November 1991; *Al-Sharq al-Awsat*, 2 November 1991

26. ABC, 16 August 1993

27. Hasan Tariq, *Rose al-Yusuf*, 22 July 1991

28. Yared M., *Jeune Afrique*, 19-25 March 1992

29. SUNA, 25 April 1991

30. Yared M., *Jeune Afrique*, 19-25 March 1992

31. *Al-Watan al-Arabi*, 4 December 1992

32. Melman Y., *Ha'aretz*, 29 August 1993

33. IRNA, 13 December 1991

34. IRNA, 15 December 1991

35. Ma'ruf Mahmud, *Al-Quds al-Arabi*, 27 January 1992

36. *Al-Jumhuriyah*, 2 August 1992; Husayn Tariq, *Roseal-Yusuf*, 10 February 1992

37. Yared M., *Jeune Afrique*, 12-18 March 1992

38. *Al-Wasat*, 16 November 1992; *Al-Watan al-Arabi*, 6 November 1992

39. Bodansky Y., *Defense & Foreign Affairs: Stategic Policy*, March 1992

40. Sa'dah Ibrahim, *Akhbar al-Yawm*, 14 November 1992

41. al-Ashri Ashraf, *Al-Ahram al-Masa'i*, 23 August 1992

42. Abu-Dahr Walid, *Al-Watan al-Arabi*, 2 April 1993

43. Mirghai Uthman, *Al-Sharq al-Awsat*, 3 July 1993

44. Finnegan M., Lambiet J.M. & Sennott C.M., *Daily News*, 25 June 1993

45. Dan U., *New York Post*, 26 June 1993

46. ABC, 16 August 1993; Material provided by Sudanese sources

47. Dan U., *New York Post*, 26 June 1993

48. Capeci J., *Daily News*, 25 June 1993; Shamir S., *Ha'aretz*, 26 June 1993

49. Myers S.L., *New York Times*, 18 July 1993

50. Miner C., *New York Post*, 21 September 1993

51. *Al-Sharq al-Awsat*, 28 April 1993

52. Material provided by Iranian and Arab sources

53. Seifman D. & Dicker F., *New York Post*, 25 May 1993; King J., Reuter, 25 May 1993

54. Shaw G., *New York Post*, 3 June 1993; Mitchell A., *New York Times*, 3 June 1993

55. Seifman D. & Dicker F., *New York Post*, 25 May 1993; King J., Reuter, 25 May 1993; Shaw G., *New York Post*, 3 June 1993; Miner C., *New York Post*, 21 September 1993

56. Sposato W., Reuters, 24 June 1993; Mitchell A., *New York Times*, 25 June 1993; *New York Post*, 25 June 1993; Caspit B., *Ma'ariv*, 2 July 1993

57. Juffe M., *New York Post*, 25 June 1993; *New York Times*, 25 June 1993

58. *Daily News*, 26 August 1993; Duke L. & Malcolm G.,*Washington Post*, 26 August 1993

59. ABC, 17 August 1993

60. Tabor M.B.W., *New York Times*, 6 August 1993; BlumenthalR., *New York Times*, 6 September 1993

61. Miner C., *New York Post*, 17 July 1993; Perl D., *Ha'aretz*, 25 July 1993; Mitchell A., *New York Times*, 1August 1993

62. Myers S.L., *New York Times*, 18 July 1993; Miner C., *New York Post*, 19 July 1993; Dan U. & Miner C., *New York Post*, 22 July 1993

63. *New York Post*, 25 June 1993; *New York Times*, 25 June 1993

64. Shamir S., *Ha'aretz*, 25 June 1993

65. Juffe M., *New York Post*, 25 June 1993; *New York Times*, 25 June 1993

66. Juffe M., *New York Post*, 25 June 1993; *New York Times*, 25 June 1993; *Daily News*, 25 June 1993

67. Reuters, 24 June 1993; *New York Times*, 25 June 1993; Broderick D., *New York Post*, 25 June 1993; *Daily News*, 25 June 1993; LeVine S., *Washington Post*, 16 July 1993

68. Unconfirmed reports by Sudanese sources

69. Mitchell A., *New York Times*, 25 June 1993

70. Miner C., Smilon M. & Pierson R., *New York Post*, 29 June 1993; Clines F.X., *New York Times*, 26 June 1993

71. Miner C., Smilon M. & Pierson R., *New York Post*, 29 June 1993

72. Reuters, 24 June 1993; *New York Times*, 25 June 1993; Broderick D., *New York Post*, 25 June 1993; *Daily News*, 25 June 1993; Stassen-Berger R.E., *Washington Post*, 30 June 1993

73. Kaspit B., *Ma'ariv*, 2 July 1993

74. ABC Nightline, 2 August 1993

75. *Washington Post*, 29 August 1993

76. *Al-Wasat*, 15 March 1993

77. Tabor M.B.W., *New York Times*, 4 August 1993

78. ABC Nightline, 2 August 1993

79. Juffe M., *New York Post*, 25 June 1993; *New York Times*, 25 June 1993

80. Mitchell A., *New York Times*, 29 June 1993

81. McFadden R.D., *New York Times*, 26 June 1993; Olojede D., *New York Newsday*, 26 June 1993; Capeci J. & Mustain G., *Daily News*, 27 June 1993; *US News & World Report*, 5 July 1993; ABC, 2 August 1993

82. ABC, 16 August 1993; Molotsky I., *New York Times*, 17 August 1993; Material provided by Sudanese sources

83. *New York Post*, 25 June 1993; Neumeister L., AP, 24 June 1993

84. Juffe M., *New York Post*, 25 June 1993; *New York Times*, 25 June 1993; *Daily News*, 25 June 1993; Miner C., *New York Daily News*, 1 July 1993; Tabor M.B.W., *New York Times*, 1 July 1993; Stassen-Berger R.E., *Washington Post*, 1 July 1993; Blumenthal R., *New York Times*, 8 July 1993

85. Juffe M., *New York Post*, 25 June 1993; *New York Times*, 25 June 1993

86. Tabor M.B.W., *New York Times*, 1 July 1993

87. ABC, 16 August 1993

88. ABC Nightline, 2 August 1993

89. Thomas P. & Duke L., *Washington Post*, 29 August 1993

90. *Al-Wasat*, 14 December 1992

91. Juffe M., *New York Post*, 25 June 1993; *New York Times*, 25 June 1993

92. Mitchell A., *New York Times*, 25 June 1993

93. Thomas P. & Duke L., *Washington Post*, 29 August 1993

94. Reuters, 24 June 1993; *New York Times*, 25 June 1993; Broderick D., *New York Post*, 25 June 1993; *Daily News*, 25 June 1993

95. Clines F.X., *New York Times*, 26 June 1993; *New York Post*, 25 June 1993

96. Blumenthal R., *New York Times*, 24 July 1993; Perl D., *Ha'aretz*, 25 July 1993

97. Tabor M.B.W., *New York Times*, 28 July 1993

98. Neumeister L., AP, 8 July 1993; Blumenthal R., *New York Times*, 8 July 1993

99. Clines F.X., *New York Times*, 26 June 1993; *New York Post*, 25 June 1993

100. Blumenthal R., *New York Times*, 24 July 1993; Perl D., *Ha'aretz*, 25 July 1993

101. Blumenthal R., *New York Times*, 30 June 1993; Juffe M., *New York Post*, 25 June 1993; Stassen-Berger R.E., *Washington Post*, 30 June 1993; *New York Times*, 25 June 1993; *Daily News*, 25 June 1993; Miner C., *New York Post*, 21 September 1993

102. Juffe M., *New York Post*, 25 June 1993; *New York Times*, 25 June 1993

103. *Jahan-ye Islam*, 2 June 1993; *Jahan-ye Islam*, 3 June 1993

104. *Al-Sharq al-Awsat*, 5 June 1993

105. Material provided by Iranian sources

106. Material provided by Iranian and Sudanese sources

107. SUNA, 13 June 1993

108. *New York Times*, 25 June 1993; *New York Post*, 25 June 1993; *Daily News*, 25 June 1993; Hardt R., AP, 24 June 1993; AP, 2 August 1993

109. Blumenthal R., *New York Times*, 30 June 1993

110. Juffe M., *New York Post*, 25 June 1993; *New York Times*, 25 June 1993

111. Perlman S., *New York Newsday*, 24 June 1993; McFadden R.D., *New York Times*, 25 June 1993; McFadden R.D., *New York Times*, 26 June 1993

112. Juffe M., *New York Post*, 25 June 1993; *New York Times*, 25 June 1993

113. Perlman S., *New York Newsday*, 24 June 1993

Chapter 7
ONLY THE BEGINING

1. Soudan F., *Jeune Afrique*, 11-17 March 1993

2. *The Times*, 4 March 1987c

3. ABC Nightline, 18 March 1993

4. *Al-Jumhuriyah*, 2 August 1992; Husayn Tariq, *Roseal-Yussuf*, 10 February 1992; *Al-Watan al-Arabi*, 6 November 1992; *Al-Watan al-Arabi*, 4 December 1992; *Al-Wasat*, 14December 1992

5. *Al-Wasat*, 14 December 1992

6. Thomas P. & Duke L., *Washington Post*, 29 August 1993; Myers S.L., *New York Times*, 18 July 1993; Miner C., *New York Post*, 19 July 1993; Dan U. & Miner C., *New York Post*, 22 July 1993

7.   Johnston D., *New York Times*, 28 June 1993; *US News & World Report*, 5 July 1993

8.   *Daily News*, 26 June 1993

9.   Miner C., *New York Post*, 28 June 1993

10. Miner C., Smilon M. & Pierson R., *New York Post*, 29 June 1993

11. Miner C., *New York Post*, 3 August 1993; Shamir S., *Ha'aretz*, 4 August 1993

12. Hedges C., *New York Times*, 16 July 1993

13. Thomas P. & Duke L., *Washington Post*, 29 August 1993; ABC,2 August 1993; ABC Nightline, 2 August 1993; Treaster J.R., *New York Times*, 3 August 1993; Shamir S., *Ha'aretz*, 4 August 1993

14. Smilon M. & Miner C., *New York Post*, 26 August 1993

15. Tabor M.B.W., *New York Times*, 4 August 1993

16. Al-Kinani Ahmad, *Al-Sha'b*, 4 August 1992

17. *Al-Wasat*, 15 March 1993

18. *Rose al-Yusuf*, 15 June 1992

19. *Rose al-Yusuf*, 22 June 1992

20. Radwan Amin, *Al-Safir*, 1 July 1992

21. *Rose al-Yussuf*, 22 June 1992; *Al-Ahram*, 17 June 1992

22. Hasanayn Abduh, *Al-Wafd*, 16 November 1992

23. Hasanayn Abduh, *Al-Wafd*, 21 November 1992

24. Siblah Majdi, *Al-Musawwar*, 4 December 1992

25. Al-Ahram Press Agency, 23 December 1992; *Al-Ahram*, 24 December 1992

26. *Al-Ahram Weekly*, 4-10 February 1993

27. Abd-al-Latif Najwan, *Al-Musawwar*, 4 December 1992

28. Al-Ahram Press Agency, 23 December 1992; *Al-Ahram*, 24December 1992

29. *Misr al-Fatah*, 23 November 1992

30. Hasanayn Abduh, *Al-Wafd*, 21 November 1992

31. Musa Ahmad & al-Zayni Hisham, *Al-Ahram al-Duwali*, 15 April 1993

32. MBC, 28 June 1993

33. *Al-Hayah*, 7 June 1993

34. Musa Ahmad & al-Zayni Hisham, *Al-Ahram al-Duwali*, 15 April 1993

35. *Al-Kifah al-Arabi*, 4 May 1993

36. Naji Muhammad, *Al-Sharq Al-Awsat*, 12 June 1993

37. *Al-Kifah al-Arabi*, 4 May 1993

38. McFadden R.D., *New York Times*, 25 June 1993

39. McFadden R.D., *New York Times*, 26 June 1993

40. Shamir S., *Ha'aretz*, 25 June 1992

41. Miner C., *New York Post*, 28 June 1993

42. Tyre P., *New York Newsday*, 16 July 1993

43. ABC Nightline, 18 August 1993

44. Johnston D., *New York Times*, 28 June 1993

45. Miner C., *New York Post*, 28 June 1993

46. *Time*, 5 July 1993

47. *Jahan-i Islam*, 4 July 1993

48. McFadden R.D., *New York Times*, 25 June 1993

49. Ilm-al-Din Riyad, *Al-Watan al-Arabi*, 19 March 1993

50. Abu-Dahr Walid *Al-Watan al-Arabi*, 2 April 1993

51. AP, 2 July 1993; Reuter, 2 July 1993; MENA, 2 July 1993; *New York Times*, 3 July 1993; Khashuqji Jamal, *Al-Hayah*, 4 July 1993; Dan U., *New York Post*, 6 July 1993

52. Khashuqji Jamal, *Al-Hayah*, 4 July 1993

53. *Al-Wafd*, 3 July 1993

54. AFP, 5 July 1993

55. AFP, 8 July 1993

56. Nakhoul Samia, Reuter, 26 August 1993

57. Sami Mariam, AP, 26 August 1993

58. AFP, 26 August 1993

59. Reuter, 27 August 1993; AFP, 28 August 1993

60. Sami Mariam, AP, 26 August 1993

61. Radio Hilverstrum Netherlands, 15 August 1993; Soderlind Rolf, Reuter, 15 August 1993; Rehnult Andreas, AP, 15 August 1993; AFP, 15 August 1993; DPA, 15 August 1993; Soderlind Rolf, Reuter, 16 August 1993; Rehnult Andreas, AP, 16 August 1993; DPA,16 August 1993; AFP, 16 August 1993; MENA, 16 August 1993

62. DPA, 16 August 1993

63. DPA, 16 August 1993; MENA, 16 August 1993; Reuter, 16 August 1993; Bajak Frank, AP, 16 August 1993

64. Reuter, 16 August 1993; Bajak Frank, AP, 16 August 1993

65. Reuter, 16 August 1993; Bajak Frank, AP, 16 August 1993

66. Reuter, 28 August 1993

67. *Ettela'at*, 13 February 1993

68. *Jomhuri-ye Islami*, 7 March 1993

69. Badamachian Asadollah, *Resalat*, 3 March 1993

70. Azizi Ahmad, *Ettela'at*, 7 March 1993

71. Badamachian Asadollah, *Resalat*, 3 March 1993

72. Azizi Ahmad, *Ettela'at*, 7 March 1993

73. *Jomhuri-ye Islami*, 7 March 1993

74. Azizi Ahmad, *Ettela'at*, 7 March 1993

75. Reuters, 15 March 1993; *Al-Anwar*, 16 March 1993

76. Radio Tehran, 18 March 1993; IRNA, 18 March 1993; Reuters, 18March 1993

77. Radio Tehran, 19 March 1993; IRNA, 19 March 1993; Reuters, 19 March 1993

78. Ladki Nadim, Reuters, 19 March 1993

79. *Jahan-i Islam*, 22 April 1993

80. *Jahan-i Islam*, 22 April 1993

81. Radio Tehran, 17 June 1993

82. Radio Tehran, 17 June 1993

83. Larijani Dr. Muhammad Javad, *Ettela'at*, 13 May 1993

84. *Jahan-i Islami*, 24 May 1993

85. IRNA, 29 May 1993

86. Iranian TV, 31 May 1993; Iranian TV, 30 May 1993

87. *Kayhan International*, 2 June 1993

88. *Tehran Times*, 2 June 1993

89. Parhizgar M., *Salam*, 2 June 1993

90. *Jahan-i Islami*, 2 June 1993

91. IRNA, 2 June 1993

92. IRNA, 3 June 1993

93. Radio Tehran, 4 June 1993

94. Radio Tehran, 3 July 1993; Radio Tehran, 5 July 1993; Radio Tehran, 6 July 1993

95. *Tehran Times*, 5 July 1993; IRNA, 5 July 1993

96. *Jahan-i Islam*, 4 July 1993

97. *Jahan-i Islam*, 4 July 1993

98. *Resalat*, 10 July 1993

99. Ziayi Hoseyn, *Kayhan*, 6 July 1993

100. *Jomhuri-ye Islami*, 10 July 1993; IRNA, 10 July 1993; Reuters, 10 July 1993

101. IRNA, 9 July 1993; Reuters, 9 July 1993

102. Radio Tehran, 13 July 1993

103 Radio Tehran, 14 July 1993

104. Radio Tehran, 19 July 1993

105. *Kayhan International*, 16 August 1993

106. Iranian TV, 26 August 1993; IRNA, 26 August 1993; Reuter, 26August 1993

107. *Al-Wasat*, 15 March 1993

108. *Daily News*, 27 August 1993

CONCLUSION

1.   Mohtashemi Ali Akbar, *Salam*, 2 August 1993

2.   *Al-Wasat*, 15 March 1993

3.   *Al-Wasat*, 6 September 1993

4.   Ahmed Gutbi Mahdi, Muslim Organizations in the United States, Haddad Yvonne Yazback (ed.), *The Muslims of America*, New York, NY, Oxford University Press, 1991, pp. 16-18

5.   *Al-Wasat*, 6 September 1993; Material provided by Arab sources.

6.   *Al-Nur,* 7 July 1993

7.   *Daily News*, 27 August 1993

8.   *Jomhuri-ye Islami*, 14 September 1993

9.   Iranian TV, 16 September 1993; Reuter, 16 September 1993

10. Azmeh Youssef, Reuter, 19 September 1993; Ladki Nadim, Reuter, 19 September 1993; Reuter, 18 September 1993

11. *Salam*, 15 September 1993

Index

A

Inform Yourself About Your Politicians Through S.P.I. Books

Recent S.P.I.
Entertainment Books

SWEETHEARTS: 156171-206-X $5.50 U.S./ $6.50 CANADA

❏ The inspiring, heartwarming and surprising stories of he girls America tuned in to watch every week in the '60's these glamorous and sexy stars who made the '60's a time to remember and long for:

Goldie Hawn & Judy Carne- "Laugh-In's" funniest girls
Mary Tyler Moore- "The Dick Van Dyke Show's" Laura Petrie
Sally Field- "Gidget's" Frannie Lawrence & "The Flying Nun's"
Sister Bertrille
Elizabeth Montgomery- "Bewitched's" Samantha Stevens
Barbara Eden- "I Dream of Jeannie"
Tina Louise & Dawn Wells- "Gilligans Island's"
Diana Rigg- "The Avengers'" Emma Peel
Stefanie Powers- "The Girl from U.N.C.L.E."

COSBY: 156171-205-1 $4.99 U.S/$5.99 CANADA

❏ The Critically Acclaimed Revealing Look at America's #1 Entertainment Legend Cosby. Packed with revealing interviews with friends, family and other stars plus sixteen pages of exclusive photos.

Chronicles Cosby's early struggle up from Philadelphia's projects and his tireless efforts to break through the color barriers in show business and build an unmatched career.

Cosby's illustrious list of triumphs in the last 25 years are revealed as well, including his marriage and family and a Grammy and Emmy award-winning TV, recording and film career, including YOU BET YOUR LIFE.

To order in North America, please sent this coupon to: **S.P.I. Books** •136 W 22nd St. • New York, NY 10011 • Tel: 212/633-2022 • Fax: 212/633-2123

Please send European orders with £ payment to:
Bookpoint Ltd. • 39 Milton Park • Abingdon Oxon OX14 4TD • England • Tel: (0235) 8335001 • Fax: (0235) 861038

Please send____books. I have enclosed check or money order for $/£
(please add $1.95 U.S./£ for first book for postage/handling & 50¢/50p. for each additional book). Make dollar checks drawn on U.S. branches payable to **S.P.I. Books**; Sterling checks to **Bookpoint Ltd.** Allow 2 to 3 weeks for delivery.
❏MC ❏ Visa # _____
Exp. date _____
Name _____
Address _____

More Adventure-Filled Historical Fiction From S.P.I.

SPI BOOKS
A division
Shapolsky Publishers, In